A HISTORY OF JEWISH LITERATURE
VOLUME X

Israel Zinberg's *History of Jewish Literature*

An Analytic Index to the *History of Jewish Literature* will appear in Volume XII.

Israel Zinberg

A HISTORY OF
JEWISH
LITERATURE

TRANSLATED AND EDITED BY BERNARD MARTIN

The Science of Judaism and Galician Haskalah

HEBREW UNION COLLEGE PRESS
CINCINNATI, OHIO

KTAV PUBLISHING HOUSE, INC.
NEW YORK, NEW YORK
1977

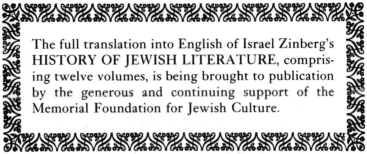

The full translation into English of Israel Zinberg's HISTORY OF JEWISH LITERATURE, comprising twelve volumes, is being brought to publication by the generous and continuing support of the Memorial Foundation for Jewish Culture.

Library of Congress Cataloging in Publication Data

Zinberg, Israel, 1873–1938.
    The science of Judaism and Galician Haskalah.

    (His A history of Jewish literature; v. 10)
    Translation of Ḥokhmes Yisroel un Galitsyaner haskole.
    Includes bibliographical references and index.
    1. Hebrew literature, Modern—History and criticism.
2. Jewish learning and scholarship—History. 3. Haska-
lah—Galicia. 4. German literature—Jewish authors—
History and criticism. I. Title.
PJ5008.Z5313 vol. 10 [PJ5019] 809'.889'24s [892.4'09]
ISBN 0–87068–491–4   76–47583

Printed in the United States of America.

Contents

Yom-Tov (Leopold) Zunz as founder of the Science of Judaism
—The "Hep-Hep riots against Jews—Ludwig Börne and *Der
ewige Jude*—*Der Verein für Cultur und Wissenschaft des Judentums*—
The youthful Heinrich Heine and his national moods—His *Al-
mansor* and *Über Polen*—The *Zeitschrift für die Wissenschaft des
Judentums*—Immanuel Wolf and Eduard Gans—*Die Wissenschaft
des Judentums* as approval for equal rights—Lazarus Bendavid on
the belief in the coming of the Messiah—Heine and his *Rabbi of
Bacharach*—The demise of the *Verein*—The apostates—Isaac
Marcus Jost and his *Geschichte der Israeliten*.

Bikkurei Ha-Ittim and its editors—Jehudah Loeb Jeiteles and the
Galician contributors—The *maskilim* as patriots—Their iso-

Contents

A Note on Israel Zinberg

DR. ISRAEL ZINBERG is widely regarded as one of the foremost historians of Jewish literature. Born in Russia in 1873 and educated at various universities in Germany and Switzerland, he devoted more than twenty years to the writing, in Yiddish, of his monumental *Di Geshikhte fun der Literatur bay Yidn* (History of Jewish Literature). This work, published in eight volumes in Vilna, 1929–1937, is a comprehensive and authoritative study of Jewish literary creativity in Europe from its beginnings in tenth-century Spain to the end of the Haskalah period in nineteenth-century Russia. Based on a meticulous study of all the relevant primary source material and provided with full documentation, Zinberg's history is a notable exemplar of the tradition of modern Jewish scholarship known as *die Wissenschaft des Judentums* (the Science of Judaism).

In addition to his *magnum opus*, Zinberg, who earned his living as a chemical engineer, wrote numerous other valuable monographs and articles on Jewish history and literature in Russian, Hebrew, and Yiddish. In 1938, during the Stalinist purges, he was arrested by the Soviet police and sentenced to exile in Siberia. He died in a concentration camp hospital in Vladivostok in that same year.

The reader who wishes a fuller introduction is invited to consult the Translator's Introduction to Volume I of Zinberg's *History of Jewish Literature.*

Foreword

In 1972 the Case Western Reserve University Press began publishing an English translation of Israel Zinberg's *History of Jewish Literature.* Zinberg, an engineer by profession, was a scholar by choice and inclination. In thirty years of intensive study in the great Jewish libraries of St. Petersburg (later Leningrad), he produced eight volumes in Yiddish portraying the course of literary creativity among the Jews beginning with the Golden Age of Spanish Jewry and continuing to the end of the last century. It was not until many years after Zinberg's death that a Hebrew translation was prepared and published in the State of Israel.

There has been no work of similar scope and magnitude in the English language, despite the fact that the Jewish reading public in Britain, South Africa, Canada, and the United States constitutes about half of the Jews in the world. Now, however, the Zinberg volumes have been beautifully translated into English by Dr. Bernard Martin, Abba Hillel Silver Professor of Jewish Studies and Chairman of the Department of Religion at Case Western Reserve University in Cleveland, Ohio. All the English-speaking lands are indebted to Professor Martin for his endeavor to make accessible a literary history such as Zinberg's, a history which depicts the intellectual strivings of the Jews, their aspirations, yearnings, and spiritual search in the medieval and modern worlds, in both of which they have played a not undistinguished role.

Special gratitude is due to the Press of Case Western Reserve University which inaugurated the challenging task of publishing this handsome and very important series of books. Each volume is an aesthetic as well as intellectual delight. The Case Western Reserve Press was aided in publication by a generous grant from the Memorial Foundation for Jewish Culture. The grant is, indeed, a memorial to the martyred Zinberg, who was arrested by the Soviet police in 1938 and deported to Siberia, where he died. We, for our part, are pleased with this opportunity to express our gratitude to the Memorial Foundation for the support which made possible the publication of the first three volumes.

Unfortunately, the economic difficulties from which many universities are now suffering has led to the dissolution of the Case Western Reserve Press and made it impossible for it to continue with the remaining nine volumes. That is why the Hebrew Union College—Jewish Institute of Religion, realizing the importance and cultural implications of this work, is cooperating with the Ktav Publishing House, Incorporated, in the publication of the remaining volumes.

The completion of this series will make available to the English-speaking world a magnificent account of the literary and cultural treasures created by the Jewish people during their millennial history.

Hebrew Union College—
Jewish Institute of Religion
Cincinnati, Ohio
April 1977

Alfred Gottschalk
President

Acknowledgments

The generous support of the Memorial Foundation for Jewish Culture, New York City, of the Morris and Bertha Treuhaft Memorial Fund, the Leonard, Faye, and Albert B. Ratner Philanthropic Fund, Mr. Samuel H. Givelber, and Mr. and Mrs. John K. Powers, all of Cleveland, is gratefully acknowledged by publisher and translator alike. Without this generosity it would not have been possible for Israel Zinberg's monumental work to reach the new audience that it is hoped a translation into English will afford. The editor and translator wishes to express his appreciation to his friend Dr. Arthur J. Lelyveld, Rabbi of the Fairmount Temple of Cleveland and President (1966–1972) of the American Jewish Congress, for his aid in securing a grant from the Memorial Foundation for Jewish Culture for the publication of this work.

The translator also wishes to express his deep appreciation to Dr. Nathan Susskind, formerly Professor of German at the College of the City of New York and Visiting Professor of Yiddish at Yeshiva University, for his invaluable help in clarifying the meaning of many terms and concepts in Zinberg's Yiddish and Hebrew text. Responsibility for any errors of translation is, of course, the translator's.

It should be noted that Yiddish books with Hebrew titles are usually rendered according to the modern Sephardic pronunciation of Hebrew.

A gift to my loyal friend
and life-companion—my wife.

—Israel Zinberg

Transliteration of Hebrew Terms

א is not transliterated

ב = b

ב = v

ג,ג = g

ד,ד = d

ה = h

ו = v (where not a vowel)

ז = z

ח = ḥ

ט = t

י = y

כ = k

כ = ch

ל = l

מ = m

נ = n

ס = s

ע is not transliterated

פ = p

פ = f

צ = tz

ק = k

ר = r

שׁ = sh

שׂ = s

ת,ת = t

ָ = a

ַ = a

ֹ, וֹ = o

ֻ, וּ = u

short ָ = o

ִי = ei

ֶ = e

ִ = i

ֵ = ei

ְ = e

ֳ = o

ֲ = a

vocal *sheva* = e

silent *sheva* is not transliterated

Transliteration of Yiddish Terms

א	not transliterated		יי	ey
אַ	a		יִ	ay
אָ	o		כ	k
ב	b		כ,ך	kh
בֿ	v		ל	l
ג	g		מ,ם	m
ד	d		נ,ן	n
ה	h		ס	s
ו,וּ	u		ע	e
וו	v		פ	p
וי	oy		פֿ,ף	f
ז	z		צ,ץ	ts
זש	zh		ק	k
ח	kh		ר	r
ט	t		ש	sh
טש	tsh. ch		שׂ	s
י	(consonant) y		ת	t
י	(vowel) i		ת	s

Abbreviations

JQR	*Jewish Quarterly Review*
JQR, n.s.	*Jewish Quarterly Review*, new series
MGWJ	*Monatsschrift für die Geschichte und Wissenschaft des Judentums*
PAAJR	*Proceedings of the American Academy for Jewish Research*
REJ	*Revue des Études Juives*
ZHB	*Zeitschrift für hebräische Bibliographie*

This volume is dedicated
to
Beatrice Hammond
whose crowning achievement is her
devotion to culture and learning

THE SCIENCE OF JUDAISM AND GALICIAN
HASKALAH

CHAPTER ONE

The Science of Judaism;
LEOPOLD ZUNZ AND HEINRICH HEINE

Yom-Tov (Leopold) Zunz as founder of the Science of Judaism—
The "Hep-Hep" riots against Jews—Ludwig Börne and *Der ewige Jude*
—*Der Verein für Cultur und Wissenschaft des Judentums*—The youthful
Heinrich Heine and his national moods—His *Almansor* and *Über Polen*
—The *Zeitschrift für die Wissenschaft des Judentums*—Immanuel Wolf and
Eduard Gans—*Die Wissenschaft des Judentums* as approval for equal
rights—Lazarus Bendavid on the belief in the coming of the Messiah
—Heine and his *Rabbi of Bacharach*—The demise of the *Verein*—The
apostates—Isaac Marcus Jost and his *Geschichte der Israeliten.*

T THE same time that the battle between the Reform party and its adversaries broke out,[1] there appeared in Berlin (in 1818) a small brochure under the rather vague title *Etwas über die rabbinische Literatur.* The name of the twenty-four-year-old author was also little known. Nevertheless, this brochure was a harbinger of a new era. It became the first foundationstone for the great structure that west European Jewry erected in the nineteenth century. *Die Wissenschaft des Judentums,* "the Science of Judaism," is the name of this structure, and Yom-Tov Lippmann (Leopold) Zunz was the author of the brochure.

---

1. See the preceding volume, last chapter.

Yom-Tov Zunz was born in 1794 in the small German town of Detmold. His father, Menaḥem Immanuel, a scholarly Jew, died when Yom-Tov was nine years old. The family was greatly impoverished, and the young orphan lived in dire poverty. He was brought up in Wolfenbüttel in a Talmud Torah for poor children which was reorganized in 1807 into a model Jewish school. The adolescent Zunz very assiduously studied both Hebrew and general subjects. In 1809 he entered the local gymnasium and completed its curriculum in 1815. During the years he spent in the gymnasium, Zunz also devoted himself intensively to Hebrew studies and was already at that time competent in rabbinic literature. In 1816 he came to Berlin, where he entered the university. He spent his first years in Berlin as a tutor in the home of Henriette Herz,[2] made acquaintances in the circles close to the Reform party, was enchanted by Israel Jacobson's preaching, and in 1817 was himself appointed a preacher in Jacobson's Reform temple. However, he was not at all a fighter by nature. His vocation was not the platform but the scholar's study—sitting in the tent of Torah, poring day and night over ancient folios. And already in his youth Zunz possessed what the battlers for culture and reform of the previous generation so greatly lacked—a sense of history.

Born on the threshold of two centuries, Zunz remained faithful to the optimistic faith of the enlighteners of the eighteenth century in the universal power of reason and common sense. He was also firmly persuaded that as soon as one grasps the true and rational through reason, it is quite easy to persuade another of the correctness of the assumptions and views that reason entails. On the other hand, he adopted from the new century the important, truly scientific principle concerning the historical approach to problems of culture. The *maskilim* of the previous generation—the Friedländers, Hombergs, and Wolfsohns—regarded the post-biblical, Talmudic literature with contempt. They perceived in it, above all, superstition and enormous conflicts with common sense. Zunz, however, saw in the post-biblical (*rabbinische*, as he calls it) literature, first of all, a mighty, two-thousand-year monument of national culture which must first be explored from beginning to end. Zunz notes that at least the gentile scholars made an attempt to explore the biblical period, but rabbinic literature was regarded with extreme hostility by most Christian savants and we, for our part, have until now contented ourselves merely with "thoughtlessness" or with *oberflächlichen Tadel*, "superficial reproof" (page 7).

2. See our History, Vol. VIII, pp. 121–22.

Zunz finds that he is standing at a boundary. The rabbinic literature continues to decline; it is moribund. The Hebrew language is becoming speedily forgotten. It is being displaced by "the German language and German culture," and this brings the demise of "rabbinic" literature even closer. This literature is already at its end. It is a completed, *closed*[3] literature. Hence, the balance must be drawn up; our past must be critically and scientifically investigated, our two-thousand-year national creativity must be critically and scientifically explored. But all the requisite preliminary studies must first be made, so that the building of the Science of Judaism can be constructed. Zunz was firmly persuaded in this connection that precisely now, in the time of enlightenment, when the government and society are thinking of radical changes in the legal condition of the Jews, Jewish scholarship, the scientific elucidation of Jewish culture and ethics, would serve as a sure guide in the solution of many highly important questions.

Zunz sets forth an extensive, well-elaborated program on how the various realms of Jewish scholarship should be investigated. The most interesting point in this connection is the following: the theses developed here actually became the program of his long life-path, the prospectus of his indefatigable, almost seventy-year-long scholarly work.[4]

In his work Zunz notes the hostility and contempt with which Jews and Judaism were discussed in German scholarly literature in former times, and he concludes with satisfaction: "Thanks, O eternal God! Such times are now past. Courageous and truth-loving writers presently disseminate true enlightenment of the people, and powerful princes and dukes aid them therein."[5]

Quite soon, however, Zunz had melancholy opportunity to become persuaded that the black shadows of the benighted Middle Ages had not yet disappeared. The national battles for liberation in Germany (1812–1814) hastened the downfall of the brilliant Napoleon, the heir of the French Revolution, and over all of Europe leaden reaction spread under the supreme supervision of the Holy Alliance. The hopes of the romantically-minded battlers for freedom in Germany proved illusory. The German people did not become free or united but remained, as before, fragmentized and divided under the despotic power of thirty-six monarchs. The German nobles and princes forgot their obliga-

3. Italicized by Zunz.
4. His scholarly work after the revolution of 1848 will be discussed in the next volume.
5. *Gesammelte Schriften*, I, 24.

tions and everything they had promised their people formerly, in the years of distress and terror; their only wish was to return to the old status, to place the people under the previous yoke. They understood very well how to render impotent the feeling of anger and discontent that had accumulated among certain strata of the urban populace. They utilized the old, tried method: making of the Jews a target for the blind wrath of the people and declaring them the scapegoat that must pay for all the injustices which the ruling classes committed against the people.

The year 1819 was, for the Jews in Germany, a year of shame and degradation. In many cities the Christian mob attacked Jewish homes with wild cries of "Hep! Hep!," plundered their property, and beat them murderously. In these riots, in which scores of Jews were killed, students and representatives of the merchant class also participated. There was also a sufficiency of Jew-haters among the learned professors who came forth against the Jews with rabid tracts and demanded that this "vermin" be driven out of the land. Some even proposed that, in order for the Jews not to increase, "the men should be castrated and the women and girls placed in brothels."[6]

The aged David Friedländer was astounded and shocked. He could not understand how such a thing could happen in the present "enlightened times, when the bright rays of healthy human reason" had driven away the medieval "prejudices." But a significantly more powerful voice was also heard at that time. The erstwhile Leib Baruch of the ghetto of Frankfurt who, under the name Ludwig Börne, was transformed into the "first German publicist," the tireless battler for democratic freedom, also issued forth with the power of his mighty talent not only against the physical "Hep! Hep!" movement, against the riots and murders, but also against "metaphysical Hep! Hep!," against the Jew-hating tracts, brochures, and ostensibly scientific treatises.[7]

Börne, however came forth as an outsider—already not as a Jew, but as a democrat and battler for freedom who understands quite well that "Jew-hatred is one of the Pontinian marshes which infect the beautiful spring-landscape of our freedom"[8] and that the urban rabble was provoked to its attacks on the Jews

6. Graetz, *Die Geschichte der Juden*, Vol. XI (1900), 328.
7. "Für die Juden" (*Gesammelte Schriften*, I, 210–215, Philipp Reclam Edition; "Der ewige Jude," *ibid.*, II, 271–302.
8. *Ibid.*, II, 273.

"to be able to say that it is not really worthy of freedom and that it is appointed to be the jailer of the Jews, since the jailers, like the prisoners, may not be allowed to leave the prison." Börne, like Friedländer,[9] is filled with hatred and contempt for "rabbinism." In the new Reform temples he perceives an attempt to reawaken in Jewish worship the mood of reverence and piety driven thence by the crude rabbinic follies *(rabbinische Alfanzereien).*[10] He is also firmly persuaded that in thirty years the Jews will remember the Talmud "only to laugh at it."[11]

Leopold Zunz also reacted to the tragic events of 1819, but in an entirely different fashion. At his initiative, there was formed in Berlin at the end of 1819 by a group of young Jewish intellectuals a *Verein für Cultur und Wissenschaft des Judentums.* The major purposes of the society were to disseminate culture among the masses of the Jewish populace, and to battle against the epidemic of conversion which was again strengthened after the riots—to battle by spreading Jewish knowledge in Jewish intellectual circles, familiarizing them through critical-scholarly lectures and editions with the Jewish past, with the foundations of Jewish culture. To this end the *Verein* planned to establish a scholarly institute. Leading the *Verein* were—besides Zunz—Moses Moser, Ludwig Marcus, and Eduard Gans, who was not only president of the association but also its talented propagandist. Soon a number of popular personalities, among them the young Heinrich Heine, joined the association.

Heine was not only a great poet but also one of the sharpest minds that young Germany possessed, truly a man with the open eye that perceives and discloses what is concealed for many, still hidden in the womb of the future. Highly characteristic, therefore, is his attitude toward historic Jewry and Judaism. He had studied much less Hebrew than Ludwig Börne. His cultured, intellectual mother, an ardent adherent of Rousseau, took care mainly that her beloved son should obtain a European education. He studied in a lyceum which had been made over from a Jesuit school within the walls of a Franciscan monastery and whose teachers were Catholic priests. But the young Heine was powerfully impressed by the tragic fate of the eternally wandering people. The romantic, richly imaginative poet was inspired by the brilliant era of proud Arabic-Spanish Jewry, and also by the stubborn martyr's struggle that German Jewry car-

9. *Ibid.,* I, 213.
10. *Ibid.,* II, 287.
11. *Ibid.,* 292.

ried on for centuries. Not without reason does he state in a letter to Moser that he is a "Jewish poet."[12] When, in 1819, he witnessed with his own eyes in Hamburg the shameful scenes of riots and pogroms, he decided to express his "great Jewish pain," his wrath against Christianity, and produced in 1820–1821 his tragedy *Almansor*.

As a work of art *Almansor* is still quite weak; only in the lovely, image-filled language does one sense the future master. The poet himself notes in his letter to the publisher that he produced his work for religious-polemic reasons, and that he deals in it, despite the medieval dress, with painful contemporary questions. The Moslems, the Moors of the fifteenth century who are compelled by the Spaniards to adopt the Catholic faith in Heine's tragedy—these represent the Jews in Christian society; and in the stormy, emotive speeches of the aged Hassan, the young poet pours out his own wrath. "Do not go to Aly's castle," Hassan cries to the young Alamansor:

> Flieh jenes Haus, wo neuer Glaube keimt.
> Dort zieht man dir mit süssen Zangentönen
> Aus tiefer Brust hervor das alte Herz
> Und legt dir eine Schlang' dafür hinein . . .
> Dorten vertauscht man dir den alten Namen
> Und gibt dir einen neu'n, damit dein Engel,
> Wenn er dich warnend ruft beim alten Namen
> Vergeblich rufe.[13]

Even then the twenty-two-year-old Heine was considerably more far-seeing than many of his generation. Typical in this respect is his work *Über Polen*, composed in the fall of 1822 after he had spent several months at the estate of his friend Graf Eugen von Breza in Gnesen in the duchy of Posen. Heine travelled through the entire region of Posen, also passed a short time in Russian Poland, and thereby had his first opportunity to become familiar with the Polish Jews, with the economic role they played in the land and with their way of life. "The external appearance of the Polish Jew," he writes, "is frightful. I shudder when I remember how near Mezhirech I saw for the first time a Polish village mainly inhabited by Jews."

In this connection Heine relates how in "former times the Polish Jews were, as far as culture and intellectual development

12. *Briefe an Moses Moser*, 1862, 6.
13. H. Heine's *Sämtliche Werke*, II, 561–62.

are concerned, far superior to the Polish nobleman, who was only competent in the crude craft of warfare and still lacked French polish." In later generations, however, the Jews of Poland declined culturally. "Their intellectual world sank ever more deeply into non-vivifying superstition, which the subtlest scholasticism set in the most wondrous forms." Heine adds:

Nevertheless, despite the barbaric fur cap that covers his head and the even more barbaric ideas with which his head is filled to overflowing, I regard the Polish Jew as far superior to certain German Jews who wear a broad-brimmed hat on their heads and carry Jean Paul[14] in their heads. In his strict isolation the Jew of Poland bears a unitary, integral character . . . The Polish Jew, with his dirty fur coat, with his beard populated by insects, with his garlic smell and corrupted language, is still dearer to me than others with all their officially certified elegance.[15]

With caustic irony Heine speaks of the Reformers, of these chiropodists, or "removers of corns from the feet," through whose "clumsiness and spidery bandages of reason" the people of Israel must bleed to death:

We no longer now have the strength to wear long beards, to fast, to hate, and—out of hatred—to endure. This is the motive of our reform. Those who have obtained their education and enlightenment through comedians or hypocrites wish to provide Judaism with new decorations and cultures, and desire that the theater-prompter should, in place of a beard, wear a white, turned-over collar. They wish to pour the Atlantic ocean into an artificial pool of papier-mâché . . . Others would have a little evangelistic Christian sect under a Jewish firm-name.

When, in 1821, Heine left the University of Göttingen and moved to Berlin, he made friends with the founders of the *Verein für Cultur und Wissenschaft des Judentums,* and in 1822 became a member of the society. He devoted himself to cultural work with great enthusiasm. He read historical lectures before Jewish young people and immersed himself in studies of Jewish history in order to write a work that might express, as he himself indicates in his letter to his dear friend Moses Moser,[16] the "tragic pain of Jews." Heine intended to write this work especially for the scholarly journal which the *Verein* established. The pro-

14. Johann Paul Richter (1763–1825), a well-known German writer.
15. *Sämtliche Werke,* II, 190–193.
16. *Briefe von Heinrich Heine an seinem Freund Moses Moser,* 1862, 11.

jected "Jewish Scientific Institute" belonged to the *Verein's* "high-flyingly grandiloquent but unattainable ideals" of which Heine speaks in his well-known *Denkwort*.[17] The only thing that the *Verein* managed to accomplish in the field of scholarship was the *Zeitschrift für die Wissenschaft des Judentums*, which appeared under the editorship of Leopold Zunz.

We noted earlier that in his youth Zunz remained loyal to the motto of the *Aufklärer* of the eighteenth century; he firmly believed that all troubles derive from ignorance and that, as soon as society is illuminated by the rays of knowledge, truth and justice will prevail over the whole world. In a private letter[18] he wrote in 1823: "To create for Jewry the condition and honor that it deserves and gradually to awaken and to unite the better powers of the Jewish people—this can take place only with the aid of scholarship or scientific knowledge, at whose height our journal must rigorously maintain itself."

The journal that was projected in 1821 was to appear in irregular issues; the first was published in March, 1822. The editorial "Über den Begriff einer Wissenschaft des Judentums" by Immanuel Wolf shows best how right Heine was when he complained that, from the largest part of the *Zeitschrift*, one can have no pleasure because of the "careless, untidy form." He therefore begs the editor "to force upon the contributors the culture of style because, without this, other culture cannot be promoted." The author of the editorial was an ardent Hegelian and proceeds from the well-known principle of Hegel that all events are only manifestations of the "dynamic and developing spirit, and it is just the gradual unfolding of the living spirit that constitutes the instructive content of world history."[19]

In a diffuse style that is difficult to digest, the writer attempts to disclose the intellectual content, "the idea of Judaism" in world history. He concludes that this idea is the concept of absolute unity that rules the universe, "the living unity of all beings in eternity" that is expressed in the word Yahweh.[20] The bearer of this revealed "divine, living, spiritual unity" in the actual physical world is the Jewish people. Through it the Jewish people, as guardian of the revealed divine idea, became the people of priests—"a people of God"—and its historic task became "to develop this idea ever further and to raise it to the

17. After the death of Ludwig Marcus.
18. The letter is quoted in *MGWJ*, 1922, 90.
19. *Zeitschrift*, p. 15.
20. *Ibid.*, 3.

universal,"[21] despite all hindrances and obstacles. In this way, the author notes, Judaism appeared "in the greatest part of world history as an important and influential moment in the development of the human spirit."[22] Such a significant factor in world history must be *scientifically* investigated. This, the author concludes, has not been done until now either by Jewish or Christian scholars, the latter of whom have treated Judaism either merely as an aid in the historical investigation of Christian theology or with the definite purpose of fighting against it and refuting it. The founders of the *Zeitschrift,* however, proceed from a completely different view. They intend to explore Judaism in all its details; they wish to create a "science of Judaism," a science that "treats its object *in and for itself,* for its own sake, not for any special purpose but out of a definite view."[23]

The author later repeats that science is "self-sufficient," i.e., has its own intrinsic value, and therefore does not need "to serve any use beyond itself." Nevertheless, he deems it necessary at the end to stress that "scientific knowledge of Jewry must, however, decide the worth or lack of worth of the Jews, their capacity or incapacity *to be considered like other citizens and to be made equal to them.*"[24]

Hence, *die Wissenschaft des Judentums* must serve as approval or authorization for equal rights.

This motif also resounds in the aged Lazarus Bendavid's essay *Über den Glauben der Juden an einen künftigen Messias* (On the Belief of the Jews in a Future Messiah). Lazarus (Eleazar) Bendavid belonged to the earlier generation, that of the Meassefim. Born in 1762 in Berlin, he studied mathematics and philosophy along with Hebrew subjects while quite young. As a convinced Kantian, he endeavored to popularize Kant's philosophy and ethics in lectures and writings. He also acquired a reputation for himself as a competent mathematician, and in this connection devoted himself considerably to pedagogical questions. For many years he was the head of the Jewish model school "Hinnuch Ne'arim" *(Jüdische Freyschule).* When, after Mendelssohn's death, the movement of conversion was intensified in the wealthy and intellectual Jewish circles of Berlin, Bendavid published (in 1793) a brochure entitled *Etwas zur Charakteristik der Juden,* in which he comes forth as a definite opponent of Jewish ritual. As a

21. *Ibid.,* 4.
22. *Ibid.,* 14.
23. *Ibid.,* 18.
24. *Ibid.,* 23 (italicized by Zinberg).

typical *Aufklärer* of Friedländer's generation, Bendavid was firmly persuaded that all the positive commandments must be abolished, for their usefulness cannot be demonstrated by common sense. Fighting against the epidemic of conversion is possible only through religious reform, through ceasing to confuse obsolete religious customs with the pure morality of the Mosaic Torah, which is, according to the author's firm conviction, in closest affinity with the ethics of Immanuel Kant.[25]

In the above-mentioned essay, which Bendavid published in the *Zeitschrift* (p. 297-330), he endeavors to demonstrate that belief in the advent of the Messiah in no way belongs to the basic principles of the Jewish religion. This belief, Bendavid asserts, is only an alien growth which the "Kabbalists" planted in Judaism in later times. Highly typical is the closing sentence of the essay: "No person can therefore take it amiss of the Jew that he perceives his Messiah in the fact that good princes grant him equal rights with all the other citizens and allow him to hope that, when he fulfills all his civic duties, he will also obtain civic rights."[26]

The other article which Bendavid published in the *Zeitschrift* "Über geschriebenes und mündliches Gesetz"[27] (On Written and Oral Law) belongs to the realm of Bible criticism. The author attempts to demonstrate with great erudition that the text of the Pentateuch is the product of a considerably later era than the generation of Moses.

Except for Bendavid and David Friedländer,[28] only men of the younger generation contributed to the *Zeitschrift*. The twenty-three-year old Eduard Gans, who was already then renowned for his keenness in the realm of jurisprudence, published several works in it. The most important of them are "Gesetzgebung über Juden in Rom, nach den Quellen des römischen Rechts (Legislation Concerning Jews in Rome, according to the Sources of Roman Law) and "Grundlinien des mosäisch-talmudischen Eherechts (Basic Principles of the Mosaic-Talmudic Law of Marriage).[29] The latter work later formed a chapter in Gan's four-volume major work *Das Erbrecht in welt-*

25. It ought to be noted in this connection that Bendavid himself, as an idealist and a man of purely ethical character, lived all his life in poverty and proudly overcame the temptation to obtain a professorial post through baptism.
26. *Zeitschrift*, 225.
27. *Ibid.*, 472–500.
28. His "Briefe über das Lesen der heilegen Schriften," published in the *Zeitschrift*, also had a very slight significance for that time.
29. *Ibid.*, 419–471.

geschichtlicher Entwicklung (The Right of Inheritance in World-Historical Development).

Of no lesser significance were the works which its editor, Leopold Zunz, published in the *Zeitschrift*. Zunz was the first in the field of scientific Jewish scholarship who noted[30] the importance of statistics for social-historical investigations. Literally epoch-making, however, was his scholarly study of Rashi ("Salomon ben Isaac, genannt Rashi," *ibid.*, 277–384).[31] With enormous scholarship Zunz managed to illuminate one of the obscurest but also most interesting moments in the cultural history of Franco-German Jewry. From scanty material scattered among hundreds of books, he erected a complete structure, provided a more or less substantive portrait of the great Parshandatha, or commentator, and his environment. He leads us into Rashi's library and tells us the sources from which the great master drew the material required for his works which had such an enormous influence on the culture of the people. To be sure, from the contemporary point of view, Zunz's monograph is certainly not free of defects, both in regard to methodology as well as crudeness of structure. It must, however, be remembered that this was the first attempt, a pioneering work which became the cornerstone of literary-historical investigation in the field of Jewish scholarship.

Heinrich Heine did not complete the long article that he projected for the *Zeitschrift*. The poet in him overcame the scholar. He decided to disclose to the world the "tragic pain of the Jew" not in arid historical documents, but in living, artistic images. The youthful Heine was a romantic poet, but a romantic poet of Jewish stock. The poets of the romantic school are distinguished by their nationalist mood. Not the cosmopolitan, the rationalist of the eighteenth century with his enthusiasm for the classical world of antiquity, dominates the world-view of the romantic poet, but the emotional man of the people who sets feeling, form-filled imagination, above "reason" and is in love with the shadows of the Middle Ages, with its gothic churches reaching to the heavens, its marvelous legends and wondrous tales. The young Heine was also in love with the medieval world of legends, because, as he himself puts it, "it is the land of poetry."[32] However, he wishes to celebrate the *Jewish* Middle

30. In his article "Grundlinien zu einer künftigen Statistik der Juden," 523–532.
31. Thanks to Samson Bloch's Hebrew translation (*Toledot Rashi*, 1840) Zunz's monograph became very popular among the Galician and Russian *maskilim*.
32. *Elementargeister*, 307.

Ages with their "tragic pain." He is impressed not only by the proud Jews of Spain in the Middle Ages but also by the bowed German Jew, marked by the yellow badge, with his stubborn, passive battle, his incessant, centuries-long wandering over the Via Dolorosa, the martyr's way of suffering and distress.

Heine cannot forgive David Friedländer his hatred and contempt for the rabbis.[33] "A partiality for rigorous and strict rabbinism," he writes, "has already lain in me for many years as a result of historical inquiries."[34] And a rabbi, a medieval rabbi of the fifteenth century, was to be the hero of Heine's novel, *Der Rabbi von Bacharach (The Rabbi of Bacharach)*, projected in several parts. With great energy and diligence Heine collected the historical material required for his novel,[35] in which not only German Jewry but also representatives of Spanish Jewry were to be portrayed. "The spirit of Jewish history reveals itself to me ever more," writes Heine.[36] And the more he immersed himself in the melancholy historical chronicles, the stronger grew the poet's indignation at militant Christianity and its leaders who persecuted the defenseless Jews with such barbaric hatred. Heine is not content with his mocking, sarcastic poem "Donna Clara."[37] He also wrote at that time the wrathful stanzas in *Almansor* in which the hero of his youthful tragedy wanders in Cordova among the rooms of the former Islamic mosque which the Christians have transformed into a Catholic monastery:

> Auf den Stufen, wo die Gläubigen
> Das Prophetenwort gesungen
> Zeigen jetzt die Glatzenpfäfflein
> Ihre Messe fades Wunder.

Later the proud Almansor dreams of standing again among the rooms of the desecrated mosque and seeing how the enormous pillars of the temple no longer wish to endure the shame:

> Und sie brechen wild zusammen
> Es erbleichen Volk und Priester,
> Krachen stürzt herab die Kuppel
> Und die Christengötter wimmern.

33. *Über Polen*, 191.
34. *Briefe an Moses Moser*, 1862, 51.
35. *Ibid.*, 99–101.
36. *Ibid.*, 99.
37. On the autobiographical motif in this poem, see his letter to Moser, 53.

With bitterness the poet turns to "Edom," the symbol of the Christian peoples:

> Ein Jahrtausend schon und länger
> Dulden wir uns brüderlich;
> Du—du duldest dass ich atme;
> Dass du rasest, dulde ich.
>
> Manchmal nur, in dunklen Zeiten
> Ward dir wunderlich zu Mut
> Und die liebefrommen Tätzchen
> Färbtest du mit meinem Blut.
>
> Jetzt wird unsre Freundschaft fester,
> Und noch täglich nimmt sie zu;
> Denn ich selbst begann zu rasen
> Und ich werde fast wie du.

Heine wrote his novel with vast enthusiasm and love. To Moser he wrote: "I carry the whole work in my breast with the greatest love. It is created exclusively out of love and not out of desire for fame. And precisely because it comes out of love, it will be an immortal book, an eternal candelabrum in God's temple, not a theater-lamp which quickly flickers out." He notes[38] that the novel will be a large, thick book, and that approximately a third of it is already finished.

The feelings that the poet lived through when he wrote his novel were poured out in the well-known poem which was to adorn the copy of *The Rabbi of Bacharach* which the poet would send to his dear friend Moser, the "Epilog von Nathan der Weise," the "correct, luxury-edition of a real man,"[39] as he is called by Heine:

> Brich aus in lauten Klagen,
> Du düstres Martyrerlied,
> Das ich so lang getragen
> Im flammenstillen Gemüt!
>
> Es dringt in allen Ohren,
> Und durch die Ohren ins Herz;
> Ich habe gewaltig beschworen
> Den tausendjähringen Schmerz.

---

38. In his letter to Moser of October 25, 1829.
39. *Ibid.*

Es weinen die Grossen und Kleinen,
Sogar die kalten Herr'n
Die Frauen und Blumen weinen,
Es weinen am Himmel die Stern.

Und alle die Tränen fliessen
Nach Süden im stillen Verein,
Sie fliessen und ergiessen
Sich all in den Jordan hinein

It is this "thousand-year pain" that cries out of the very first pages of Heine's novel, in which the rabbi of Bacharach is compelled to flee on Passover night from a blood-libel and, waiting at the gates of a strange city, turns to his wife, the wondrously beautiful Sarah, and says "How badly protected is Israel! False friends guard his gates from without, and his guardians within are folly and fear." And when the life-loving Spaniard of Abravenel's stock, enchanted by Sarah's beauty, proposes to be her knight and to carry her colors, the beautiful Sarah replies:

Noble lord! If you would be my knight, you will have to battle against whole peoples, and in this battle one can win very little gratitude and honor. And if you would also carry my colors, you would have to sew a yellow badge on your cloak or wrap yourself in a blue-colored scarf; for these are my colors, the colors of my house, that which is called the house of Israel and is very miserable and ridiculed in the streets . . .

Heine's novel, however, was not fated to appear in the world. In his letters to Moser, the poet and novelist always asks how things are going with the *Verein* and wonders why his friend writes him nothing of it.[40] Moser's silence is quite easy to explain. At the time that Heine was writing his novel, the long death-agony of the *Verein* began. Reaction in the Prussian lands continued to grow. The hopes for the grant of civic rights which the Jewish bourgeois and intellectuals carried about were destroyed by reality in the cruelest fashion. The Prussian government, led by its deeply pious king, through whose initiative there was established in Berlin the "Society for the Promotion of Christianity among the Jews," deliberately refused to ameliorate the civic disabilities of the Prussian Jews, in order "to capture souls" and to force the Jews to obtain human rights

40. *Briefe an Moses Moser*, 1862, 59, 68, 103, 118.

through baptismal water. The representatives of the Jewish youth who founded the *Verein für Cultur und Wissenschaft des Judentums* felt their affinity to the Jewish stock instinctively only but were unable theoretically to establish their connection with Jewry.

In this connection, another factor must be taken into consideration: Hegel, who was the guide and intellectual leader of that era and whose philosophical ideas, as we noted above, dominated the contributors to the *Zeitschrift*, had a certain contempt for the role of Judaism in world history. According to Hegel's *Philosophie der Geschichte*, Judaism is a "vanquished" point of view, because in it the "subject," i.e., man, never comes "to a consciousness of his personality."[41] Christianity is the loveliest flower which the world-spirit *(Weltgeist)* has produced in the realm of religion, for "the nature of God's pure spirit is first revealed to man in the Christian religion."[42]

This, to a certain degree, facilitated the process which the political and social circumstances of that time evoked, namely, the mass conversions, the "epidemic of apostasy" in the bourgeois and intellectual circles of the Jews. This epidemic also appeared in the camp of the *Verein für Cultur und Wissenschaft* and led one member after another to the baptismal font. The leader and chief propagandist of the *Verein*, the talented Eduard Gans, was one of the first who fled the battlefield and obtained a professorial appointment through baptism. Twenty years later, when Gans was already dead, the friend of his youth, Heinrich Heine, could still not speak dispassionately of Gans' "defection." "It is a firmly established obligation," Heine writes in his memorial address after the death of Ludwig Marcus, "that the captain of a ship is the last to leave the vessel that is about to sink; Gans, however, saved himself first."

But neither did Heine himself stand the test. As we know, his parents at first hoped to make of their son a successful businessman, and the young man worked for a time in the banking business of his millionaire uncle in Hamburg. Like most great poets, however, Heine manifested very slight abilities in the realm of business; thereupon, his family decided that the unsuccessful merchant should study jurisprudence. Because the economic situation of his own parents was very difficult, Heine was supported at the university by his millionaire uncle Solomon Heine. This wealthy banker was a very decent person but with

---

41. *Vorlesungen über die Philosophie der Geschichte*, 1840, 240.
42. *Ibid.*, 393, 399ff.

many caprices, and it irritated the proud and sensitive Heine enormously that he had to obtain support from his capricious uncle who looked with contempt on everyone who was unable to "make a living" and to win an honored place in society through his own powers. "I decided," Heine writes to Moser, "to try everything, only not to have to obtain help any more from my uncle."[43] Another time he writes, "I do not under any circumstances wish any further favors from my uncle."[44] Hence he wished to take his doctoral examination as quickly as possible and become a certified lawyer. "I would rather eat my mid-day bread from Themis' scales [of justice] and not from my uncle's charity bowl."[45]

However, Themis' scales were not so easy to obtain. In Germany at that time only jurists of Christian faith could practice law. Heine's family was not at all opposed to his converting to Christianity. As early as 1823 he wrote to Moser that, in connection with his "lawyering," "baptism comes into discussion." No one, Heine writes, was opposed to this, except himself. He even concludes that, should he officially go over to Christianity, he would be able to devote himself more to "the defense of the rights of my miserable brethren." Nevertheless, Heine notes, "I consider it beneath my dignity and a stain upon my honor" to let myself be converted in order to obtain a position in Prussia.[46] I now understand very well, he adds, the words of the Psalms: "Master of the universe, give me my daily bread, so that I may not blaspheme Your name."

Nevertheless, Heine committed that which he considered "beneath his dignity." When he writes of Gans' "defection," he adds that "originality and virtue" seldom live peaceably together and "turn their backs to each other peevishly." Heine also exemplified this. In 1825, before taking his doctoral examination, he let himself be baptized, and soon repented the act.

"I assure you," he writes to Moser, "if the laws permitted stealing silver spoons, I would not have had myself baptized."[47] Two weeks later he confesses to his friend that he regrets his conversion,[48] and adds: "He who torments me most is always myself." "I am glad," he writes further, "that old Friedländer and Bendavid are already aged and will soon die. Thus, we are

43. *Briefe an Moses Moser,* 1862, 21, 29–30.
44. *Ibid.,* 101.
45. *Ibid.,* 79.
46. *Ibid.,* 37–38.
47. *Ibid.,* 155.
48. *Ibid.,* 163 and 177.

at least certain of them, and men will not be able to say of our time that not a single truly decent person was to be found among us."[49] After his conversion he visited the temple in Hamburg on the Sabbath and tells Moser that he listened there with great pleasure and enjoyment to Dr. Salomon's sermon against the converted Jews "who abandoned the faith of their fathers only in the hope of possibly obtaining a position thereby."[50]

Heine's feeling of degradation because he had also attempted "to obtain something, to haggle something through baptism"[51] embittered him even more against reactionary Prussia and filled him with animosity and wrath toward the Christian church. "My love for human equality, my hatred for the clergy," he writes to Moser,[52] "has never been as strong as it is now." Upon reading the memoirs of the well-known Russian traveler V.M. Golovnin, in which the life and customs of the then still very little known Japanese are portrayed, Heine exclaims enthusiastically: "Nothing in the world is so repugnant to the Japanese as Christianity; I would like to be a Japanese. Nothing is so hated by them as the cross; I wish to be a Japanese."[53] And, filled with resentment and regret, he hurls these wrathful verses at himself:

> Und du bist zum Kreuz gekrochen
> Zu dem Kreuz das du verachtest,
> Das du noch vor wenig Wochen
> In den Staub zu treten dachtest!
> —————————
> Gestern noch ein Held gewesen,
> Ist man heute schon ein Schurke.

After his conversion Heine continued to work on his *Rabbi of Bacharach*. Soon after his baptism he writes (July 1, 1825) to Moser: "In the meantime it goes very slowly with *The Rabbi*. Every line must be fought for. Nevertheless, I continue to work, filled with the consciousness that only I can write such a book and that it is a useful, God-pleasing undertaking." "I hope at the end of this year," he writes further, "to be finished with *The Rabbi*. It will be such a book as will be called a *source* by the Zunzes of all

49. *Ibid.*, 178.
50. *Ibid.*, 155.
51. *Ibid.*, 177.
52. *Ibid.*, 206.
53. *Ibid.*, 228.

centuries." "If I only obtained leisure to finish writing *The Rabbi,*" he writes half a year later. And on February 14, 1826, he reports from Hamburg, "I also wish to complete *The Rabbi* here."[55] He even attempted to weave into the novel his personal experiences of that time. It is not difficult to detect autobiographical features in the young Spaniard Don Isaac of the family Abravanel, whom the poet characterizes with the words: "In his heart a Jew but, from the wantonness of luxury, he let himself be baptized."[56] The rabbi of Bacharach warns the frivolous Spaniard, "Be careful, Don Isaac . . . The water (you know whereof I speak) is your misfortune, and you will perish." Don Isaac regrets his act and, like Heine himself, expresses his compunction in a poem that he sends to the young Jehudah Abravanel, who later gained fame with his *Dialoghi di Amore.*[57]

Nevertheless, *The Rabbi of Bacharach* remained unfinished. As a converted Jew, himself an apostate,[58] Heine did not have the courage to come forth before the Christian world with a work such as *The Rabbi.* He left the uncompleted manuscript in his mother's house, where a great misfortune took place: during a fire the manuscript was burned. The author himself had a copy of only the first three chapters, and sometime later published these as a fragment.

Yet Heine did not forget the statement he had made to his intimate friend Moser that he was a "Jewish poet." He did not forget that, along with the poet of the Bible, he had sworn the oath: "If I forget thee, O Jerusalem, let my right hand forget its cunning!" This, however, already pertains to the later period, and we shall have occasion to speak of it in subsequent chapters.

Along with the moribund *Cultur Verein,* the *Zeitschrift für die Wissenschaft des Judentums* also succumbed. The third number with which the first volume closed, appeared in June, 1823. With this number the existence of the *Zeitschrift* also ended. On May 4, 1824 Zunz wrote to Ehrenberg: "What will become of the *Zeitschrift* no one knows, least of all myself. There is no money, no workers, no articles, no correspondence."[59] Quietly and unnoticed, the *Verein* dissolved. Some of its members were transformed into brand new Christians. Others despairingly lost their courage and came to the conclusion that they "were strug-

---

55. *Ibid.,* 168.
56. *Ibid.,* 228.
57. See our work, Vol. IV, Chapter One.
58. The verses quoted earlier are written under the title "An einen Abtrünnigen."
59. *MGWJ,* 1922, 95.

gling for a long lost thing." Zunz alone remained faithfully at his post. When, decades later, Heine told of the erstwhile *Cultur Verein,* he spoke enthusiastically of the "excellent Zunz:" "A man of speech and action, he created and had an effect where others merely dreamed and despairingly surrendered their efforts."[60] Witnessing the collapse of the *Verein* and the conversion of many of its members, Zunz declared with assurance:

> The only thing that will not be washed away by this deluge and will have an abiding existence is *die Wissenschaft des Judentums* . . . and I confess that my whole consolation and strength is my engagement in this science. All the storms and bitter experiences cannot deflect me from my way. I have done what I considered my duty. Because I saw that I was a solitary voice crying in the wilderness, I ceased to preach, but not because I began to disavow what I had previously preached.[61]

To tell the truth, Zunz, in fact, did not cease to "preach." Indeed, soon after the *Zeitschrift* was silenced, he undertook a work that is recognized as one of the most important foundation-stones of the mighty structure about which he dreamed— *die Wissenschaft des Judentums.* This work is entitled *Die gottesdienstlichen Vorträge der Juden,* and with it Zunz intended, above all, to "preach." We noted in the last chapter of the ninth volume that the Prussian government forbade preaching in German in the synagogues.[62] Zunz, who at that time was enthusiastic about religious reform and himself served for a period as a preacher in Jacobson's Reform temple, decided to "enlighten" the Prussian government and show that the prohibition is contrary to the historical traditions of the Jewish people, since for thousands of years it has been a firmly established custom among Jews that sermons in the vernacular are given during worship. It was this that was to be demonstrated by his major work *Die gottesdienstlichen Vorträge.*

60. *Denkwort an Ludwig Marcus.*
61. Adolf Strodtmann, *H. Heines Leben und Werke,* Vol. II, 1884, 275.
62. The following fact is worth noting: When in the Reform temples the Reformers endeavored to displace the language of the Bible by the language of the country, and the Prussian government proscribed German sermons in the synagogue, the *Hovevei Sefat Ever* made an attempt occasionally to give sermons in Hebrew. Such a sermon was given by a certain Aaron Rosenbach on the Sabbath of the 25th of Nissan, 1821 "in the circle of several friends and admirers of this language in the premises of the *Humanität-Gesellschaft* at Cassel." The lecture, which was given in the rhetorical language of the Meassefim, was so pleasing to the auditors that they begged him to print the sermon and, indeed, in the same year it was published in Roedelsheim under the title *Ruaḥ Da'at Ve-Yirat Adonai.*

Zunz collected material for his book, which first appeared in 1832, with indefatigable diligence for years. During this time a friend of Zunz's youth managed to complete a monumental work that ought rightfully to be considered the true foundation of modern Jewish historiography. This scholar was named Isaac Marcus Jost.

Jost obtained his primary education, along with Zunz, at Wolfenbüttel in the reorganized Jewish model school. Later he studied at Göttingen and Berlin. In Berlin the young man frequently visited Henriette Herz's salon. David Friedländer's rationalist ideas and hatred for "reactionary rabbinism" had a strong influence on the future historian, and throughout his life[63] Jost remained loyal to the ideals of the Berlin Haskalah. While still quite young he undertook to write a multi-volume Jewish history from the time of the Hasmoneans to the modern age. In 1820 the first volume appeared. One of the major tasks Jost set for himself in his work was "eliminating and battling against prevalent errors and prejudices."[64]

Typical of his outlook is the title of his work. His history begins, as we have indicated, from approximately the second century B.C.E., when the kingdom of Israel with its capital city of Samaria had already long been destroyed. Jost himself, indeed, notes several times that "the people of the Israelites had not been in existence for a long time" and that "only Judea still existed."[65] Nevertheless, on the title-page of his work he wrote *Geschichte der Israeliten,*[66] because he recalled very well the contentions of Friedländer in *Sulamith* that the word *Juden* has nationalist overtones. The Jews, Jost insists, existed as a people only for fifteen centuries.[67] Along with the destruction of the Second Temple also occurred the "dissolution of the Jewish nation."[68] Now the bearers of the Torah of Moses represent merely an "extended religious association."[69]

In the introduction Jost promises that his work will hold fast to the principle: "the most scrupulous precision and impartiality."[70] And, indeed, he does endeavor to be impartially objective.

63. Jost was born in Bernburg in 1793 and died in 1860 in Frankfurt-am-Main, where he spent the last twenty-five years of his life as a teacher in the local school known as the Philanthropin.
64. *Kultur-Geschichte,* 1847, VII.
65. *Op. cit.,* Vol. II, 164, 241.
66. *Geschichte der Israeliten seit der Zeit Maccabäer bis auf unsere Tage.*
67. *Ibid.,* Vol. II, 3.
68. *Ibid.,* 237.
69. Jost, *Kultur-Geschichte zur neueren Geschichte der Israeliten,* 1847, 270.
70. Jost, *Geschichte,* Vol. I, XI.

However, beneath this objectivity appears very clearly the arid *Aufklärer* of Friedländer's school with his servile self-depreca-tion before the Christian world. This brings it about that Jost speaks . with extreme contempt of *Josippon* ("nothing but a clumsy piece of work")[71] and terms the colorful *Shevet Yehudah*[72] a "miserable book"[73] that does not even deserve to be men-tioned. On the other hand, he considers, without the slightest historical sense, the legends woven around the birth and life of the founder of the Christian religion as firmly reliable, historical facts. Two to three hundred years after Isaac Troki, the author of *Hizzuk Emunah*,[74] Jost reports as a historic event the story of how Mary fled with her child to Egypt, since it was foretold through a spirit of prophecy that the redeemer would very soon be born in Bethlehem and the cruel Herod therefore com-manded that all children under the age of two be slaughtered.[75] The other legends about Jesus are treated in the same spirit.[76] Again, indeed, for the sake of objective "impartiality," Jost mocks the Talmudic legend about the gnat that bored into the brain of "the wicked Titus,"[77] whom he does not tire of crown-ing with all kinds of praises and laudations ("the stout-hearted Titus," "the noble Titus," etc).

Jost does the same in regard to the Romans in general. They are called the "magnanimous Romans" (Vol. II, 343), "the free-thinking Romans" (*ibid.*, 344). He also stresses that, while the Pharisees and scholars, with their piety and rigorous views formed a "slavish religious mentality," the Romans "liberated the spirit ever more and spread abroad art and science."[78] In general, the Pharisees, as well as their spiritual heirs, the rabbis of the later generations, are despised by Jost no less than by Friedländer, for they (the Pharisees and rabbis) aroused and strengthened separatism and isolation among the "Israelites." They brought about all the troubles that our ancestors had to endure in exile. That all the sufferings of the Jews derived from the "separatism" which the Pharisees preached is in no way doubted by the objective Jost, for he sets forth the fundamental thesis that the situation of the Jews in every country was a direct consequence of the manner in which they conducted themselves

71. *Ibid.*, Vol. II, 237.
72. See our *History*, Vol. V.
73. Jost, *Geschichte*, Vol. II, Supplements, 109.
74. See our *History*, Vol. VI, pp. 105ff.
75. Jost, *op. cit.*, Vol. I, 266, 269, 270.
76. *Ibid.*, 295–300.
77. *Ibid.*, II, Supplements, 101.
78. *Ibid.*, 343.

there.[79] For him it is "crystal clear" that in the Jews themselves "lies the ground of their fate, not outside them."[80] Wherever the Jews did not live isolated and apart and, remaining loyal to their religion, freed themselves from peoplehood i.e., national uniqueness, they were regarded as equals and enjoyed equal civic rights.[81] So it was in Syria, where Jews were "according to their own conviction Syrians,"[82] and in the Persian Empire, where the "majority of the Jews were Persians" of the Mosaic faith, and in other lands where the Jews considered themselves not a people but a "religious association."[83] And if the Jews in Rome had "manifested better will" and endeavored to be loyal and devoted citizens and to occupy themselves "with science and art," then—Jost asserts—the "free-thinking Romans" would certainly not have seen any hindrance in the Jewish faith "to placing the Jews on an equal plane with all and to endowing them with equal civic rights."

It is for this reason that the Zealots, who fought with extreme obstinacy against the Romans and defended the freedom of their fatherland, are so despised by the sedately bourgeois Jost. The Zealots, in his portrayal, were true wretches. They were "absurd seducers of the people," "wild rebels" who "thought only of tyranny" and of the "overthrow of the established order."[84] Here Jost relies blindly on the ancient historian Flavius Josephus and completely forgets what he himself several times notes: that one should rely only with great caution on the author of *The Jewish War*. The leaders of the Zealots, John of Gischala and Simeon ben Giora are portrayed by Jost as bloodthirsty murderers and tyrants who, with "shameless impudence," occupied themselves only with robbery and deception.[85]

Nevertheless, with all its defects, Jost's work has a definite cultural-historical significance as an important pioneering work. Jost assumed the difficult, arduous task of collecting the building material required for Jewish history. In his work he employed new, hitherto little used, or completely unknown sources. He was the first who attempted to utilize the Talmud and Midrashim as historical sources. One must agree completely with Jost himself when he humbly noted in his old age that his

79. *Ibid.*, 344.
80. *Ibid.*, 336.
81. *Ibid.*, 341.
82. *Ibid.*, 294.
83. *Ibid.*, 336–338.
84. *Ibid.*, 2, 3, 21, 137, 138, 145.
85. *Ibid.*, 92, 94, 137, 138, 139, 154, 157ff.

history should be considered "preparation of the material for future historical writing."[86]

However, in the course of the years during which Jost's nine-volume history appeared,[87] important events took place in the realm of Jewish culture and science. These events did not occur in Prussia but in the neighboring Slavic lands. This was a harbinger that in east European Jewry also a new era was beginning. The Berlin Haskalah thereby obtained correction; in the new environment it gradually altered its form and also obtained a new content. Of this in the subsequent chapters.

86. *Kultur-Geschichte*, 1847, VI. See also Jost's article in *Kerem Ḥemed*, IX, 132–135.
87. The last volume appeared in 1828.

CHAPTER TWO

Bikkurei Ha-Ittim;
JEHUDAH MIESIS' *KINAT HA-EMET*

Bikkurei Ha-Ittim and its editors—Jehudah Loeb Jeiteles and the Galician contributors—The *maskilim* as patriots—Their isolated situation—Prestigious *maskilim* and the local "officials"—Jehudah Leib Miesis and his *Kinat Ha-Emet*—Echoes of the past century—Friedländer's and Homberg's approbations—Harbingers of a new world-view.

 N THE previous volume we noted that the young poet Shalom Cohen carried about the idea of reviving the organ of the Berlin Haskalah that had been suspended since 1797. His attempt to accomplish this in Germany itself had very slight success, and the renewed *Ha-Meassef* was silenced in the middle of its third year (in 1811). Cohen, however, did not forget the ideal of his youth, and when, in 1820, he settled in Vienna as a proof-reader and corrector in the well-known press of Anton von Schmid, he decided to make a new attempt: to establish a Hebrew periodical that would serve as a platform for the Berlin Haskalah. The Christian entrepreneur Schmid had a good business in his Hebrew press and, therefore, gladly agreed to the proposal of his capable proof-reader. Vienna itself at that time was actually not much more favorable for a Hebrew journal than Berlin. There also the Jewish bourgeoisie of that age and its intelligentsia were already assimilated to a very considerable degree and no longer required the propaganda of a Hebrew journal. But Vienna had an extensive *Hinterland*. It was the capital city of an empire to which such provinces as Galicia, Bohemia, and Hungary—all with a compact Jewish populace which still lived according to the old, patriarchal fashion—be-

longed. Here was an extensive field for Haskalah propaganda.

In the fall of 1820, under the editorship of Shalom Cohen, the first volume of the annual almanac *Bikkurei Ha-Ittim*[1] appeared. The businessman Anton von Schmid, however, was concerned that the almanac provide the reader with practical information, and *Bikkurei Ha-Ittim* therefore appeared in its first years as a supplement to the "complete" Israelite calendar, *Ittim Mezuma-nim*. On the title-page it is also noted that the supplement is "a useful and instructive business- and entertainment-book for a New Year gift for educated housefathers and housemothers and as a prize-book for industrious youth."[2]

Shalom Cohen did not consider it necessary to inform the reader about the program of the new journal. His highest ideal, after all, as we previously noted, was *Ha-Meassef.* The new organ was conceived not as a *continuation* of *Ha-Meassef;* it was merely to repeat it, to familiarize the Jewish youth of the Austrian provinces with the memorial of the Berlin Haskalah which had already then become very rare.[3] Cohen, therefore, set himself the task of reprinting in the new journal "summaries of the most beautiful essays from *Ha-Meassef.*" And, indeed, at the head of these "summaries" he printed "Naḥal Ha-Besor," which was to be regarded as the program for *Bikkurei Ha-Ittim.*

The editor, indeed, strives to be loyal to the program of "Na-ḥal He-Besor." In the first volumes of *Bikkurei Ha-Ittim* "biographies of great Israelites" were printed in the same crude style and of the same "scientific" quality as in the *Ha-Meassef* of Königsberg. In it, too, were published poems of praise to kings and officials, with the difference that in *Ha-Meassef* Frederick II and Joseph II were celebrated and in *Bikkurei Ha-Ittim,* Franz I. Also in *Bikkurei Ha-Ittim* "moral narratives" and idylls in Hebrew and in German with Hebrew letters were published—all in the style of *Ha-Meassef.*

Nevertheless, as early as in the first years of *Bikkurei Ha-Ittim*

1. The full title was: *Bikkurei Ha-Ittim Hem Peri Tevuah Li-Shenat 5581 Ha-Kollelim Kamah Devarim Neḥmadim Ve-Inyenei Madda Ve-To'elet No'adim Le-Virkat Horim Le-Hovil Shai Li-Veneihem Ha-Shome'im Le-Kolom Le-ma'an Yishma Haḥam Ve-Yosif Lekaḥ.* In later years the title was somewhat abbreviated. On the title-page of the eighth volume we read: *Bikkurei Ha-Ittim, Minḥat Bikkurim Le-Reshit Shenat 5588 Ḥibbur Divrei Haḥamim VeHiddotam Ve-Inyenei Madda Ve-To'elet Le-Da'at Ḥochmah U-Musar, Le-Havin Imrei Vinah.*

2. In later years the German text on the title-page was also abbreviated. It is merely noted: "As a New Year gift for the instruction and entertainment of cultured Israelites." The "business" part falls away, and *Bikkurei Ha-Ittim* appears only as "a useful and instructive book of entertainment."

3. See our *History,* Vol. IX, p. 263. Incidentally, the text there is erroneous. Instead of "the erstwhile admirer of *Meassef,*" it ought to read "the ardent admirer of *Ha-Meassef.*"

—even if contrary to the will of the editor himself—there already appeared moods quite foreign to *Ha-Meassef.* In the poetry section of *Ha-Meassef* the most honored place was occupied by translations of Gessner, Ramler, and other old German poets. In *Bikkurei Ha-Ittim,* however, the favorite poet is Schiller. Schiller's emotive style, the echo of Rousseau's ideas on equality and fraternity and the humanitarian-didactic tendencies heard in many of his lyric and epic poems, won the hearts of the Jewish *maskilim.* Already in the first volume of *Bikkurei Ha-Ittim* are printed three translations of Schiller's: a fragment of "Die Glocke" ("Hatzlaḥat Ha-Bayyit"), a chorale from the "Braut von Messina" and "Die Macht des Gesanges." It is worth noting that all three translations were submitted by Galician *maskilim.* Indeed, it was thanks to the contributors from Galicia that *Bikkurei Ha-Ittim* in its later years managed to liberate itself to a significant degree from *Ha-Meassef's* old-fashioned garments and to obtain its own individuality, its unique style.

To be sure, the managers and editors of *Bikkurei Ha-Ittim* were not Galicians. After Shalom Cohen, who edited only the first two years of the journal, it was edited by the *parnass* of Prague, Moses Landau. Landau acquired a reputation only as a wealthy publisher. He himself was a talentless writer with very weak literary taste. More significant in this respect was the later editor of *Bikkurei Ha-Ittim,* Jehudah Loeb Jeiteles, an erstwhile contributor to *Ha-Meassef.*[4] Jeiteles was a man of extensive knowledge[5] who occupied himself considerably with philology, composed a textbook of the Aramaic language (*Mevo Leshon Aramit,* 1813), and wrote a commentary to several biblical books.

---

4. Born in Prague in 1773, died in Vienna in 1838.

5. Apparently Jeiteles was an ardent adherent of religious reform. In the elegy that he wrote (1829) after the death of the well-known communal leader Israel Jacobson (see our *History,* Vol. IX, pp. 243ff.) he notes especially:

> So you ordained, O Jacob, man of great accomplishment
>   and virtue!
> You saw your brethren perplexed, groping about in the
>   way.
> They would seek prayer without heart and whose meaning
>   they do not understand.
> You wrapped yourself in honor and rescued it from the
>   darkness of night.
>
> (*Bikkurei Ha-Ittim,* 5590)

Along with this the following comment is made: "With the establishment of Jacobson's temple, the ground was laid for the improvement of worship in many of Germany's Israelite communities."

He also composed witty epigrams, fables, satires, and didactic poems.[6] In addition, he was the author of *Sibah Be-Eretz Ha-Hayyim*, a tract against the Frankists of which we spoke in the previous volume.

Only under Jeiteles' editorship did *Bikkurei Ha-Ittim* cease to be merely the echo of *Ha-Meassef*. It still chanted paeans to the Berlin *Ha-Meassef* and asserted that "all the gates of knowledge were opened through *Ha-Meassef*, and in all corners its plants bloom."[7] The admirer of *Ha-Meassef*, however, already obtained its own voice and, in its last years, brought into the Haskalah movement a new ideological tendency of broad scientific and scholarly scope.[8] The new tendencies were introduced mainly by the contributors from Galicia. The Galicians, living under quite different circumstances and in a unique environment, made for the Berlin Haskalah, which they so revered and extolled, a new commentary in which there were seeds of a quite different worldview.

In the previous volume[9] we noted the social and cultural circumstances which contributed to the fact that in certain east Galician centers, especially Brody and Tarnopol, circles of *maskilim* that were not only materially but spiritually connected with Berlin and other important German centers were established. But the spiritual and intellectual milieu in which the Galician *maskilim* in the times of *Bikkurei Ha-Ittim* lived was very different from the environment in which the representatives of the Berlin enlightenment had lived and struggled. The *Aufklärer* of Berlin inhabited a European environment, together with the rising bourgeois industrial strata. They breathed the

6. A collection of his poems, together with a panegyric biography of his father, the physician Jonah Jeiteles, was published by Jehudah Jeiteles under the title *Benei Ha-Ne'urim* (1821). The second part of the collection remained in manuscript (see *Bikkurei Ha-Ittim*, VIII, 267).

7. *Bikkurei Ha-Ittim*, VIII, 155–156. However, the following point is worth noting in this connection: *Bikkurei Ha-Ittim* also considers it necessary to stress that the *Ha-Meassef* of recent years has strayed from the right way and groped about on false paths. In *Sibah Be-Eretz Ha-Hayyim*, a dialogue between Naftali Herz Wessely and the Hebrew language (published in the sixth volume, 5586) Hebrew complains of the Meassefim that they "have turned away quickly from the way that you marked out for them . . . They also were among the troublers, destroyers and wreckers from whose midst they came. Diligent seekers of the good and of wisdom ceased completely, and were followed by singers of passionate love songs and lovers of the fruit of the vine," etc. (7–8).

8. *Mivbar Ha-Meassef* was printed in *Bikkurei Ha-Ittim* only until the eighth volume, in which extracts from the fourth year's run of *Ha-Meassef* (5558) are presented. In the later volumes of *Bikkurei Ha-Ittim* only new material is given.

9. Vol. IX, last chapter.

humanitarian, enlightening ideals imported from France into the salons of Berlin. The drive for equality, for living "no worse than anyone else," strengthened the desire to be liberated as quickly as possible from the "legacy of exile," from "superstition" and medieval "prejudices." And the struggle between the older generation and the younger, enlightened one, between the "fathers" and "sons," ended with the total victory of the latter. The new generation triumphantly stormed the old-fashioned bastion of the fathers, and the old forfeited one position after another.

Quite different was the situation in Galicia. From an industrial point of view, Galicia was the most backward province in all of Austria. It was not the European world that surrounded the circles of the *maskilim* in Galicia, but the compact, old-fashioned Jewish masses. Not the ideas of the French enlighteners, not the materialist philosophy of the Encyclopedists, dominated their minds, but the world of ideas of the youthful Hasidic movement which conquered one center after another on its triumphal march. The mercantile bourgeois community of Brody long opposed the propaganda of Hasidism. In the 1780's *Toledot Yaakov Yosef* and other Hasidic works were publicly burned there. By the beginning of the nineteenth century, however, and especially in its second decade, Brody was also a Hasidic center. The Galician *maskilim* at that time found themselves in a situation similar to that of the first Hasidim in the Lithuanian centers forty years earlier: tiny circles surrounded by a hostile environment.

The inimical attitude toward enlightenment and European education on the part of the Hasidim[10] was especially intensified in Galicia by unique local circumstances: people there still remembered vividly how, and through what means, Herz Homberg and his collaborators had attempted to "enlighten" the Jewish masses. The "normal schools" were closed in 1806, but the hatred of the people for the "enlighteners" remained long afterward. In addition, one must take account of the following point: in Prussia in Mendelssohn's times the occupant of the throne was the "philosopher" Frederick II, who considered himself a genuine freethinker and gloried in the fact that he permitted critical discussion of religious questions. At the end of the second decade of the nineteenth century in Roman Catholic Austria and in all of Europe, however, it was Metternich's leaden reaction that prevailed. To be sure, the *maskilim* in

10. See Vol. IX. pp. 234ff.

Austria at that time also strongly endeavored to display their patriotism and praised the "enlightening government" to the skies. As illustration, it suffices to give several quotations from *Bikkurei Ha-Ittim,* taken from articles written by the editor himself, Jehudah Loeb Jeiteles.

Jeiteles ends his rather long essay on the education of children entitled "Devarim Nechoḥim"[11] with the following conclusion:

Understand, you men of faith, that by giving your children a normal education you will fulfill the will both of the Father in heaven and of your exalted king. The gracious will of the king and his high officials is well known to everyone: all their goal and desire is that we should improve our way through normal and proper education of children. Thereby you will attract the graciousness of the government, because it will perceive that your good will is to improve that which previous generations had corrupted. And the surrounding peoples will say with praise: An understanding people are the Jews, and they are intensely devoted to the peace of the realm.

When the well-known American Jewish communal leader Mordecai Manuel Noah came foreward in 1825 with his project for establishing a separate Jewish state in North America and addressed Jewry in a special proclamation on the subject, Jeiteles published this proclamation in *Bikkurei Ha-Ittim.* However, he deemed it necessary to accompany it with sarcastic gibes and with comments strongly colored with patriotism. "Does this community leader not know," he asks,

that his summons will find a response only among a few people? The Jews now live under the protection of gracious and merciful kings who spread their grace over us, along with all other peoples, alike. And who will be so foolish as to abandon the land of his parents, his property and possessions, and seek a refuge in a strange land?

"My brethren, children of Israel," Jeiteles exclaims with feeling,

we shall live in our dear land. We shall serve our king in reverence. We shall do his will and fulfill all his commands in the future, as until now, with our whole heart. We shall be in a faithful bond with the people amongst whom we live, and in their light will we march on the path of enlightenment. We shall be good and useful according to the wish of our king, and it will be well for us and the whole house of Israel now and evermore.[12]

11. The article was composed by Jeiteles as early as 1816, but he published it only thirteen years later (*Bikkurei Ha-Ittim,* 5589, 133–149).
12. *Bikkurei Ha-Ittim,* 5587, 49.

The Attitude of the Government toward the Maskilim

These passages are highly characteristic not only for the Galician *maskilim* but, as we shall see further on, for the Russians as well. Slight in numbers and in power, surrounded by a hostile environment, the *maskilim* saw their only protection in the external power, the government. They did not wish, and perhaps also were not able, to realize that the government regarded the "superstition" and "stubborn wildness" of the Jewish masses with hatred and contempt for quite different reasons than they, the *maskilim*. The government was not a promoter of culture and rationalist enlightenment, but a pietistic zealot of Catholic Christianity and a major representative of certain feudal class interests. The *maskilim*—in any case, a considerable segment of them, who belonged mostly to the wealthier mercantile circles —refused, in their patriotic zeal, to recognize the true causes of the catastrophic economic situation in which the Jewish masses in Galicia found themselves, and therefore asserted that these "enjoyed" the favors of the "gracious and merciful kings."

Metternich's government, however, was a quite unsteady support for the enlightened *maskilim*. It did, indeed, regard the "superstition" and "obscurantism" of the Jewish masses contemptuously, but it also looked with suspicion on the rationalist-minded "enlighteners." The leaders of orthodoxy and the Hasidim understood very well how to exploit this in their battle against the *maskilim*. The latter did find a certain support—but this only the wealthy ones—among the local officials. The government functionaries in the Galician centers—Brody, Lemberg, etc.—were mostly not from the local populace but sent there from Vienna and other German provinces. As persons educated in the German language and culture, they felt quite alien in Polish-speaking society. Hence, it is not surprising that they would find themselves in rather friendly relationships with the enlightened Jewish merchants and men of wealth, who had been raised on the Berlin Haskalah, read the German classics with enchantment, regarded the language of their "fatherland" as very precious, and proclaimed it their mother tongue. The fact that wealthy *maskilim* were respected by the government, by the local officials, had a certain influence on the development of Haskalah literature in Galicia.

We observed in the previous volume[13] that of all the anti-Hasidic polemic works which the Galician *maskilim* composed, only the satire of the affluent merchant and maecenas Joseph Perl was actually printed. He alone had the courage to issue forth publicly, even if under a pseudonym, with his *Megalleh*

13. See our *History,* Vol. IX, pp. 240ff.

Temirin, for the Hasidim were afraid to attack him—the rich merchant who was so influential among the local officials.[14] The same phenomena was repeated several years later in the case of the wealthy *maskil* of Lemberg, Jehudah Leib Miesis.

Born into a very rich and prestigious family in 1798,[15] Jehudah Leib Miesis, while still quite young, became an ardent battler for Haskalah and a bitter opponent of the Hasidim and the orthodox Jews. He would generously support every *yeshivah* student who was eager to obtain knowledge, and thanks to his material assistance, numerous young people from Galicia had the opportunity to complete their studies in Austrian and German universities.[16] Along with this, he was also indefatigable in his battle against "fanaticism and superstition." We shall have opportunity further on to note the contempt with which the eighteen-year-old Miesis issued forth against the aged rabbi of Lemberg, Jacob Ornstein. Miesis was a battler by nature with a great deal of temperament and a huge thirst for knowledge, but with rather mediocre capacities. He read much and was familiar with the medieval Hebrew philosophical works as well as with modern German scientific literature—but all this superficially and without proper criticism. With his anti-historical, narrowly rationalist world-view, he still stood with both feet in the eighteenth century. He was an enormous admirer of the aged David Friedländer and, indeed, did not diverge from the latter's universe of ideas by a hair's breadth.

We noted in the previous volume[17] that the twenty-two-year-old Miesis published David Caro's polemic work *Techunat Ha-Rabbanim*, along with his notes. This, however, could not assuage his lust for battle. Filled with the militant spirit of youth, he undertook to battle on his own account for the ideals of Haskalah that were so dear to him and to storm the fortress of Hasidism and "superstition" that he so despised. It was this that he intended with his *Kinat Ha-Emet* (Vienna, 1828) which made a rather strong impression in the orthodox circles as well as in those of the *maskilim*.

14. On how Joseph Perl used to exploit his influence among the officials, see Vol. IX, p. 240.
15. Most of Miesis' biographers do not note the year of his birth. M. Weissberg and others merely indicate that he was born "at the end of the eighteenth century." According to the report of Max Erik (*Etiudn Tsu Der Geshikhte Fun Der Haskole*, 1935), there is in the White Russian state library in Minsk a copy of *Kinat Ha-Emet* on which the physician of Rymanow, Samuel of Slavuta, noted a month after Miesis' death (1831) that the author died in Lemberg at the age of thirty-three.
16. See M. Letteris, *Zikkaron Ba-Sefer*, 115.
17. P. 259.

Jehudah Leib Miesis

Like all battlers for Haskalah, Miesis was an ardent admirer of Maimonides[18] and therefore wrote his work in the form of three discussions "in the world of souls" between Maimonides and his fervent disciple Solomon Chelm, the author of *Mirkevet Ha-Mishneh*.[19] Chelm merely raises questions; the chief speaker is Maimonides. In his mouth the author places his own favorite ideas.

Miesis does not tire of repeating how every *maskil* is obliged to enlighten his ignorant brethren, to disclose to them the truth in plain, clear words, so that they need not grope in darkness.[20] First of all, a battle must be carried on against the barbaric belief in spirits, demons, and magic, from which all troubles derive.[21] This benighted superstition, Miesis complains, has become especially strengthened among the people in recent times with the spread of the "sect of the *Beshtnim*," of these "wicked men and doers of evil," these "schemers and workers of iniquity," who, under the mask of piety, commit the vilest deeds.[22] The founder of this sect, Miesis asserts, was a tremendous ignoramus, did not understand a single sentence either in the Talmud or in the Bible, but his heart was filled with falsehood; in addition, he was a terrible pursuer of honor and glory.[23] This sinful man was soon joined by false, base people who also obtained a desire to play a prominent role and, like him (the Baal Shem Tov), to rob and plunder the people through swindlery. But they were not content with this and literally flooded the world with their writings, which are filled to overflowing with such follies and absurdities that they disgust every sensible man.[24]

But whence did the foolish belief in magic spirits and demons enter among Jews? Miesis poses this question several times, and his answer is one ready-made from the rationalist eighteenth century: Men of deceit and swindlery arose who had a bit of knowledge in the "science of nature" and, seeing how foolish and ignorant the multitude was, they understood how to exploit their knowledge to lead the multitude by the nose with their false tricks (*ibid.*, 48). This was still not sufficient for these swindlers. In addition, they composed numerous books filled with

18. See *Kinat Ha-Emet*, 14: "There has never been in Israel a man who did so much good for them in the matter of enlightening their understanding as Maimonides. For only he aroused them from the slumber of their folly and awakened their minds."
19. See our *History*, Vol. VI, 241ff.
20. *Kinat Ha-Emet*, 6, 9, 18ff (we quote according to the first edition, 1828).
21. *Kinat Ha-Emet*, 6, 9, 28.
22. *Ibid.*, 7.
23. *Ibid.*, 22–23.
24. *Ibid.*, 26–27.

incantations, trickeries, and deceits. These books, written by swindlers and frauds, fell into the hands of fools and simpletons who believed every word they contained, perceived stupendous mysteries and profound wisdoms in them, and themselves began to believe that they also could perform great feats through incantations. So they, for their part, added all kinds of follies. Thus, "swindlery, lying, and foolishness spread in Israel."[25] Many of the superstitious follies, Miesis stresses, were also adopted by the Jews from the peoples among whom they dwelt, for, he explains, the "class of priests and clergy" of every people always endeavored to entice the people into crooked ways and to blind their understanding, just as the deceivers used to do among us Jews.[26]

For all the superstitions, all the idolatries among various peoples, we are indebted to the "swindlerish priests." They ordained all kinds of precepts and laws, and pretended that thereby they were fulfilling the commandment of the gods. It was the priestly class who fabricated all this with their deceit, in order to blind the eyes of the rabble, to enlarge their own fortune, and to obtain great honor and glory.[27]

Miesis dislikes speaking in veiled fashion, through hints and allusions; he expresses himself openly and clearly. He himself notes that one can come foreward with the argument: Is it not the case that, in some of the statements of the teachers of the Talmud, it is definitely noticeable that they also believed in demons? To this he replies: "We are not obliged to listen to their words in these matters." Furthermore, he adds, not all who passed among us as scholars and great men were in fact authentic scholars. Many of them spent all their years only over the Talmud. Of all other sciences and wisdoms they had not the slightest knowledge, especially the natural sciences, with whose aid alone one may have some notion of the laws of the world.[28]

Miesis issues forth openly and sharply against the slogans to which the rabbis and leaders of the generation clung so tenaciously: "The custom of Israel is Torah," or "A custom is stronger than a law." He does not tire of pointing out that many Jewish usages are "contrary to common sense and the ways of the world" and are truly a plague for the Jewish people. There is, he asserts, no other nation that carries such mountains of

25. *Ibid.*, 51–52.
26. *Ibid.*, 53–54.
27. *Ibid.*, 33–34.
28. *Ibid.*, 46–57.

customs, ordinances, and all kinds of prohibitions as we Jews. This reaches such a point that every sensible man among us is literally disgusted by these ways which the Jewish people now follow. And who does not know that the hatred for Jews that exists among some of the peoples is chiefly because of the barbaric customs through which we become a mockery and object of laughter?[29]

Our Torah, Miesis emphasizes, is built "on the foundations of reason." The commandments of the Torah were created in wisdom. In time, however, to the essential customs without which no community can get along, there were admixed, by foolish and evil men, barbaric practices and noxious commandments whose purpose not everyone can comprehend.[30] Miesis endeavors to explain to the reader why and to what end these harmful usages were instituted. For him it is clear that numerous foolish customs were introduced among the Jews by deceivers and frauds who were the "teachers and heads of the people." They did this only out of greed for honor, power, and greatness; all their thought and action was directed only to the end that their name should be praised and hallowed by the people, that they should be looked upon as truly "holy ones on high."[31]

But it was not merely frauds and deceivers who were among the teachers of the people, Miesis asserts, but also plain fools. Countless customs were multiplied among us by so-called sages who were without sense, for among us Jews there were in every time and place enough "fools and men poor in understanding" who, in their folly, made the people stumble and led them on crooked paths. And these fools and simpletons who were void of knowledge and of whom it is said that "a carcass is better than a *talmid ḥacham* (scholar) who has no understanding"—these, in their folly and benightedness, created one restraint after another, one separation after another, and devised ever new, wild ordinances and customs.[32]

Miesis argues that one ought to adopt a critical attitude toward every practice. He should first of all raise the question: Of what use can this custom be under present conditions, and for what purpose was it instituted? If it brings no utility, it ought to be abolished. Everyone ought to be given to understand how

29. *Ibid.*, 79.
30. *Ibid.*, 80.
31. *Ibid.*, 94.
32. *Ibid.*, 95, 102. Among the foolish customs, Miesis also lists the many prayers, supplications, and liturgical hymns, most of which were written "in the language of stammerers and are filled with vain and false words."

pernicious it is.[33] For one must remember, our author repeats, that the whole purpose and goal of the Torah is only "usefulness for our people," the maintenance and perfection of our people in social life.[34]

Miesis does, indeed, declare that among other nations also there was a sufficiency of wild superstition and foolish customs, for among them also were "fraudulent priests" who used to lead the people astray. Many pernicious ideas and customs were in fact taken over by the Jews from the nations of the world. The question, however, arises: Why is the Jewish people more foolish than all other peoples? Why do all the sciences bloom among other peoples? Why do there appear among them each year by the hundreds useful books filled with science and wisdom, and among us are printed only "books filled with words of wind"—stuffed with all kinds of silliness? Why are the notions of morality and religion among Jews so distorted and crippled? Why are important things considered insignificant, and why is foolishnesses accorded major importance among them?[35]

Extremely characteristic is our author's answer to this question—characteristic not only for him but for the entire initial Haskalah period, when the representatives of ideas and spokesmen were the Friedländers and the Wolfsohns.

Miesis turns to history. And this rationalistically-minded *maskil* gives us a very unique picture of the cultural evolution through which the Jewish people passed on its long historical path. In fact, in his view, there was nothing—neither culture nor evolution. For, according to Miesis' conception, immediately after the era of King David and his son Solomon, the spiritual, intellectual, and moral decline of the people commenced. The Jews served idols, refused to know anything of science, and committed the vilest deeds, until Nebuchadnezzar's armies destroyed the kingdom. In exile they became even more ignorant and boorish. They took over many foolish customs and ideas from the peoples among whom they lived, and when, in the time of Cyrus, they returned to their ruined land, they brought with them the old idolatrous notions of former times and fresh ones besides which they had obtained in exile.[36] Things were no better at home in their own land in the period

33. *Kinat Ha-Emet*, 81, 88–89, 93.

34. *Ibid.*, 190–191.

35. *Ibid.*, 119.

36. *Ibid.*, 121: "They brought with them there all the vain views that cleaved to their hearts from the worship of idols and those corrupt views that they acquired in exile."

of the Second Temple. In the times of the wicked Antiochus Epiphanes idolatrous concepts were again strengthened and Jews adopted many "corrupted views." Thereafter an era of controversy and wars which lasted "virtually throughout the period of the Second Temple" began. In such restless times, the Galician *maskil* notes, the Jewish people had no opportunity to acquire knowledge. Later, following the destruction of the Second Temple, when apostasies and oppressions began, the Jews certainly had neither opportunity nor desire to occupy themselves with any sciences, and in exile they became even more deeply sunk in the swamp of folly and ignorance than before.[37]

In the Arabic-Spanish period there were among the Jews men of knowledge and science, but these, like all the learned in former times, addressed themselves in their works only to the elect few, not to the ignorant people, and therefore wrote in a philosophical-scientific style. But they also had to suffer more than enough persecutions, for then also, as in the present day, there were among Jews many simpletons, fools, frauds, false and base men who played the role of pious and holy persons and were regarded by the multitude, which believes in everything blindly and uncritically, as scholars and great sages. These fools and deceivers fabricated all kinds of libels against the learned investigators who fought for truth; they persuaded the multitude that the scholars were heretics and violated all the precepts of the Torah, and that one may therefore not take their writings in hand.[38]

After the author of *Kinat Ha-Emet* had portrayed the Jewish history of culture, or—more correctly—the Jewish lack of culture, in such black colors, he proceeded to the other nations of the world. Here he presents an entirely different picture. Here is a portrait glittering with the loveliest, most brilliant colors. Yes, among the peoples of the world in whose midst Jews lived, especially among the European nations, things were quite otherwise. It was not only that among them all the melancholy factors and hindrances were not prevalent, but, on the contrary, their historical circumstances contributed greatly to the dissemination of science and culture. First of all, from very ancient times, from even before the Second Temple, there existed many higher academies or universities where people studied languages and science, and everyone who wished to do so could

---

37. *Kinat Ha-Emet*, 122: "Through this, the majority of them were sunk in the abysses of folly and even greater ignorance than that in which they were drowned before."
38. *Kinat Ha-Emet*, 125.

obtain, unhindered, knowledge and wisdom from the greatest scholars and scientists—and that without payment.

Aside from this, one must take into consideration the fact, well known to everyone, that the Christian clergy had to know Greek well in order to be able to read their religious books written in that language and, as a result thereof, were also able to become familiar with the works of Plato, Aristotle, and the other Greek thinkers and thereby obtain much useful knowledge. Many of the Christian clergy and of the kings also were great lovers of culture and science, devoted themselves to them seriously, and also established institutes of culture for the people. Furthermore, they themselves wrote works on various branches of science, generously supported scientists and scholars with their fortunes, and did not allow the rabble and the pietists to do any harm to the men of knowledge. And if there were such kings as had no desire to protect the ideological battlers for truth from the persecutions of the foolish fanatics, the persecuted found protection in other lands under "gracious kings, lovers of reason" who not only allowed the oppressed scholars to write and publicly preach whatever their heart desired but associated with them in fellowship and supported them generously.

It is also known to everyone, Miesis notes in this connection, that virtually all the Christian scholars and men of science who battled for truth and preached against the besotted pietists and deceivers deliberately wrote in a very simple and plain language, the language which the masses of the people spoke at the time, so that everyone, both men and women, should readily understand.[39] Among the other factors which contributed to the enlightenment and culture of the people among the nations of the world, the author of *Kinat Ha-Emet* also lists theater presentations and belletristic works ("the stories that are called by them *romana*").

How, then—Miesis asks—can the Jewish people be helped? By what means can one rend the heavy veil of foolishness and benightedness in which our brethren are wrapped?—The Galician *maskil* has a ready-made answer: Reforming the educational system among Jews, familiarizing the youth now growing up not only with the Bible and the Hebrew language, but also with European languages, with the elements of natural science, ethics, psychology, and history. There should be written in simple Hebrew or in the vernacular (Yiddish) as many compositions as

39. *Kinat Ha-Emet*, 130–134.

possible that will do battle against the false ideas and barbaric customs prevalent among us, so that we may no longer be a mockery and laughter "in the eyes of the scholars and officials of the peoples."[40] Miesis, indeed, emphasizes that he wishes to be one who practices what he preaches, and notes that his *Kinat Ha-Emet* is composed "in simple language."

Kinat Ha-Emet is, in fact, distinguished from the other writings of the first Haskalah period in being written without rhetorical flourishes, without quotation of verses and fragments of verses from the Bible. Miesis also avoids Talmudic expressions, wishing to write simple Hebrew. His literary resources, however, were too limited for him to be able to create his own style, and he writes in a wooden language. One not infrequently encounters in him such awkward phrases as "there did not arise in them the spirit of desire to occupy themselves with any wisdom," or "undoubtedly he also was a simpleton all his days," etc.

One must not forget, Miesis declares, another important task: to battle against the so-called "wisdom of the Kabbalah" and especially the *Zohar*. Let the "enlightened among our people arise and show through the Torah and reason" that all the *Zohar*'s talk is "falsehood and vanity," that it is filled to overflowing with nonsense and heresy.[41] Let all know that the wisdom of the Kabbalah is disseminated "by the hands of fools and deceivers" who misled and made the Jewish people stumble with their foolishness, in order to make their own names great and that they might do with the confused and erring whatever their hearts desired.

One must not, the author of *Kinat Ha-Emet* admonishes, be content merely with showing that Moses de Leon himself fabricated everything in the *Zohar* and fraudulently declared that Rabbi Simeon ben Yoḥai was its author. No, it must also be demonstrated clearly and distinctly that the basic ideas presented in the *Zohar* and all the other Kabbalist works, whether the older or the later, are nothing but falsehood and folly, and that most of them derive from the idolatrous notions prevalent among Jews in former times.

To be sure, our author's attempt to demonstrate this scientifically is not quite successful, and the pages of *Kinat Ha-Emet* dealing with this matter (139–147) show merely that the author is not greatly familiar either with the "wisdom of the Kabbalah" or with philosophical matters in general. Nevertheless, he is

40. *Ibid.*, 134.
41. *Ibid.*

quite certain that every sensible person who merely attempts to compare the views of the Kabbalists with the ideas expressed in the works of the ancient idolatrous people *(be-sifrei ha-goyyim me-ovedei avodah zarah)* will soon be convinced that the Kabbalah has drawn everything from this corrupted source. Moreover, the later Kabbalists in each generation added many new items of foolishness.[42]

It is easy to imagine the intense wrath that Miesis' polemic work provoked immediately after its publication (Vienna, 1828) in the Hasidic and orthodox circles. Against the wealthy and prestigious author, who was highly regarded and influential among the local officials, the orthodox were afraid to come forth publicly. Only three years later, when the thirty-three-year-old Miesis suddenly died during the cholera epidemic in 1831, did his enemies express all their wrath and thirst for vengeance over the corpse of the heretic whom they despised so intensely. With hooting and laughter, with "trumpets and coronets," and with wild cries of jubilation, the young author of *Kinat Ha-Emet* was brought to burial in a Jewish cemetery.

It was not only in orthodox circles, however, that Miesis' work found definite opponents but also in the camp of the *maskilim*. Soon after the publication of *Kinat Ha-Emet*, Solomon Jehudah Rapoport issued forth sharply in the pages of *Bikkurei Ha-Ittim*[43] against Meisis' critical method. Other prominent representatives of the enlightening circles also expressed their dissatisfaction with the views put forth in *Kinat Ha-Emet*. In order to paralyze these critical attacks which might, as the author himself notes in his statement written in German, frighten away the common reader "in whom reason has not yet won its rights" and who will lose his desire to become familiar with his book, Miesis applied to prominent authorities—first of all, to the octogenarians David Friedländer and Herz Homberg. Indeed, it was their *haskamot*, or approbations, that he published at the head of the collection of letters which he printed in the eleventh volume (1830) of *Bikkurei Ha-Ittim*.[44] The aged Friedländer assures Miesis that through "earnest study" of his *Kinat Ha-Emet*, the "Israelites" will obtain "a treasure of new insights and

42. *Ibid.*, 147, 151.
43. *Bikkurei Ha-Ittim*, 1829, in the preface to the monograph on Nathan, the author of the *Aruch*, IV–V: "To gag mouths speaking wantonness that increase and break forth day by day, all of whose wisdom is their mocking of true scholars, without knowledge of the course of their [i.e., the scholars'] life and all the great things they achieved in their day . . ."
44. *Bikkurei Ha-Ittim*, XI, 126–142.

knowledge" that is difficult to find "in the much older writings of their own scholars." Incidentally, Friedländer notes, quite correctly, that he himself "in earlier years composed plans similar to yours." This, in fact, is the sharpest criticism of Miesis' work. He, the thirty-year-old, actually occupied the same anti-historical standpoint as the eighty-year-old Friedländer, and apparently had no notion of the great changes that had taken place in the realm of philosophical and historical scholarship in the period of these fifty years.

But the approbations of the Friedländers and Hombergs could be of little avail. Not against Miesis himself but against his world-view, against his anti-historical rationalism and his scientifically ungrounded critical method, came forth a thinker who stood at the peak of the culture and science of his day—the most important personality in the era of Galician *Haskalah*. Naḥman Krochmal was the name of this great thinker. Of him in the chapters that follow.

CHAPTER THREE

Naḥman Krochmal
and Solomon Rapoport

Naḥman Krochmal's childhood—The young Krochmal as guide and teacher—Solomon Rapoport and his enlightening circle in Lemberg—The rabbi of Lemberg Jacob Ornstein and the "verdict of excommunication" against the *maskilim*—The attack against Krochmal and his "Defense"—Penitents among the young *maskilim*—Krochmal and Rapoport against the penitents—Rapoport's *Ner Mitzvah*—Rapoport and Bick; two world-views—Bick "the apostate"—Love for Israel and love for mankind—Rapoport's scholarly works.

AHMAN KROCHMAL was born February 17, 1785, in Brody into a wealthy merchant family. His father, Shalom Krochmalnik, while still quite young and working in a large silk business, used to travel to Leipzig and Berlin, where he had opportunity to meet frequently as a businessman with Moses Mendelssohn who, as is known, also worked in a silk factory. In consequence of his frequent journeys, Shalom Krochmalnik was a bit "worldly" and "contemporary." Nevertheless, he gave his young Naḥman a strictly traditional education and upbringing. His pious wife gladly paid six ducats as annual fine for not letting her son attend the local "normal school" so that he might not—God forbid—become a heretic.[1]

1. Zunz, *Gesammelte Schriftten*, II, 150.

The young Naḥman, however, did become "infected" with heresy. On the very richly endowed and affluent youngster an eye was cast by the local *maskil*, Dov Baer Ginzberg,[2] and thanks to him the intellectually curious Naḥman, while still quite young, became familiar with Haskalah literature. When he was fourteen, he was married off by his parents to the daughter of Shmerel Hobermann, a rich man of Zolkiew. The young son-in-law settled in the home of his wealthy father-in-law who supported him. Dov Baer Ginzberg gave him a letter of recommendation to Zolkiew, to the teacher of the local normal school, Baruch Tzevi Ney. This acquaintanceship was of considerable significance for Krochmal's intellectual development. Ney was an educated man, had a very extensive library, and was pleased to see his new young acquaintance use it so eagerly.

The most fruitful years of learning now began for Krochmal. For a period of ten years, supported by his rich father-in-law, the young man studied languages and sciences with indefatiguable industry. Aside from Hebrew, Aramaic, Arabic, and Syriac, he thoroughly studied Latin, Greek, German, and French. These languages served as a key providing him the possibility of penetrating into the most varied realms of knowledge. The Jewish scholars and thinkers who had been his favorites from his early youth—Maimonides, Ibn Ezra,[3] and Azariah dei Rossi—contributed not a little to the fact that he concerned himself chiefly with two realms of knowledge: philosophy and history.

Aside from the thinkers of antiquity, he diligently studied Spinoza, Mendelssohn, Lessing, Solomon Maimon, and especially Kant, who had a very great influence on him not only as the brilliant author of *The Critique of Pure Reason* but also as a teacher of ethics. Later he systematically studied the new German philosophers—Fichte, Schelling, and especially Hegel. Krochmal also devoted himself not a little to poetry. But the young *maskil* who was raised on Talmudic literature was most pleased by poetic works in which there is some moral lesson, that have "something to tell us." His favorite poets were, of the

---

2. See our *History*, Vol. IX, p. 215. Some bibliographers note, incidentally, that a great influence was exercised on Krochmal not only by Ginzberg but also Mendel Levin (Lefin). This, however, is not correct. When Levin settled in Galicia (around 1808), Naḥman Krochmal was already an adult with extensive knowledge.

3. About these two scholars Krochmal wrote many years later: "Who among all those in whom the spirit of the Lord began to throb in the wisdom of Israel [i.e., the Science of Judaism] did not draw it first from the sap of the intelligence of these two excellent wells?"

ancient, Horace, and of the modern, Gotthold Ephraim Lessing, author of *Nathan the Wise.*[4]

Krochmal's enormous intellectual exertions, however, were beyond the powers of his weak, sickly body. He became seriously ill. With great effort and after long struggle, he managed to overcome his illness, but his physical powers were permanently broken. Thin, emaciated, leaning on a stick, he would wander like a shadow over the streets, and the good women would piously shake their heads and say: "it is the *kelipah* sitting in him, because he carried around heretical books."

Krochmal's mind, however, was not broken. He became the center around whom all those who were eager for knowledge in Zolkiew and the entire region grouped themselves. He impressed others and drew them to himself not only with his rich knowledge but also through the magic of his powerful moral personality. Not only adults but even eleven and twelve-year-old children would come to him. For them, too, he would find appropriate words, intimate contact, and with joyous gratitude they would recall decades later the happy moments they spent in their childhood with the "enlightener" of Zolkiew.[5]

Krochmal would carry on his discussions with the intellectually curious young people on the open field, in the forest outside the town, because the sickly "enlightener" had great need of fresh air. Like the ancient Peripatetics, the Galician *maskilim* used to imbibe the doctrine of their young teacher under the open skies, walking over the meadows and gardens. And the disciples would later remember with the greatest enthusiasm these promenades with Krochmal around the region of Zolkiew. "I still recall," Solomon Jehudah Rapoport reminisces after Krochmal's death,[6] "the precious times when I used to go to be with him for a day or two or for a whole week, or he used to come to me, and we would walk about over the field. Sweeter than all the pleasures in the world were these walks to me. One was not to be sated with his wise conversation. Every word of his was filled with knowledge." The scholarly discussions on the open field are recalled with no lesser enthusiasm by Samson Bloch[7] and the poet Meir Letteris.[8] Many young people of strongly pious and Hasidic families who thirsted for knowledge

4. See Krochmal's statement quoted by M. Letteris in his *Zikkaron Ba-Sefer*, 70.
5. See the recollections of Letteris in *Zikkaron Ba-Sefer*, 34–35.
6. *Kerem Ḥemed*, VI, 47.
7. In the preface to the first part of *Shevilei Olam*.
8. *Zikkaron Ba-Sefer*, 57–58.

were afraid openly to show themselves with Krochmal and his associates; hence, they would visit him secretly at night, so that no one might notice.

But the opposite side was also not silent. In the year 1815 the opponents of the *maskilim* suddenly came foreward with the ancient weapon, the "verdict of excommunication." This attack, which greatly agitated the enlightening circles in Galicia, also had a considerable influence on Krochmal's life.

The attack against the *maskilim* broke out in the major city of eastern Galicia, Lemberg. At the head of the local *maskilim* was Krochmal's admirer who has already frequently been mentioned, Solomon Jehudah Rapoport, commonly known by the acronym *Shir.* Rapoport was five years younger than Krochmal (he was born in Lemberg June 1, 1790). His father Aaron Hayyim, an average householder and man of learning, raised his son according to the old order. Gifted with a phenomenal memory, Solomon Rapoport, while quite young, was renowned as a great scholar in Talmudic and rabbinic literature, and the keen scholar Aryeh Leib Cohen, author of *Ketzot Ha-Hoshen,*[9] selected him as a son-in-law.

The greatest influence on Rapoport's intellectual development was exercised, as he himself indicates, by Maimonides and Naḥman Krochmal. "A thousand thanks," Rapoport feelingly calls out, "to you, Rabbi Moses, my teacher and guide. The little that I possess I owe to you. If not for your doctrine and support, I would have perished, naked and without knowledge, like the majority of our unfortunate brethren."[10] Of no lesser significance than his acquaintance with Maimonides' work was Rapoport's personal friendship with Krochmal, whom he first came to know when the latter travelled to Lemberg to seek a cure for his illness among its doctors. "It is already thirty years," Rapoport wrote after Krochmal's death,[11] "since I came to know him; as a result of his words, the spirit of knowledge and understanding awakened in me, and I was almost transformed into another person." Rapoport studied German with the help of Mendelssohn's translation of the Pentateuch. He was taught French by an officer who lived in the same house as he.

Rapoport spent whole nights over the monumental work of the French scholar Pierre Bayle, *Dictionnaire historique et critique,* and studied the German classical writers Lessing and Schiller with great enchantment. The Torah scholar became a *maskil,*

9. Novellae to *Hoshen Mishpat,* in two parts.
10. *Zikkaron Ba-Sefer,* 125; *Kerem Hemed,* I, 76–77.
11. See his article in *Kerem Hemed,* VI, 47.

himself attempted to write verses and rhetorical pieces, and in 1814, when the power of the brilliant Napoleon was broken and he was confined on the island of Elba, Rapoport issued a brochure entitled "Techunat Ir Pariz Ve-I Elba," an account in rhetorical style of the Napoleonic epic.

Rapoport's house became the place of assembly for the *maskilim* of Lemberg: the later renowned satirist Isaac Erter, the then still quite young Jehudah Leib Miesis, Benjamin Tzevi Notkish, Leib Pastor, Mordecai Tzevi Jolles, and many others. The temperamental and witty Rapoport, who was also endowed with extraordinary talent as an orator, never grew weary of carrying on with his friends hours-long scholarly discussions, peppered with clever comments and keen conceits. Under the influence of Bayle's acute criticism and of personal converse with Krochmal, the young Rapoport used to allow himself more or less free comments to, and explanations of, certain passages in Scripture. Reports of these "heretical" conversations gradually spread through the city and agitated the orthodox and Hasidic circles. In addition, there were purely personal motives.

The leader of the Lemberg community was Rabbi Jacob Meshullam Ornstein, who acquired a great reputation with his keen commentary on the *Shulḥan Aruch* entitled *Yeshuot Yaakov*. However, the extremely erudite Rapoport, with his phenomenal memory, was critical of the renowned composition of the local rabbi, and in the circle of his own friends would frequently point out that the author of *Yeshuot Yaakov* borrowed a good deal from other writers but did not think much of reporting things "in the name of him who said them," i.e., of noting the sources whence he drew his wisdom and learning. This reached the rabbi's associates. It especially enraged the rabbi's son Mordecai Ze'ev—a wild zealot with an aggressive temperament. He and his colleagues decided to avenge themselves, to settle accounts with the "sect of the wicked," the heretics. The moment was a highly suitable one. The star of the "heir of the great Revolution," the brilliant Corsican, had just set tragically, and the heavy reaction of Metternich spread its leaden wings over all of Europe.

On a dark night there was posted on the doors of the great synagogue of Lemberg, in the name of the rabbi,[12] a "verdict of

---

12. The genteel and moderate Samson Bloch even asserts (in the preface to the second part of *Shevilei Olam*) that the ban appeared without the rabbi's knowledge. The same thing is asserted by Meir Letteris in his *Zikkaron Ba-Sefer*, 45. The Galician Jacob Ḥayyim Korn who wrote under the anagram Yehalek categorically rejects this version and declares definitely that the ban was explicitly posted with the knowledge of the rabbi of Lemberg (*Ha-Kol*, V, 382).

excommunication" against the leaders of the local *maskilim*. The text of the ban has not come down to us. Only the German translation of this document in the government archives has been preserved. The translation, however, is given by the opposite side, by the *maskilim* in their complaint to the government, and S. Bernfeld's suspicion (in *Toledot Shir*, 17) that the *maskilim* did not faithfully translate the "verdict of excommunication" but in places deliberately falsified the text in order to make their opponent, the orthodox rabbi, ridiculous in the eyes of the officials is perhaps justified. In the German version that has been preserved, the ban begins as follows:

Dear brethren of the household of Israel. It is known that for a certain time now culture and education, and also the study of the German language, have begun to spread among us. Those chiefly responsible are two well-known young people, Solomon Rapoport and Hirsch Notkish. They publicly recite Scripture in German translation, and with the commentary of the philosopher Moses Mendelssohn. They also agitate among all their friends and acquaintances, urging them to study languages and sciences. Therefore, with the authority of the Torah and of the holy rabbis, we decree against them and against their colleagues and against all who hold with them, the great excommunication . . .

The ban created an enormous sensation. The *maskilim* appreciated quite well the great danger that this public declaration of war posed to them. A tiny circle surrounded by a compact mass of enemies and opponents, conscious and unconscious, they could hope only for the aid of those "outside the camp," the external government-power. The *maskilim* promptly appealed to the local authorities, noting that the Austrian government had already, in the time of Joseph II, forbidden the rabbis to use the ban as a mode of punishment. The *maskilim*, in fact, managed to persuade the local officials to compel Rabbi Jacob Ornstein publicly, in the great synagogue, to revoke the ban and declare that the verdict had been posted without his knowledge. And when the old rabbi, who was renowned among the orthodox as a great scholar, made his statement in a weak and trembling voice, the young Jehudah Leib Miesis triumphantly cried out: "Louder, rabbi, louder; we cannot hear you!"[13]

The *maskilim*, however, were quite far from victory. The shame which the aged rabbi suffered embittered the orthodox even more, and the supposedly revoked ban actually became the

13. *Ha-Kol*, V, 382.

battle-signal for the entire clerical camp to issue forth in a "holy war," to persecute the *maskilim* and the "heretical" literature that derived from Moses Mendelssohn of Dessau. They did not dare persecute the wealthy and prestigious Jehudah Leib Miesis, but the poor Isaac Erter, who earned a living from giving Hebrew lessons, had to flee from Lemberg to Brody. The above-mentioned David Caro relates that approximately fifty young householders who were suspected of associating with the *maskilim* and reading heretical books were forcibly divorced.[14]

The orthodox Jews of Lemberg knew quite well that the spiritual and intellectual leader of the Galician *maskilim* was Naḥman Krochmal. Hence, they considered it a very important duty to discredit him publicly, to declare him a "heretic and denier." The Hasidim in Lemberg learned that Krochmal was on friendly terms with a Karaite *ḥacham* who lived not far from Zolkiew in the village of Kukizow. Through all kinds of tricks they managed to obtain a copy of a letter by Krochmal to the Karaite *ḥacham*. The letter was of a quite innocent character. Nevertheless, the orthodox found a tremendous "heresy" in it. Krochmal assured the Karaite, who rejected the Oral Law, that he is worthy of the world-to-come because he is a pious, God-fearing man and fulfills the commandments of the Torah with all his heart.

This letter was circulated by the opponents of the *maskilim* in numerous copies with the appropriate commentaries to the effect that Krochmal has been corrupted and wishes to go over to the Karaites. Krochmal felt compelled to reply to this attack, and in the form of a letter to an acquaintance of his, Ze'ev Dov Schiff (the letter is dated 13th of Tammuz, 1816), he wrote his "Ketav Hitnatzlut," or "Defense."[15] In a calm, sedate tone he tears the petty accusations of his opponents apart like spider webs. This "plague of the Hasidim," who not long ago were themselves degraded and persecuted, now that they have become stronger and have power in their hands—"their hearts have grown arrogant to the point of becoming perverted; and may the Merciful One preserve us from the persecuted who has become a persecutor." This "Defense," a masterpiece of epistolary style, was distributed by Krochmal's friends in many copies over all the study-houses, and even in the orthodox circles it

---

14. *Ha-Kol*, V, No. 26, 396.
15. The "defense document" was several times reprinted: first in *Sulamith*, V, later in Letteris' collection *Ha-Tzefirah* and his *Zikkaron Ba-Sefer*. Subsequently it appeared as a supplement to the editions of *Moreh Nevuchei Ha-Zeman*.

made a great impression with its tone and persuasive power.[16]

Not all, however, had Krochmal's moral strength. Many youths who tended toward Haskalah, young sons-in-laws maintained in the homes of their fathers-in-law, were terrified; hence, they humbly submitted for burning the heretical books they possessed, and promised to follow the right way in the future. Some went even further. They realized that the enlightening circles, weak and small in number, were persecuted by the orthodox, but that in the Hasidic conventicles there was liveliness and cheerfulness. The young Hasidim rejoiced, told wonderful tales, drank "tikkun," danced and sang—all because "the *rebbe* commanded rejoicing." So, these young people who had been attracted to Haskalah did not stand the test and "repented," binding themselves again to the majority—the Hasidic masses.

This phenomenon found its unique resonance in Hebrew literature. Literary documents have been preserved that characterize most clearly the contemporary intellectual leaders of the Galician Haskalah, as well as the environment in which they were active. These documents were written in the form of letters. In the previous volume we noted that, in the first efflorescence of Hasidism, the leaders of the movement used to circulate among their followers open letters and proclamations in which various social and religious-ethical questions were treated. These letters were reproduced on the spot in many copies, and thus spread over the whole region. Some of these letters belong to the most significant buildingstones of Hasidic literature, e.g., *Likkutei Amarim (Tanya)* of Shneur Zalman of Lyady. A similar picture presents itself among the *maskilim* of Galicia. The letter-style was the favorite literary form there, and we shall see further on how in Galicia there even appeared journals in which all the material is presented to the reader in the form of "precious letters" *(iggarot yekarot)* that the "sages of the time" sent to each other.

Shortly after the "Defense" in connection with the Karaite, Krochmal issued forth with another letter addressed to one of the young *maskilim* of whom he had learned that the youth allowed himself to be frightened by the aggressive Hasidim and surrendered to them for burning Haskalah books that he owned.[17] This letter is very important also for an understanding of Krochmal's character. The sickly philosopher and historian

16. For interesting details, see *Zikkaron Ba-Sefer*, 53.

17. According to Letteris (see his biography of Krochmal in the second edition of *Moreh Nevuchei Ha-Zeman*, 23), the name of this *maskil* was Abraham Goldberg.

was, indeed, a retiring person and a pursurer of peace, but only to a definite limit. The feeling of self-respect, the proud consciousness of his own moral personality, did not permit him to yield where it was a question of defending his intimate worldview, the ideals that he had fought out through difficult struggle.

Krochmal writes:

A sound of the *shofar*, the noise of war, have my ears heard. A band of Hasidim[18] of your town have surrounded you, lurked for you at night, attacked you and threatened you with excommunication and persecutions, so that you might cease to follow the way of understanding and be content with their follies. Hearing this, my heart boiled up, but I was even more bewildered to hear that they frightened you and that your terror was so great that you meekly agreed to hand over to them some of your good and proper books for burning, and that you begged the foolish wretch who is their leader like a boy who cries under the rod. My dear friend, you have behaved foolishly and acted very unjustly . . . I simply do not know what has become of you. You are quite young, only in the springtime of your life, and it is unlovely for you to be a coward. At the age of twenty you ought to be a fighter and not tremble and be afraid before a petty little man . . . You know me for a man of peace who has no desire to carry on war. Yet if it is really true, as they say, and the fanatical pietists boast here, and the shameful thing actually happened; if they really terrorized you with "excommunication, ban, and ostracism," and forced you to surrender many of your books for burning, this must be avenged upon them . . . and they must be proceeded against with the axe of the government's laws.[19] And I am certain that they will be punished for this sin . . .

"Do not give in to them and do not be afraid of them," Krochmal declares at the end;

otherwise you will become a mockery not only among those who follow the right way, but even in the eyes of the pietists themselves. For it is clear to everyone that excessive fear and humility before a morally worthless person is proof of a flabby spirit and of a lowly soul fashioned by nature itself for enslavement and subjection. Whoever wishes to be chosen and raised over the multitude of the people, with their erroneous notions and lowly qualities, must be a courageous, militantly active man who is ready to fight like a lion for his ideals against antagonists and attackers. But if he should always put before himself the question—What do the creatures say, what do the pietists think, and what do the enemies devise?—this would merely darken his

18. Krochmal does not use the word *Hasidim* but *Mithasedim*.
19. I.e., relying on the law prohibiting the use of the punishment of the ban.

thought and confuse his mind. And if the most important of the sages of our people had had this timorous quality, we would not have their best treasures, and their most precious works would never have seen the light of the world. For all of them knew quite well how much pain and suffering they would endure for their published works. And the best proof is the rabbi and teacher, the light of Israel, Rabbi Moses ben Maimon, who publicly declared in his introduction to *A Guide for the Perplexed* that he knows very well that his work "will satisfy and inspire only the chosen individual and will incite tens of thousands of fools." And if you look into the matter carefully, you will see that so it was with other great scholars, from recent generations back to the great prophets. The multitude always follows the lead of any false priest, hypocritical pietist and Tartuffe, sorcerer and trickster, of any least miracle worker, *baal shem* and *baal shed*. And against anyone who tries to oppose them, they incite "the wild beast without eyes and with many sharp mouths," as the rabble is called by the Prussian King Frederick II.[20]

In these militant tones of the Galician battler are heard quite sharply the echoes of Maimonides' intellectual aristocratism, with its arrogant contempt for the "foolish, ignorant multitude."[21]

Typical also are the letters written at that time to terrified young *maskilim* by Krochmal's disciple and colleague, Solomon Jehudah Rapoport. In 1815 he composed an essay entitled *Ner Mitzvah* which he undoubtedly intended originally to publish at once.[22] Apparently, however, he also became frightened of the *Mitḥasedim* (Hasidim), and the essay remained in manuscript, disseminated merely in copies. It was published only after Rapoport's death (*Naḥalat Yehudah*, 1868, 1–25).

Ner Mitzvah is addressed to a former disciple of Rapoport's from Hrubieszow, a young *maskil*, the son of a rabbi, of whom Rapoport had heard that he had become a penitent and was associating with the Hasidim. The whole essay is filled with hatred and bitterness toward the Hasidim. The "great men and saints of the Hasidim" are divided by Rapoport into two categories: (1) deluded dreamers, men without knowledge and understanding, who, with their overheated fantasy, have imagined that the holy spirit rests on them; and (2) vile frauds who, from their youth on, have devoted all their thought only to cheating

20. The letter is printed in *Kerem Ḥemed*, I, 90–92; by Letteris in *Zikkaron Ba-Sefer*, 65–69; and *Kitvei RaNaK*, 416–418.
21. See our *History*, Vol. I.
22. Testimony to this is provided, for instance, by the following expression: "And, behold, I say before the sons of my people and before the sun: to every reader in whose eyes these words of mine will appear strange" (*Naḥalat Yehudah*, 21).

people and to dazzling and misleading the multitude. "The Hasidim," Rapoport complains, "have devised new laws of which our ancestors had no notion. These new laws have poisoned the cup of faith, intoxicated the whole people of Israel, and let it sink into the swamp of folly. These laws have made us a mockery and laughter among all the surrounding peoples. My heart mourns at the ruin of my people."[23]

This bitter hatred for the Hasidim remained with Rapoport throughout his life. Twenty-five years later, when he was already rabbi in Prague, he speaks with no less venom about "these *Mithasedim*, the troublers of the people," the "fiery serpents who burn with the sulphur of their mouths every *maskil's* name."[24]

No less typical is another letter of Rapoport's, written several months later to another youthful friend.[25]

This young *maskil* had also become shaky. The Hasidim had importuned him both with good and with evil. They threatened him and cast fear upon him, but at the same time argued and tried to persuade him to join their company. So this *maskil* who stood at the crossroads turned to Rapoport and begged him for help and moral support. Rapoport, in his reply, deplores the fact that the young *maskil* did not study the German language which is the key to all the treasures of science. He advises his young friend to "drink from the pure source from which all the enlightened of Israel have drawn and still draw now, but whose true depths they have still not fathomed—that is, our master who illuminates our darkness, Rabbi Moses ben Maimon, may his rest be in paradise. Rapoport stresses:

In his books and essays you should immerse yourself. So your eyes will be enlightened. They will make your neck strong as iron and your forehead firm as copper against every attacker and frightener. And you will mock the arrows of the antagonists . . . You should also familiarize yourself with Maimonides' letters, for in all his words you will see a great light and much instruction that refreshes the soul.

Rapoport points out in this connection that if his disciple from Hrubieszow had obeyed him and diligently studied Maimonides' work, he would not have been caught in the net of the *Mithasedim*.

However, several years later Solomon Rapoport had opportu-

---

23. *Nahalat Yehudah*, 14, 21–22.
24. *Kerem Ḥemed*, VI, 43.
25. The letter was first published in *Kerem Ḥemed*, I, 75–77; reprinted by Letteris in *Zikkaron Ba-Sefer*, 122–25.

nity to be persuaded that even Maimonides' work cannot always protect one from the net of the *Mithasedim*. One of the most brilliant representatives of Galician Haskalah, Rapoport's relative, the finely educated, clever, and universally loved Jacob Samuel Bick,[26] in his middle years[27] abandoned the banner of Haskalah and publicly declared his sympathy with the *Mithasedim*, the "rebels against the light." To dramatize his rebellion against the acknowledged guides of the *maskilim* and his disavowal of the ideals of Haskalah, he demonstratively sold his copy of *A Guide for the Perplexed*.[28]

Bick's "apostasy" made an enormous impression in the world of the *maskilim*. Among them, after all, it was absolutely clear and certain that all troubles derive from superstition and ignorance, and that the only remedy is education and enlightenment, for these shatter the power of darkness and assure the reign of clear common sense. And now, suddenly, the incomprehensible has occurred—something impossible to understand with common sense: one of the most prominent *maskilim* and enlightened men becomes a penitent, associates with the Hasidic sect, speaks with greatest respect of the *rebbes*, the "frauds" and "rebels against the light."

How great is my astonishment," Jehudah Leib Miesis writes[29] to a friend of his who had reported Bick's apostasy.

I would not have given it credence, had I not read it in your letter . . . Who could have believed this of a man who always strove that all his thinking and acting should be only "according to reason and righteousness"? To whom could it even have occurred to go to such a person and say: A time will come when you will turn away from wisdom, associate with foolish men, and walk together with the *Beshtnim*.

"How great is my distress," Miesis writes further; "we and science have lost a faithful friend, and the sect of the fools and the *Beshtnim* will rejoice as over a great prize."

Miesis consoles himself with the thought that perhaps this is merely pretense. "It may be," he writes,

26. See our *History*, Vol. IX.

27. Samson Bloch notes in his letter to Bick of 1830: "It is now six years since your eyes began to grow dim (*Kerem Hemed*, I, 121; *Ha-Meassef*, I, 1862, 181). Bick's "apostasy" therefore, took place in 1823–1824.

28. *Ibid.*

29. The letter is published in *Bikkurei Ha-Ittim*, XI, 131–142. Bick's name is not even mentioned in the letter. It is beyond doubt, however, that it is he who is spoken of here.

that our friend deliberately clothed himself in the garments of Hasidism in order that they should trust him, and that he might thereby learn their secrets, and the leaders of the sect of the *Beshtnim* will no longer keep anything hidden from him. I have no doubt whatever that our friend will come back to us and confess his sin, for since the world has been in existence no understanding person has turned away out of conviction from the path of wisdom and science; and if such a thing has happened, he returned after a time to the right way. However, we may not wait long, we must apply all our powers that he [our friend] may return as soon as possible to the way of wisdom, so that we not become a mockery and laughter in the eyes of those who hate understanding. I cannot bear this, for I fear that young Jews who are just beginning to educate themselves will learn from our friend and abandon the way of life and set out, like him, on the paths of foolishness.

A significant cultural-historical interest pertains to the letters which Solomon Rapoport and Jacob Samuel Bick wrote to each other and which have been preserved. We noted in the previous volume the enthusiasm with which the Meassefim took up the ideals of fraternity, equality, and love of mankind proclaimed by the French "enlighteners." With no less feeling does *Bikkurei Ha-Ittim* reflect these ideals. Max Nordau's father Gabriel Suedfeld feelingly calls out in his poem "Ha-Shivvui" (*Bikkurei Ha-Ittim*, 1827, 81–84): "Before God, all men are brothers, all—without distinction—equal." Baruch Schönfeld translates Schiller's well-known poem "An die Freude" with the emotive proclamation:

> Seid umschlungen, Millionen!
> Diesen Kuss der ganzen Welt![30]

In the intellectual Jewish circles of the larger Prussian cities the abstract slogan of equality and fraternity led, as we have observed, to assimilation. But the Galician environment, with its compact orthodox masses, was at that time a very unsuitable ground for assimilation. The unconscious national feeling still found, as we shall see further on, significant support in the heightened interest in historical investigations. Symptomatic in this respect is Rapoport's preface to his Hebrew translation of Jean Racine's play *Esther*,[31] in which he speaks with emotion of "love of the nation," love for the children of "your solitary mother Zion."

30. *Bikkurei Ha-Ittim*, VII, 100.
31. Published under the title "She'erit Yehudah" in *Bikkurei Ha-Ittim*, VIII, 171–254.

These emotive words, however, could not satisfy Jacob Samuel Bick, for Bick and Rapoport were men of different worldviews. We spoke at length in the third volume of the obdurate cultural struggle that took place between two camps of the Jewish intelligentsia: the rationalists, on the one side, with their battle-slogan, "Sovereignty of the intellect!," and, on the other side, men whose guide in life was sentiment, emotion, and the act of will based on these. This battle was now reflected in the encounter of two representatives of the same camp.

In the previous volume we noted how, many years earlier, Bick had approached the question of the folk-language quite differently than the *maskilim* in general.[32] In this particular also he differed with Rapoport who, like the majority of the *maskilim*, was a definite opponent of "jargon."[33] These two *maskilim* disagreed in the sharpest fashion regarding the motto "Love for the people." Bick cannot understand how Rapoport can speak of love for the people, affection for the children of the "solitary mother Zion," and at the same time passionately hate the "sect of the Hasidim" who, at that time, constituted the majority of the Galician Jewish population. He writes to Rapoport: "You so love the German poet Schiller and eagerly translate his poems. Why, then, have you not memorized for yourself his cosmopolitan verse, "Diesen Kuss der ganzen Welt," and do not fulfill it in regard to the Jewish people. Embrace and kiss all our Jewish brethren with your whole heart and soul, even if you must pay therefor with both reason and soul."[34]

Bick no longer believed in the basic motto of the Haskalah—that through enlightenment and culture the Jewish community will be saved from all troubles. Typical, incidentally, is his statement in a letter to the future editor of *Kerem Ḥemed,* Samuel Leib Goldenberg: "I do not wish to clothe my words in the garment of rhetoric. What good is beauty to us when tears pour from the eyes of our brethren, turned to us with a plea to feed their children perishing from hunger?"[35] Bick expressed his intimate thoughts in his memoirs, which unfortunately were lost,[36] and when his fellow-*maskilim* became familiar with some fragments they were greatly dissatisfied with his "heretical" ideas. To Rapoport Bick writes:

32. See our *History*, Vol. IX, pp. 222–23.
33. See *Bikkurei Ha-Ittim*, VIII, 11: "Why the Judeo-German language in the land of Poland?," asks Rapoport. "Either the holy language or Polish."
34. *Otzar Ha-Safrut*, III, "Orot Me-Ofel," 27.
35. *Kerem Ḥemed*, I, 68.
36. See our *History*, Vol. IX, p. 222.

You have complained of me and charged me, who truly loves to kindle as much light as possible in the holy sanctuary, of preaching obscurantism. In your haste you have forgotten that whoever extinguishes a candle out of fear of an attack by strangers, or of robbers, or of an evil encounter, or so that a sick person may fall asleep—such a one is free of guilt.

Bick lost faith in the notion that the ideals of Haskalah could actually bring salvation to the greatly suffering Jewish masses in Galicia. He arrived at the conclusion that the Hasidism so despised by the *maskilim* at least provides the masses the comfort they require, and is concerned that "the sick man be able to fall asleep peacefully." Against this Rapoport, with his militant nature, issued forth most sharply. He writes to Bick: You charge me with forgetting the fundamental law of tolerance because I hate the "men of your sect" (i.e., the Hasidim). But I understand by this motto that for convictions alone one may not punish another or persecute him and especially not—God forbid—kill him. This, however, cannot at all move me, out of tolerance, not to allow myself to express my view on any ignorant fool, on any swindler and seducer. God illuminated our reason so that we might bestow as much light as possible on the multitude groping in darkness, not that we should kiss every fool, even when this kiss "paralyzes reason and soul." We will not make ourselves crazy and jump about like goats because we are surrounded by crazy men. And this is in no way inconsistent with the notion of tolerance.[37]

Bick, Rapoport writes to his friend Leib Holish about him,[38] always speaks of love of Israel and forgets about love of mankind in general. He believes that true love of Israel must consist in hatred for all other peoples, for everything that comes from the outside. I, however, consider such love the greatest hatred. It has always brought us only evil. It has intensified the hatred of all other nations for us. It has thrown us into pitch blackness for hundreds of years. Our hands became powerless to do good, and we became a burden among our neighbors in all lands. I do not say—God forbid—that the house of Jacob is not precious to me. I swear to you by the God who gave me my soul that I am devoted wholeheartedly to the children of Jeshurun. I love my people with all my powers, and am prepared to endure everything to the end of my years for its welfare. But all my many

37. *Otzar Ha-Safrut*, III, "Orot Me-Ofel," 29–30.
38. *Kerem Hemed*, I, 83–84.

years of investigation in the realm of Jewish history have persuaded me that not by isolating themselves from all other peoples, not by refusing to participate in their culture, will our brethren obtain the high level destined for them. Only when they endeavor to take over from every people the useful and good will they truly surpass all with their pure and true faith and will, indeed, become a "wise and understanding people."

Rapoport reverts to the same question in the poem he wrote for Bick in his album.[39] Dear friend—the poem begins—you always speak of bliss and rest for the people of Israel. However, you come foreward with counsel that is very far from me and with which I cannot agree. To you the people's long slumber is dear and precious, and all your concern is only not to disturb its sleep. But my thoughts are distant from yours. I love my people with all the palpitation of my soul. To it belong my life and all my powers. I cannot, however, like you, calmly witness its degradation. All my thought and striving is to bring light into its darkness. I will provide it the best judgment as a gift. I will lay at its feet the loveliest treasures of various people. In whatever language I find sparks of wisdom, I will collect them for my people and replant them in their language. Perhaps they will awake from their sleep. Their eyes will see the bright light and they will understand that wisdom must be drawn from all sources. For only then can the highest stages be reached.

In the preface to *She'erit Yehudah* quoted above, in which Rapoport emotively declares that every *maskil* ought, with all his forces, to arouse in his brethren the sparks of love for his people and its faith, he notes that he himself, "the small and young one among my people," despite the fact that he is so beset with worries about a livelihood and spends so much time as a day-laborer,[40] devotes every one of his free moments to national interests and has set himself the task of producing a monumental work, *Anshei Shem*, which is to include an account of the life and work of all the famous men among the Jews from the post-Biblical era on. And, indeed, soon, in the course of three years, there appeared, one after the other, in *Bikkurei Ha-Ittim* Rapoport's six monographs on great medieval Jewish scholars[41]—

---

39. *Bikkurei Ha-Ittim*, VIII, 278–281. Bick's name is not noted here, but it is indubitable that he is the "beloved friend and relative" to whom the poem is addressed.
40. Rapoport was for many years overseer and cashier in the [Jewish] community-tax office in Lemberg.
41. *Toledot Rabbenu Saadiah Gaon Ve-Korot Sefarav* (*Bikkurei Ha-Ittim*, IX); *Toledot Rabbenu Natan Ish Romi Baal He-Aruch Ve-Korot Sefaro* (*Ibid.*, X); *Toledot Rabbenu Hai Gaon Ve-Korot Sefarav* (*Ibid.*); *Zeman U-Mekom Rabbi Eliazar Kallir Ve-Inyenei Piyyutav* (*Ibid.*); *Toledot*

works which brought him fame as one of the major builders in the field of the Science of Judaism.

On the modern reader the structure of Rapoport's monographs does not make a particularly favorable impression. The numerous notes occupy far more space than the monographs themselves. It must, however, be borne in mind that Rapoport was a true pioneer in his field. The era with which he deals in his works (10th-12th centuries) was in his time genuinely "virgin territory." And Rapoport did, indeed, manifest literally brilliant acuteness in this field. With great industry he collected the requisite material, piece by piece, from little grains of sand and kernels. Out of casual remarks, at times with the aid of astute interpretations of single words, scattered over hundreds of compositions, chronicles, and responsa, he managed to assemble the cultural-historical material that he required. Where others saw merely a heap of sand and ashes, he understood how to obtain the most precious pearls. In the most confused and highly corrupted texts the keen scholar managed, with his intellectual power, to obtain the historical truth, to clarify facts that had remained unknown before him.

It suffices to give one example out of hundreds. In Volume II of our *History* (p. 6) we touched upon the old legend according to which the first disseminators of Jewish knowledge in the Rhineland provinces were the family Kalonymos whom the "French king Carlo" brought with him from Lombardy and settled in Mainz. In the Jewish sources there is great confusion on this matter. It is difficult to decide which Charles is meant here, whether Charles the Great (Charlemagne) or Charles II (the Bald). Again in certain sources a considerably later date, when both Charlemagne and Charles II had long been deceased, is noted. Rapoport in one of his notes (to "Rabbi Nathan Baal He-Aruch") demonstrated with great acuteness that the date is erroneous, and in this connection came to the correct conclusion that it happened in the times of Charles the Bald. To be sure, since Rapoport was a pioneer in a still totally unexplored field, it also happened at times that, with all his keenness, he came to false conclusions, e.g., in his work on Eleazar Kallir, where he allowed himself to be led astray through overly refined conjectures and arrived at quite erroneous conclusions regarding the time and place of the famous liturgical poet's activity.

From the point of view of their literary form, also, Rapoport's

---

Rabbenu Ḥananel ben Rabbenu Ḥushiel Ve-Rabbenu Nissim Bar Yaakov Mi-Medinat Kairouan (*Ibid.*, XII).

cultural-historical works are a significant phenomenon in Hebrew literature. They are written in a scientific but clear and easily comprehensible style, without superfluous rhetorical flourishes of the kind noticeable in his earlier works. Along with this, however, one senses that he has before him not an arid pedant but a man with considerable publicistic talent. For Rapoport intends something besides purely scientific purposes. He gives a scientifically grounded reply to Miesis' polemic attacks, to his hatred and contempt for the Jewish Middle Ages. Not with polemic debates but with the persuasive force of historically based and critically elucidated facts, Rapoport attempts to show that in the Dark Ages of medieval Europe there were among Jews thinkers and scholars who stood at the peak of contemporary culture.

Rapoport's scholarly works created a great sensation in learned circles. The European-educated and university-trained scholars saw with astonishment the Galician Jew, working as an overseer of the kosher meat-tax, opening for them completely new sources of investigation. Zunz speaks in the preface to his *Die gottesdienstlichen Vorträge der Juden,* which appeared in 1832, with high enthusiasm of Rapoport's scholarship and the great acuteness revealed in his cultural-historical investigations. He also notes, incidentally, that he quotes Rapoport in his work over a hundred times. "A man according to my heart has arisen in Israel," Samuel David Luzzatto of Padua exclaims emotively in his letter to Rapoport;[42] "you are my brother and I will praise you, my father and I will exalt you." "Rapoport's six biographies that have appeared in *Bikkurei Ha-Ittim,*" writes Franz Delitzsch,[43] "are treasures of diamonds for everyone undertaking to write the history of Jewish literature." Even decades later the historian Heinrich Graetz considers it necessary to note:

The chronology, the historical geography, the literary history, and many other branches that are so important to the critical exploration of the course of history—all these were, until that time, either not treated at all or in a very superficial way, and only through Rapoport obtained redress; he was the first to ground them and to note their true significance. The keenness with which he associates matters that appear at first glance to be completely at variance, and separates precisely what seems to be in close affinity; the critical criteria which he created and with whose aid he manages to distinguish the genuine from the false, historical events from common legends—all this exercised such

42. *Iggerot Shadal,* 165.
43. *Zur Geschichte der jüdischen Poesie,* 1836, p. 119.

a great influence that he is quite justifiably considered, next to Krochmal, the founder of the Science of Judaism. What Jost and other predecessors produced is ephemeral in comparison with his investigations, as common chit-chat is in comparison with a well thought-out,
strictly articulated, and artistically constructed speech.[44]

Rapoport's biographies made him famous. He undertook to
produce a large work, *Anshei Shem*, that would include accounts
of the life and work of all the great Jewish figures of the post-
Biblical era. His craft was single, solid bricks, formed from the
best material, and artistically polished building stones, but not
an entire structure. In the numerous notes that accompany
Rapoport's works are whole treasures of cultural-historical material, but all this as raw material that still requires the skilled
hand of the master builder, the architect.

Rapoport sensed the new spirit of the youthful nineteenth
century, the breath of the historical world-view. However, he
lacked the synthetic approach to historical development, and the
general problems relating to the philosophy of history remained
alien to him. But what Rapoport was not able to carry through
was undertaken by his teacher and friend, Naḥman Krochmal,
in the latter's life's work—*Moreh Nevuchei Ha-Zeman*.

44. *Die Geschichte der Juden*, XI, 1900 edition, p. 450.

CHAPTER FOUR

Krochmal's
Moreh Nevuchei Ha-Zeman

The modern *Guide for the Perplexed*—Maimonides and Krochmal—
Krochmal and German Idealistic philosophy—Concerning Hegel's
influence on Krochmal—The self-knowledge of the World-Spirit and
the self-consciousness of the human personality—Krochmal's cultur-
al-historical method—*Kinat Ha-Emet* and *Moreh Nevuchei Ha-Zeman*—
The "ruler of the nation" and "god of the nation"—The uniqueness
of the Jewish people—The significance of *Shechinah Be-Yisrael*—
Krochmal's view regarding the national spirit of the Jewish people—
The significance of *Kerem Ḥemed*—Its actual editor—Eliakim ben
Jehudah Ha-Milzahgi (Mehlsack) and his *Ravyah*—The "seers" and
Emek Shoshanim.]

HE "VER-
DICT of ex-
communicati-
on" of which
we spoke in
the previous
chapter made
a strong im-
pression on
Naḥman
Krochmal. We
noted how
sharply he is-
sued forth
against the
young *maskil*
who allowed
himself to be
frightened by the Hasidim and surrendered his Haskalah books
to them for burning. Krochmal himself, however, was by no
means a fighter by nature. Not without reason does he mention
Mendelssohn's words written by the German-Jewish philosopher to a friend of his: A man is not obliged always to speak the
truth openly, but he may not say what is contrary to the truth.

The multitude, which to Krochmal, the spiritual and intellectual aristocrat, was like "the wild beast without eyes and with many sharp mouths," cast fear on him. He even wished at first to withdraw completely to the sidelines and occupy himself with mercantile pursuits.[1] In the sixth volume[2] we quoted the reproving words that Mendel Levin, the typical enlightener, directed against Krochmal because the latter was a shy, retiring person, and though the man with the capacity to bring light to the people and whom God had appointed to open the eyes of those groping in darkness, to free souls languishing in prison, he sat locked up in his room, content with having accumulated much knowledge for himself, and his hand refused to wield the pen.[3]

Krochmal, however, was not impressed by Levin's words. In fact, the latter's complaints were justified only in regard to Krochmal's written teaching. We pointed previously to the single-minded enlightening role that Krochmal played in Galicia as a result of his personal intercourse and the conversations he used to carry on not only with grown-up young people thirsting for knowledge but even with twelve-year-old children. All this, however, was by word of mouth. Krochmal had a very different attitude toward the printed word. "Since my youthful years," he declares, "I cling to the counsel that the wise Joseph Solomon Delmedigo of Candia gave: 'Before teaching others what I know, I would first learn what I myself still do not know.'" He used to refer to himself ironically as "the eternal student." It always seemed to him that he still had too little knowledge. He was still ever the "seeker."

Nevertheless, the time finally came when Krochmal himself became persuaded that he could no longer remain in retirement and "content himself with having amassed much knowledge for himself." To this Miesis' *Kinat Ha-Emet* and Jacob Samuel Bick's penitential mood contributed not a little. *Kinat Ha-Emet* resounded like a monition. Krochmal saw how the Jewish intelligentsia of his generation, the modern "seekers," were standing at the crossroads. The old and traditional could no longer provide satisfaction; new ways had to be sought. One could no longer be content with Bick's program: "to extinguish the light" and let the sick man continue to sleep. For the rays of light

---

1. Krochmal, however, was little suited for business and lost a considerable part of his fortune in it.
2. See our *History*, Vol. VI, pp. 277–78.
3. Mendel Levin's speech was first published in *Kerem Ḥemed*, I, 74–75.

penetrate even through the closed shutters, arouse from sleep, and show how dark and narrow it is in one's own domain. And when one has no teachers of one's own, he seeks guides from the outside. But outsiders must bring about alienation and abandonment, an uncritical or negative attitude to one's own national culture, and thereby increase the number of "frivolous mockers" who are no less repugnant to Krochmal than the "fools who believe in everything."

"As in earlier generations," Krochmal notes,

it was dangerous to reveal the hidden, so at present it is dangerous to keep hidden what has already been disclosed by others . . . Once, for instance, it could be considered a firmly established truth that the whole book of Psalms, even the chapter beginning "By the rivers of Babylon," was composed by King David through the holy spirit. But this can in no way satisfy the contemporary reader. He has already learned that in the European world great doubts have been expressed about this. Will he uncritically take these views, accept the correct along with the false?[4]

It was perhaps not known to Krochmal that virtually the same words had been uttered by one who lived in "earlier generations," and that this person, like himself, was an ardent admirer of Maimonides. In Volume II of our *History* (p. 109) we observed that the translator of *A Guide for the Perplexed*, Samuel Ibn Tibbon, in his *Maamar Yikkavu Ha-Mayyim,*[5] a philosophical commentary on *maaseh bereshit,* considered it necessary to note:

Let people not complain of me that I have uncovered too much of that which our sages commanded be held secret. God is my witness that I did this only for His honor, because I was persuaded that the mysteries which our prophets and sages in their day considered it necessary not to reveal are now disclosed to the nations of the world, and they explain according to these revealed truths all the profound matters that are concealed in the Torah and in the words of the prophets.

Krochmal discovered that the Jewish intelligentsia of his age stood at the same crossroads as in the generation of Maimonides, when minds were confused, and with the best will could not fulfill the ancient principle, "It is good that you should take hold of this, and withhold not your hand

---

4. See the introduction to *Moreh Nevuchei Ha-Zeman;* see also *ibid.,* Gate Eleven, pp. 107 and 119 (we quote according to the second edition, 1863).

5. The work remained in manuscript and was first published in 1837 in Pressburg.

from that" (Ecclesiastes 7:18), and not notice any contradictions between the two worlds—the Talmudic-rabbinic world and the general scientific world.

And Krochmal, the shy, withdrawn scholar, the sickly and debilitated man who was frequently unable even to hold a pen in hand,[6] decided to become a guide for the groping and "searching," to create a new "Guide for the Perplexed" that might be a lighthouse for his generation as Maimonides' *Guide* had been for former generations.[7] Of the difficulties that confronted him in this connection Krochmal wrote to Samuel David Luzzatto in 1836:[8]

It is now much more difficult than in Maimonides' times to speak openly before all of matters touching principles or what are considered principles. Maimonides expressed his views regarding the mysteries of the Torah for those Jews who lived in the Arabic lands and in neighboring Provence; of the remaining Jewish communities he took no account whatever, so slight at that time was the bond between these communities. Now, however, the situation is quite different. How does one obtain the possibility of speaking a language and using words such that they will be able to penetrate equally into the hearts of, and possess the same persuasive power in regard to both the Italian and the Oriental Jews, as well as the enlightened German Jews and the pietists of the Polish lands? And now the relationships, too, are not as they once were. No matter how distant the communities are from one another and how different their views, they are, nevertheless, in frequent contact. They know of one another, dislike one another, and each asserts that if all agreed with it, we would promptly be saved.

It is characteristic that Krochmal in this connection leaves untouched one important point—apparently because of his great reverence for Maimonides. This is the *language* in which the medieval philosopher's *Guide for the Perplexed* was written. Krochmal writes of Maimonides: "Apparently, he spoke his words on the mysteries of the Torah only in the ears of the Jews

6. In 1831 Samuel David Luzzatto writes to the editor of *Kerem Hemed:* "I am sorely grieved to hear that the distinguished scholar Rabbi Naḥman Ha-Kohen is so weak in body that he cannot write letters save without strain" (*Kerem Hemed*, I, 72).

7. *Moreh Nevuchei Ha-Zeman*, Gate Thirteen, 160: "And we have already repeated that our intended goal is actually similar to the goal of the rabbi in his book *The Guide* for the people of his time, and in what pertains to the way of inquiry we follow in his footsteps without any difference, aside from the difference between the people of his generation and the confusions that fell on them and the remedy necessary for these perplexities, and between the situation of the present generation and the state in which they exist."

8. The letter was first published in *Michtevei Venei Kedem*, 1866, 65–67; reprinted in *Kitvei RaNaK*.

who lived in the lands of the Arabs."[9] The word "apparently"
is quite superfluous, for the *Guide* is obviously written in Arabic,
in the tongue accessible only to those Jews educated in Arabic
culture. Krochmal, however, considered it impermissible in
principle for himself to create the new "Guide" in any language
other than Hebrew, in which he perceived the national tongue
of the Jewish people. And when he speaks of the fact that the
major part of the literature that the Greek-speaking Jewish community produced in Alexandria was lost, he considers it necessary to note immediately in this connection: "This is undoubtedly their [the Alexandrian Jews'] punishment for the fact that
they abandoned their national holy language; let later generations remember this and take a lesson therefrom."[10]

Not, however, in language alone is Krochmal's work distinguished from Maimonides' *Guide for the Perplexed.* Krochmal's
method, his whole philosophy, is quite different.

We have noted a number of times how alien to Maimonides
was the *historical* approach to problems of culture. All the laws
and rules, as well as the reasons for the precepts, are considered
by the medieval thinker exclusively from the rationalist point of
view. This could satisfy the Jewish *Aufklärer* of the end of the
eighteenth century, but not Naḥman Krochmal, who sensed so
deeply the new *historical* spirit of the nineteenth century. Not
without reason was Azariah dei Rossi one of his favorite guides
even in his earliest student years,[11] and in his later years he
studied with great diligence the classic work of the Italian Gio-
vanni Battista Vico, *Scienzia Nuova*, which appeared in 1822 in
Weber's German translation.

Krochmal proceeds from the cultural-historical point of view
and speaks with bitter sarcasm of the "silly people of our community" who demonstrate their "enlightenment" by denying
everything, both the existence of Moses and the books of prophecy, and express their doubts: "Perhaps some swindling rabbi
composed them."[12] He sets himself the task of investigating the
genesis, the "root and source" as he expresses it, and under what
conditions and for what reasons the ideas, customs, and laws,

9. *Ka-nireh dibber devarav be-sitrei Torah rak be-oznei ha-yehudim she-yashevu be-malchut ha-aravim.*
10. *Moreh Nevuchei Ha-Zeman*, Gate Twelve, p. 127.
11. The author of *Meor Einayim* is frequently quoted in *Moreh Nevuchei Ha-Zeman*. See
ibid., 39, 126, 186, 190.
12. *Moreh Nevuchei Ha-Zeman*, Gate One, 2. It is beyond doubt that these words, as well
as several other passages—e.g. page 186 in Gate Fourteen, where a "scholar of this latter
time" is mentioned—were directed against the author of *Kinat Ha-Emet.*

which these "silly people of our community" attack with such mockery and laughter, were formed. The work planned by Krochmal, *Emunah Tzerufah*,[13] was to have consisted of two parts —the first, of a historical nature, of eighteen to twenty chapters,[14] and the second, a philosophical section. The sickly Krochmal, however, did not manage to complete his work. He finished only seventeen chapters, fourteen for the first part and three for the second. Nevertheless, this unfinished work is one of the most remarkable monuments that Jewish thought produced in the realm of Judaism in the modern period.

Krochmal's philosophy was purely idealistic, since, after all, he was an ardent admirer of Maimonides and was educated on classic German Idealist philosophy. The greatest impression on him was made by Kant and Hegel; their influence is very strongly discernible in his life's work. Johann Gottlieb Fichte affected him not with his philosophical system but mainly with his famous *Reden an die deutsche Nation,* in which he gives a brilliant philosophical elucidation of the national question. Some scholars[15] attempt to stamp Krochmal with the title Hegelian and portray him as a loyal disciple of the renowned German thinker. This, however, is not correct. To be sure, in many highly important passages of *Moreh Nevuchei Ha-Zeman* one senses Hegel's influence quite clearly. For instance, when Krochmal considers *being* and *non-being* in a purely dialectical fashion, not as two extreme antitheses but as two moments of one and the same unbroken phenomenon;[16] or when he explains how quality passes over into quantity.[17] But missing from Krochmal are precisely the most important points of Hegel's philosophy, namely, the dynamic power of historical development, the dialectic of contrasts and contradictions, the doctrine concerning the triad of thesis, antithesis, and synthesis, of the struggle of the existing with the new forms which are born out of it and become, with iron inevitability, its destroyer and gravedigger, and the teaching that precisely through this process of destruction human society passes to higher levels of development. All this is

13. For the title *Moreh Nevuchei Ha-Zeman* (Guide for the Perplexed of our Time), Krochmal's work is indebted to Leopold Zunz, who edited and published it after the author's death.
14. See the above-quoted letter to Luzzatto.
15. E.g., J.L. Landau in his German work, *Nachman Krochmal ein Hegelianer,* 1904; also S. Bernfeld in *Dor Hacham,* 15.
16. *Moreh Nevuchei Ha-Zeman,* Gate Fifteen, 214–215.
17. *Ibid.,* 218. Even Philo's philosophical world-view obtains, in Krochmal's interpretation, a Hegelian coloration (*ibid.,* end of Gate Twelve).

untouched by Krochmal, and Rawidowicz[18] is quite correct in concluding that the Galician thinker considers the course of history not from the dialectic but from the purely genetic point of view.

Other extremely important elements of Hegel's "philosophy of history" obtain in Krochmal a quite different interpretation and thereby also a new, more concrete and realistic content. Hegel teaches in his *Philosophie der Geschichte* that the essence of world history is the objective development of the Absolute Idea, the development through which the universal spirit comes to its full self-consciousness, to knowledge of itself.[19] But while Hegel considers the historical nations, kingdoms, and "folk-spirits" *(Volksgeister)* only as definite stages in the self-consciousness of the Absolute Spirit and perceives the sole significance and value of the historical process precisely in the fact that "the World-Spirit knows itself," Krochmal was chiefly interested in the process itself: how national cultures are formed and created, how the national community raises itself in its historical development from the lowest states of culture to the highest. Whereas Hegel perceived in the state the supreme disclosure of the objective spirit, the most perfect incarnation of divine wisdom in the life of mankind, Krochmal saw the exclusive spiritual power of the Jewish community precisely in the fact that it outgrew the institution of the state and that its national culture was not bound up with the narrow boundaries of any definite territory. Krochmal's chief interest in history lies not in the idea that, through its course of development, "the universal spirit comes to its full self-consciousness, to knowledge of itself," but in the fact that, through exploring and gaining knowledge of cultural-historical processes, the *human personality* arrives at "self-consciousness."

It is absolutely essential, the philosopher of Zolkiew declares, to explore as far as possible and to become familiar with the past of our people, with its major experiences, with its encounters and relationships with other societies and environments, and with the views, tendencies, hopes, and demands that were thereby produced in various periods. This is necessary, Krochmal asserts, because in it is revealed the essence of the collective national spirit; only thereby can we clarify and recognize our own nature, and can the past serve us as a guide for the future.[20] Krochmal, however, knew quite well how unfamiliar and back-

18. In his introduction to *Kitvei RaNaK.*

19. Hegel, *Die Philosophie der Geschichte,* second edition, 23, 79ff.

20. *Moreh Nevuchei Ha-Zeman,* Gate Twelve, 127. See also the end of Gate Ten: "Inquiry into all these things is excellent and precious, so that we may be wise in our end."

ward his readers were in regard to historical questions. Even scholars and savants were certain that the patriarch Jacob had studied in the *yeshivot* of Shem and Eber; that Othniel, one of the first "judges" of the Bible, had, through ingenious *pilpul*, renewed many forgotten laws; that King David's heroic warrior Amasa used to go to the *bet ha-midrash* every day girded with his sword.[21] Every law in the *Shulḥan Aruch* was "a law given to Moses at Sinai," and whoever wished to show that the Psalm beginning "By the rivers of Babylon we sat and wept" was not composed by King David through the holy spirit, but by a poet of the era of the Babylonian Exile, was a heretic and denier. "There is no greater harm," declares Krochmal, "than to confuse times and events;" and he concludes that upon him lies the obligation to remove this confusion, to become the guide for the "perplexed of the time."

In a calm, sedate tone that would satisfy both the "truth-seeker" thirsting for knowledge and the only slightly prepared reader, the Galician thinker attempts to analyze the *Massorah* and Scripture in the light of scientific criticism. He is not content with the fact that he, the first among Jewish scholars, gives a masterly overview, from the cultural-historical standpoint, of the period of origin of the major biblical works[22] and of their significance as historical documents. He dwells at considerable length on the history of the evolution of Jewish culture from the Babylonian exile to the close of the Talmud. He was the first historian who shed light on the most obscure period in Jewish history—from Zerubbabel and the first return to Palestine to the Hasmoneans. With great acuteness and clever intuition, Krochmal employs as valuable historical material numerous statements, moral lessons, *aggadot* and ordinances scattered throughout the old Talmudic literature. Also the peculiarities of the language, certain lexicological elements, are successfully employed to determine the time when a certain decision or regulation was accepted.

Literally epoch-making are the chapters (XIII-XIV) in which Krochmal attempts to provide a scientific analysis of how, in the

---

21. *Moreh Nevuchei Ha-Zeman*, Gate Thirteen, 161.

22. Several scholars note that Krochmal, in his historical-critical analysis, avoids discussing the question of the final redaction of the Pentateuch. This, however, is not quite correct. Cautiously but quite assuredly he lets the reader know that certain parts of the Pentateuch belong to a later era. See, e.g., Krochmal's indication: "And know that the blessing of Jacob to his sons was basically prophesied for the present time" (Gate Eight, 29). He also indicates that the two *tochahot*, or lists of "anathemas," belong to a later time (Gate Nine, 34).

course of generations, the Oral Torah (the *halachah* as well as the *aggadah*) developed from the times of Ezra the Scribe to the codification of the Talmud. Whereas in the field of Bible criticism Krochmal had predecessors among Christian European scholars, in the realm of the Talmud he was a true pioneer and an acknowledged guide for later Talmudic scholars.[23] All his work is written in a calm, scholarly tone, without any rhetorical flourishes, in a succinctly formulated, somewhat old-fashioned language that reminds one of the ancient philosophical books of the Ibn Tibbons and the profound Ḥasdai Crescas.[24] With vast learning and model systematic order he provides a clear picture of how the Oral Torah evolved in the course of generations under the direct influence of the gradually altered way of life. With irresistible logic Krochmal attempts to make obvious even to the orthodox reader that "if one had a clearer notion of the primitive conditions of life under which the Jews lived in the times of the Judges, and even in the era of the kings of Judah, he would then first properly understand how little they then required the numerous *halachot* that are regarded as 'laws given to Moses at Sinai.' "[25]

When one compares the corresponding "gates" of Krochmal's *Moreh Nevuchei Ha-Zeman* with the pages in *Kinat Ha-Emet* in which Miesis gives a general overview of Jewish cultural history, one first clearly sees how great is the distance between historical-critical, genuinely scientific scholarship and superficial, dilettantish, rationalistic theories drawn at third hand, without independent critical elucidation.

Krochmal, however, is not content merely with history. He also undertakes to make clear to the reader the moral lesson, the philosophy of history. It is not only Jewish tradition that he considers a product of a generations-long process of evolution of cultural-national creativity, following definite laws; according to the philosopher's conception, the national principle in

23. Interesting in this respect is the passage in the memoirs of A.H. Weiss, the author of the classic *Dor Dor Ve-Doreshav*, in which he writes of the influence Krochmal's work had on his own research (*Zichronotai*, 121, 123; see also *Dor Dor Ve-Doreshav*, Vol. II, 204).
24. Only in the subsequent chapter, Gate Fifteen, "Derech Ha-Hitzonim," in which the Jewish-Christian Gnostics and the teachers of Kabbalah are treated, does Krochmal occasionally lose his scholarly objectivity. Because the Kabbalah gave intellectual nourishment to the Shabbetai Tzevi movement and to Hasidism, which Krochmal so despised, he underscores that the theosophical ideas of the Kabbalah derive mainly from the sects which separated from Judaism.
25. *Moreh Nevuchei Ha-Zeman*, Gate Thirteen, 161, 162–163. The reader must, in this connection, come to the logical conclusion that these laws are a product of considerably later generations.

general occupies the central point in every cultural-historical process. Every national society, Krochmal declares, when, on its historical life-path, it develops its spiritual powers by stages, places upon all the cultural elements it gathers in itself the unique stamp of its spirit, of its personal version of the "I." Indeed, all these individual, specific colors and nuances that the cultural treasures obtain among every people are the essence, the nature, of the nation. The concretized symbol of the uniqueness characterizing the national spiritual powers—this is the "god of the nation," or the "ruler of the nation," as it is termed in Talmudic literature. Each nation must traverse a long, arduous way from the most primitive stages of culture until it creates its "god"—the reflection and limited conception of the Absolute Spirit *(Ha-Ruhani Ha-Muhlat).*

Each nation, like every other living organism in nature, traverses—according to Krochmal—three developmental stages: the stage of efflorescence and growth; the stage of highest development of strength and activity; and the stage of decay and dissolution.[26] With the decline of the national culture, the philosopher stresses, the nation also decays. For the essence of the nation is, after all, its *spiritual* uniqueness; and if the spirit withers, the society promptly disintegrates.[27] The spirit, however, is immortal, and everything a national culture has that is truly valuable, that is not strictly associated with the ephemeral limitations of time and place, is taken up into the treasures of universal culture.[28]

Among all the civilizations of the ancient world, Krochmal notes, that of the Jewish people was unique. Every other people's civilization disclosed itself in limited, partial forms. In one, the supreme criterion, the measure of all values, was beauty; in another, power; etc. According to these concepts were also formed the "gods of the nation" that every people produced. But the Jewish people, at the higher stages of its cultural evolution, was not content with the limited and one-sided; it turned exclusively to the absolute and universal. The national genius of the Jewish people dwelt not on the separate disclosures or revela-

---

26. *Moreh Nevuchei Ha-Zeman*, Gate Eight, "Am Olam U-Mo'adav."

27. *Moreh Nevuchei Ha-Zeman*, Gate Seven, 22: "Only that spirit in itself and *alone* gives birth to, and sustains, that bond during the entire period of the nation's existence . . . The character of a nation does not consist in the fact that it is a nation but in its spiritual essence . . . No human group or society can exist the moment this bond is dissolved."

28. *Ibid.* "They thereby become the heritage of the whole human species and its universal spirituality that is realized in it and becomes its light forever."

tions of the World-Spirit but on its all-embracing limitlessness and abstract necessity. Thus the national god of the Jewish people became the Absolute Spirit and the Infinite *(Ha-Ruḥani Ha-Muḥlat Veha-Ein Sof)*. The most characteristic aspect of the national culture of the Jewish people consists in the fact that, in the course of its historical development, it outgrew narrow national boundaries and rose to universal compass. In this, Krochmal adds, lies the secret of the words so frequently repeated in the Torah: "And I will dwell in your midst;" "For I am with you;" "And My spirit abides among you." This is the meaning of the symbolic expression *Shechinah Be-Yisrael*,[29] the Divine Presence in Israel.

Krochmal deems it necessary to underscore a number of times that the evolution which the Jewish people traversed from the ephemeral and limited national to the universal and absolute is a product of a cultural-historical process lasting many generations. But as soon as this process came to its end, the fate of disintegration common to all other peoples could have no dominion, thanks to the spirit of the universal and absolute, over the Jewish people. The spirit of the universal and absolute to which this people raised itself made it immortal, independent of the boundaries of state and definite territory. Therefore when the "triad" of development of Jewish history ended and Nebuchadnezzar's armies destroyed the Kingdom of Judah, the life-path of the Jewish people did not thereby cease, as was the case among other peoples. The fate of this singular people spun itself further; immediately there began the historical development process of a new "triad."

Krochmal defines three such "triads" in Jewish history. The first link of the second triad, the time of efflorescence and growth, was, according to the Galician thinker, the period spanning the first return of the Jews to Palestine from the Babylonian exile to Alexander of Macedon; the "period of strength and activity" ends with the death of Alexander Jannaeus' wife, Queen Salome; the third period, that of decline and dissolution, ends with the destruction of Betar and the failure of Bar Kochba's revolt. Krochmal considers the period of the codification of the Mishnah as the beginning of the third "triad;" the heyday period commences with the appearance on the world arena of Moslem-Arabic civilization and lasts to the time of Maimonides; from the thirteenth century on begins the period of decline. Not quite clearly, but only from hints and allusions in that part of

29. *Ibid.*, 23–24.

Moreh Nevuchei Ha-Zeman that was written, can one conjecture that, according to Krochmal, the first period of a new "triad" in Jewish history began close to his time, toward the end of the eighteenth century, with the first shoots of Haskalah.

This, however, is indicated only through allusions. Also unclarified are several other very significant points in Krochmal's philosophy. It is difficult to determine whether the author deliberately did not wish clearly to elucidate certain details in order not to enrage the "fools among the believers," or whether he intended to speak of them at greater length in the second, philosophical part of his work, which, because of his premature death, he did not manage to write.

It is worthwhile in this connection to dwell on an important point. We noted previously that Krochmal's philosophy was idealistic. While he frequently underscores the importance of cult and religious ritual,[30] nevertheless, as a loyal disciple of Maimonides, he indicates that "knowledge of God" is a higher stage than "service of God," for only through seeking God, by means of religious philosophy, can one attain the supreme unity, the Absolute. In every individual, as well as in every national society, Krochmal declares, there are, even at the lowest stages of culture, sparks of God-knowledge and, through a long historical evolution, these obscure, not quite defined sentiments and aspirations develop to the exalted, to the level of *emunah toriyyit* (Torahitic faith) of a positive religion, whose definition, according to the philosopher, is knowledge and grasp of the absolute truth, the primal cause of everything, through which and in which alone it obtains the significance of real existence.[31]

Elsewhere[32] Krochmal says: "The final goal of the world cannot be other than the spirit revealed in it and through it." "The spirit and its essence," "the universal spirit," "the Absolute Spirit:—these are terms that our author employs repeatedly. But he does not once attempt, in the "gates" which he managed to write, to clarify what he actually understands by the "Absolute Spirit." He merely indicates in the sixth "gate" that only

---

30. At the end of Gate Six, and also his article in *Kerem Hemed*, IV, 269–270. Krochmal perceives the significance of the cult not only in the fact that it serves as a means of regulating and hallowing the life of the community. Its importance lies, in his view, chiefly in the fact that through it the innermost spiritual consciousness of the community expresses itself in active, concrete deeds, and thereby greatly aids the unity and cohesiveness of the collective.

31. *Moreh Nevuchei Ha-Zeman*, Gate Six, 17–18.

32. *Ibid.*, Gate Fourteen, 187.

through its active, accomplished deeds does the World-Spirit arrive at self-knowledge. But we already know that, in Krochmal's cultural-historical conception, every civilized people creates its god and preserves him in its spiritual treasures. And even though the people succumbs, its spiritual treasures pass over as a legacy "to the whole human species and to its universal spirit."[33] The Jewish people, according to Krochmal's philosophy, in its conception of God as creator went even further: "He is the Creator of all!" In its cultural ascent it produced the concept of the universal, the all-embracing World-Spirit. The possession that it is attained, "the staff of its inheritance" *(shevet naḥalato)* is—"The Lord of hosts is His name!"[34] The "Lord of hosts" is the God of Israel, the "Absolute Spirit," the national spirit of the Jewish people. The thought of the old Maharal of Prague that the Jewish people is the man-God in whom the whole human species, the entire cosmos, attained its definite form, its goal and purpose,[35] obtains in Krochmal a modern, "Hegelian" interpretation. Hegel's doctrine about the self-knowledge of the World-Spirit is here elucidated from a very unique point of view: through the conception of God as Creator and the awareness of Him, the national community comes to self-knowledge, to the disclosure of its cultural powers.

Not without reason did Krochmal regard with such an ironic smile the debates that took place among the Hegelians after the death of their great teacher. In one of his letters written to his elder son, he relates how the controversy between Leo (a then well-known historian) and Hegel's disciples had at first caused him great chagrin, but later he laughed at himself, wondering why he who, after all, was so remote from the whole quarrel, takes it all to heart. Yes, the giant is dead, but "one would not like to have the poor followers come to Brody."[36]

Zunz, who quotes this letter, remarks in this connection: "The Hegelians and their opponents had no notion whatever of the fact that somewhere in Galicia a Polish Jew sits and issues a sharp, annihilating judgment on them."

As we have already noted, *Moreh Nevuchei Ha-Zeman* remained uncompleted. On July 31 (Rosh Ḥodesh Menaḥem Av)[37] 1840,

---

33. *Ibid.*, p. 22.
34. *Ibid.*, p. 23.
35. See our *History*, Vol. VI, Book One, Chapter Four.
36. See Zunz, *Gesammelte Schriften*, II, 157–158.
37. Solomon Jehudah Rapoport used this date in the epitaph that he wrote after the death of the friend of his youth: "Menaḥem (Naḥman) departed on the first day of Menaḥem (the month of Av); I have no comforter (menaḥem)."

Krochmal died at Tarnopol in the arms of his elder daughter, with whom he spent the last two years of his life.[38] Before his death he had directed that his unfinished manuscript be sent to Zunz in Berlin. Zunz greatly esteemed the Galician thinker and scholar, and through his initiative the community of Berlin, half a year before Krochmal's death, invited him to occupy the position of rabbi in the Prussian capital. Krochmal emphatically declined, indicating that with his philosophy and his "theological investigations," he considers it impossible "ever to occupy a position as a counselor of conscience" and to concern himself "with directing the religious affairs of a community."

Zunz fulfilled the wish of the deceased thinker, but because he was extremely busy with his own investigations, *Moreh Nevuchei Ha-Zeman* was published only eleven years after its author's death. In the course of this period significant changes took place in the Galician centers of Haskalah. Of Krochmal's most important fellow-battlers, some left Galicia, others completed their life's way. The major journal produced on Galician soil was silenced. The heyday of Galician Haskalah came to an end, and other centers occupied the foreground.

In the year that Krochmal died, Rapoport left Galicia. We noted earlier that Rapoport supported his family by serving as an official and cashier in the city kosher meat-tax office. He suffered greatly from the fact that this position took up a great deal of his time and little leisure remained for scholarly work. In his well-known letter to the rabbi of Zolkiew, Tzevi Hirsh Chajes, Rapoport complains that he experiences the frustration of the legendary Tantalus: he sees before his eyes the refreshing springs of knowledge but cannot reach them. He therefore envies Chajes for the fact that, as a rabbi and head of a community, he can sit quietly engaged in study of Torah and in worship.[39] Krochmal, with his philosophy, as we have observed, considered it impermissible to become the religious leader of a community. Rapoport was not so scrupulous. Moreover, he had to suffer a great deal from the local orthodox Jews who, led by the rabbi's son Mordecai Wolf Ornstein, persecuted him and even leased the town meat-taxes with the definite purpose of taking away his position and leaving him without a livelihood.[40]

In 1838 Rapoport's wish was fulfilled. With the aid of his friend Joseph Perl, who, in consequence of his wealth and influence among the local officials, played a very prominent role in Tar-

---

38. Previously he spent several years in his native town of Brody.
39. *Otzar Neḥmad*, I, 23.
40. See *Iggerot Shir*, 1885, p. 49.

nopol, Rapoport was appointed a rabbi in that community. This made an enormous impression in the Haskalah circles. They considered it a great victory that a *maskil* and scientific scholar should occupy the rabbinic chair in a prominent Galician community. Rapoport was greeted with odes and poems of praise, and it was noted with pride that in the place of "misleaders" and "ignorant teachers" who used to be entrusted "with pasturing the holy sheep," there has now been chosen a "strong man, mighty to seek out and uproot the thorns of his vineyard and to plant the truth."[41]

The joy, however, was soon marred. The orthodox Jews of Tarnopol regarded the "heretical" rabbi with great hostility. An intense controversy, with denunciations and persecutions, broke out.[42] Rapoport's situation in Tarnopol deteriorated after Perl's death in 1839. He became convinced that he could no longer remain in the Galician city. At this critical juncture his friends came to his aid and, in consequence of their intercession, he received from the community of Prague an invitation to occupy the rabbinic office there. Two weeks after Krochmal's death, Rapoport left Galicia. The Prague community received him with great honor. Nevertheless, he soon became convinced that he had been mistaken: his hope that, in the rabbinic chair, he would be able to engage uninterruptedly in scholarly work evaporated. Communal affairs demanded a great deal of his time. Moreover, there was another important factor. As a religious leader of a community in which the orthodox still played a rather significant role, Rapoport was afraid of being reminded of "the sins of his youth" and of being suspected of "heresy." This brought it about that, with his move to Prague, the period of decline in Rapoport's scholarly work actually began.[43]

41. *Kerem Ḥemed*, IV, 253–259.

42. A one-sided description of this controversy is to be found in *Kerem Ḥemed*, IV, 241–252. A more objective portrait is provided by S. Bernfeld in his *Toledot Shir*.

43. Rapoport, in fact, himself admits this in his old age in his letter of 1860 to Samuel David Luzzatto: "You know, my brother, how formerly I made known to many my desire for some rabbinic post. One thing I have asked, that will I seek: to dwell in the house of the Lord all the days of my life, to contemplate the pleasantness of the Torah, to investigate the antiquities of Israel and their signs and wonders, to explore the words of our ancient sages, may their memory be for a blessing, to disperse the darkening clouds from those who bring many to righteousness [i.e., the *maskilim*], and to demonstrate their glory like the splendor of the firmament and the stars forever and ever. However, to my distress, I saw that after my desire had been fulfilled, how greatly my imagination had misled me. For indeed, I could do more and achieve more in writing down my investigations and inquiries when I was a free man without masters than I was able to engage in such things from the time that I became a servant to many masters. For not authority does a teacher of true religion and a rabbi in Israel take upon himself, but rather enslavement" (*Iggerot Shir*, 216).

The official of the kosher meat-tax office in Lemberg contributed more to Jewish literature and scholarship than the rabbi and head of the community in Prague. Contributing to this was the fact that the important journal of which Rapoport was the actual editor—the already frequently quoted *Kerem Ḥemed*—was also silenced soon after his move to Prague.

As early as 1817 Jacob Samuel Bick in Brody had made an attempt to unite the Haskalah circles around a literary center and began to issue a journal called *Olat Shabbat* in which, besides the editor himself, the aged Mendel Levin, Naḥman Krochmal, Solomon Rapoport, Isaac Erter, Abraham Goldberg, and the then still very young poet Meir Letteris participated. The journal was circulated not in print but in handwritten copies in a very limited number. How many issues of *Olat Shabbat* appeared is not known, because not a single copy has been preserved; the only source that mentions the journal is Letteris in his *Zikkaron Ba-Sefer* (page 133).

Four years later, as we already know, Shalom Cohen established in Vienna *Bikkurei Ha-Ittum,* in which contributors from Galicia mainly participated. Only as a result of the Galician Rapoport and his important scholarly articles, did this journal obtain enduring literary-historical significance. *Bikkurei Ha-Ittim* had a relatively substantial number of readers because the same copy was read by scores of persons. The number of subscribers, however, was quite limited, and the publisher and printer Anton von Schmid, after the publication of the twelfth volume (1832), declined to issue *Bikkurei Ha-Ittim* further. This was a great blow for the Galician *maskilim,* but a young *maskil* from Bolechow, Samuel Leib Goldenberg, a son of a wealthy family who had married in Tarnopol and was supported by his affluent father-in-law, promptly came to their aid.

The well-to-do son-in-law had very slight literary capacities; on the other hand, he was a competent entrepreneur and organizer. As soon as he learned that *Bikkurei Ha-Ittim* would cease publication, he undertook a new journal which, however, was to have a character quite different from that of *Bikkurei Ha-Ittim.* He excluded the belletristic part, and to the great regret of the young, newly hatched *maskilim,* refused to publish poems and rhetorical pieces. In 1833 the first volume of his journal appeared under the title *Sefer Kerem Ḥemed Kolel Iggarot Yekarot*—a collection of important letters "which the scholars of our time have written to each other on matters of religion and scholarship."

We observed earlier[44] what an exceptional role the letter-form

44. See above, p. 52.

played in the literary creativity of the Haskalah circles. Rapoport writes to Samuel David Luzzatto:

For me, one hour spent in writing scholarly letters to good friends is more precious than whole days of scholarly labor on work that I am preparing for the press; for in regard to a printed book, I cannot know into what hands it will fall, whether the reader will be a sensible man or an ignorant person quite incapable of appreciating the value of all my trouble and accumulated knowledge. And even in the case of the understanding reader, I have no idea whether my words will please him or not. Every author is content beforehand with the knowledge that, out of a thousand readers, there will be only one of the kind whom he desires, and to this one his words are directed. But in a special letter the reader, after all, is known to me, and I know beforehand that my trouble will not be in vain; for the addressee is the desired reader-friend, the one chosen out of a thousand, and I know that I will soon receive a reply with a candid statement whether my words are right or whether I am mistaken. Hence, I learn far more from a letter especially written to me than from a book printed for thousands.[45]

In Haskalah circles it was an accepted custom that the same letter would be distributed by the writer in copies to all his close friends,[46] and each of these would, in turn, circulate it further to his friends. Goldenberg therefore conceived the idea of applying to the most important representatives of Haskalah and requesting them to send him their correspondence, so that he might "plant" these letters of friendship in his "pleasant garden" *(Kerem Ḥemed)*.[47] Goldenberg was actually only the publisher. He did not believe himself called to edit the letters of the "scholars of our time." He even points this out in the "Introduction of the Publisher," in which he asserts that he "does not undertake to be the master and judge of the works which these scholars of the generation send to him; he is also not responsible for the views the authors plant in his garden . . . He only looks at them, warms himself at the great scholars' light."

Goldenberg, in fact, kept his word. He did not express any

45. *Iggerot Shir*, 28.
46. See Letteris' note in *Ha-Tzofeh Le-Vet Yisrael*, 92.
47. Vol. I–1833; Vol. II–1836; Vol. III–1838; Vol. IV–1840; Vol. V–1841; Vol. VI–1841; Vol. VII–1843. Ten years later Senior Sachs in Berlin made another attempt to continue *Kerem Ḥemed*. Only two volumes appeared: Vol. VIII–1854, and Vol. IX–1856. In the same year (1856) the *maskil* of Brody, Isaac Blumenfeld, began to issue the journal *Otzar Neḥmad*, also a collection of "precious letters from the sages of our time" in which the same contributors as in *Kerem Ḥemed* participated, in Vienna. Four volumes appeared: Vol. I–1856; Vol. II–1857; Vol. III–1860; and Vol. IV–1863.

views to his contributors, and he, who belonged to the right wing of the Haskalah movement, even published without any editorial comments or statements in the second volume of *Kerem Ḥemed* (pp. 85–94) such a sharp article as Peli's on the "latter codifiers" *(Posekim Ha-Aharonim)*. The latter codifiers are those since Joseph Karo's and Moses Isserles' times. With hatred and bitterness the unknown author, who conceals his identity under the pseudonym "Peli," speaks of these halachic codifiers who, as he asserts, despised every branch of science and regarded poetry and elegant style with disgust. They always went backward and not forward, and groped like blind men in the dark. Since the exile from Spain, our people have declined fearfully in Torah, as well as in science and in virtue. Our authors have written, in vast numbers, books without any order or style. Their language is confused and corrupt, their reason benighted. Who gave them authorization to multiply each day new laws, new severities of which the *Rishonim* (the earlier codifiers) had no notion whatever? Long as the exile are the compositions of the *Aharonim*, for among them are mixed, together with the laws, many things that have no relationship whatever to these laws, and frequently in them are sanctioned customs that derive from the most corrupt source—from the *Zohar* and the Kabbalah, which completely altered the Torah and the religion. How did they manifest no reverence for the honor of the Torah and permit themselves to degrade it to the ground by mingling its divine precepts with such pernicious and wild things and, moreover, asserting that they derive from one and the same source?

Moses ben Maimon, the godly man, in his *Mishneh Torah* wished to give the people a definitive religious code. What would he have said had he seen these whole mountains of books produced after him in this realm? Not to explain Scripture was the goal of these authors, but to demonstrate how ingenious their *pilpul* is, what keen minds they have. It was their drive for honor and power that produced this whole misfortune. Through them was the Torah so degraded. These authors obscured it and distorted its beauty. Through their innumerable severities they pushed away with both hands the weak and tottering, and these declared in terror: "It is impossible to fulfill God's commands, for they press down like an iron yoke; it is not possible to bear them."

Peli speaks with special wrath of Rabbi Moses Isserles,[48] whom he declares to be "the father of the strict interpreters,"

---

48. See our *History*, Vol. VI, pp. 29–39.

who become "a stumbling block and an obstacle" for later generations.[49]

Excitement was also produced in the learned circles by the letter of Rapoport mentioned above to his friend Leib Holish and published in the first volume of *Kerem Ḥemed,* where he discusses the mode of learning in the times of the Amoraim in Palestine and Babylonia. Rapoport gives a melancholy cultural-historical portrait of that era, and dwells especially on the regrettable order of learning in the well-known Talmudic academy in Pumbeditha where the fruitless and overly subtle *pilpul* was especially favored.

Kerem Ḥemed, however, did not long remain without an actual editor. From the third volume on, it was edited by the keen Solomon Rapoport. His name did not appear on the title-page. Even his own numerous articles appeared anonymously,[50] but in the Haskalah circles it was known very well who the real leader of *Kerem Ḥemed* was. Rapoport's name attracted the most significant Hebrew writers of that age. To be sure, in *Kerem Ḥemed* also, as in *Bikkurei Ha-Ittim,* the majority of the contributors were from Galicia.[51] But in *Kerem Ḥemed* scholars from Italy, Bohemia, Germany, Russia, and other lands participated. Studies in the most varied realms of scholarship were printed: exegesis, archaeology, Talmudic learning, history, astronomy, mathematics, and treatises on medieval literature in which many important scholarly and poetic works of the Middle Ages were published for the first time. Critical articles, sometimes written in a sharply polemic tone, also appeared in *Kerem Ḥemed.* In this respect the sixth volume, which consists in largest part of Rapoport's polemic articles, is especially characteristic.

We noted earlier the enthusiasm with which Solomon Rapoport's critical-historical investigations were received in scholarly circles. Quite unexpectedly, however, a whole group of young *maskilim* issued forth against Rapoport, doing so impudently, with pointedly polemic attacks. This was not a battle of ideas of "fathers and sons," of the younger generation against

49. According to Halberstam and Wachstein this sharp article was composed by the Italian Hillel di Laturah (see *Die hebräische Publizistik in Wien,* 1930, p. 229).

50. For the list of Rapoport's works published in *Kerem Ḥemed,* see *Die hebräische Publizistik in Wien,* 1930, pp. 175–178. The most important of these is his excellent study of the Ten Tribes and Firkovich's falsifications in regard to the medieval monuments found in Chufut-Kale (*Kerem Ḥemed,* V, 197–232).

51. M. Weissberg already noted in his *Aufklärungs-Literatur in Galizien* (p. 63) that, among the eighteen contributors who participated in volumes II and VI, fourteen were from Galicia.

the older, backward generation. These young people were of very limited knowledge and slight talent, but with great ambition and youthful impetuosity. Through great clamor and a literary scandal they hoped to make a name for themselves, to become "household words."

In 1837 four *maskilim* of Lemberg, Jacob Bodek, Jacob Mentsh, Menahem Mendel Mohr, and Nahman Fishman, published a collection of critical articles entitled *Ha-Ro'eh U-Mevakker Sifrei Mehabberei Zemanenu* (The Seer and Critic of the Books of Contemporary Authors).[52] In it the works of Zunz, Rapoport, and Luzzatto are criticized. The "seers" issue forth with special sharpness against Rapoport. Personal motives are discernible in their crude attacks, and this is also confirmed by the fact that they participated in the persecutions Rapoport had to suffer in Tarnopol.

At the same time another more pointed and serious critic issued forth against Rapoport. This was Eliakim ben Jehudah Ha-Milzahgi (Mehlsack) of Brody. Born into a prestigious rabbinic family,[53] he was raised on Talmudic literature and, with his brilliant capacities, acquired enormous learning in it. He was also a great scholar in Kabbalah, writing a large commentary to the *Zohar* and translating the great mystical work from Aramaic into Hebrew. He also wrote a commentary to *Pesikta Rabbati* and composed many other works.[54] All these, however, remained in manuscript, for he was a very poor man[55] and furthermore, as he himself testifies,[56] a very retiring person; of his work, as of his great knowledge, only his closest friends were aware.

Even with his difficult material situation, Milzahgi managed to obtain a certain amount of European culture and was familiar with German scientific literature. Soon after Zunz's *Die gottesdienstlichen Vorträge der Juden* was published, Milzahgi wrote a whole composition with *hassagot* or notes in which he disputes many of Zunz's conclusions and also criticizes some of the as-

52. Two years later the second number appeared (in Ofen). In this number only three "seers" participated, since Jacob Mentsh soon left the group.
53. His father was a rabbi. His father's sister's son was the well-known Rabbi Zalman Margolioth. His relative also was the well-known rabbi of Lissa, Jacob Harif.
54. Milzahgi himself notes: "I composed many books." His commentary on the *Zohar* was written even before 1821.
55. "And I, burdened with troubles, obtained a livelihood painfully from my labor, supported myself with suffering from the work of my hands, and I had not the wherewithal to buy books," Milzahgi frequently complains.
56. *Ravyah*, folio 22a (through a printer's error the folio is marked 19).

sumptions made by Rapoport on which Zunz relies in his works. Especially brilliant is the keen criticism to which he subjects Rapoport's conjecture, set forth in his work on the liturgical poet Eleazar Kallir, that in many of Kallir's hymns his name is indicated through all kinds of *gematriot.*[57] This work also remained in manuscript, and Milzahgi's name would have been lost entirely if his townsman, the *maskil* Berish Blumenfeld (born in 1779, died in 1853), who acquired a reputation with his German translation of Job (published in 1826 with a commentary and with a long introduction), had not taken pity on him. At his own expense, Blumenfeld published (in Ofen in 1837) Milzahgi's "notes" under the title *Sefer Ravyah.*[58]

Ravyah created a sensation in Jewish learned circles. "*Ravyah* will live and not die," Samuel David Luzzatto exclaimed enthusiastically,[59] and Zunz confessed that some of Milzahgi's "notes" to his *Die gottesdienstlichen Vorträge der Juden* are completely correct. Rapoport's attitude, however, was different. With all his brilliant capacities, he had one very serious defect: he always stubbornly insisted on his own view.[60] He defended every idea that he had ever expressed with steel-like firmness, even when others demonstrated with the sharpest proofs that he was mistaken and the idea he had expressed was false. So it was, for instance, with his conjecture about the time and place in which Eleazar Kallir lived and worked. Many scholars, on the basis of weighty arguments, definitely rejected Rapoport's conjecture. The latter, however, continued to maintain his view with great obduracy. The same phenomenon was repeated with the *gematriot* that Rapoport supposedly found in Kallir's liturgical poems. Zunz promptly admitted that, after Milzahgi's "notes," he no longer believed Rapoport's conjecture. Rapoport, however, refused to give in. He asserted that precisely the arguments of *Ravyah* first properly convinced him of the correctness of his theory regarding the *gematriot.* And in his polemic articles that occupy approximately three-fourths of the sixth volume of *Kerem Ḥemed* he settles accounts with Milzahgi, "together with all the youths." He includes him in the company of the "seers" and with the young Menaḥem Mendel Rosenthal, who came forth in 1839 with an impudent tract entitled *Emek Shoshanim*

57. *Ibid.*, folios 16–19.
58. *Ravyah*, an acronym from Rabbi Eliakim ben Jehudah Ha-Milzahgi.
59. *Iggerot Shadal*, 602.
60. Krochmal notes the defects of Rapoport's character in a letter of 1836: "It is not to be denied that the virtues of his intellect were ten times stronger than the virtues of his heart" (*Kitvei RaNaK*, 424).

against Rapoport, whom he accuses of "having dishonored the sages of the Talmud."

The article which the young Rosenthal so sharply attacked was written by Rapoport in the 1820's.[61] In the 1830's, when he already entertained the idea of occupying the rabbinic chair in a larger community, Rapoport avoided any animadversions against the rabbis or rabbinic literature. It was only his hatred for the Hasidim that he considered it unnecessary to conceal, and in his articles in *Kerem Hemed*[62] also he speaks of the *Mithasedim* as of a "band of transgressors," who have "all turned aside, are contaminated together, all hypocrites and evil-doers, all abomination and scheming, . . . They have done corruptly, committed abominable deeds; there is none who does good—not a one." Rapoport declares the Hasidic conventicles a "cave of criminals" in which "abominable and despicable persons" who are "a true shame for the human species" dwell.[63] With great anger he speaks in his eulogy after Krochmal's death about the *Mithasedim* who mercilessly persecute everyone who strives for culture and knowledge.[64]

Rapoport used to attack the Hasidim in his articles only incidentally. Two other contributors to *Kerem Hemed*, however, set as their task to carry on a systematic, bitter warfare against the "sect of the Hasidim." These were Joseph Perl, already known to us, and the ingenious author of *Ha-Tzofeh Le-Veit Yisrael*, Doctor Isaac Erter.

Of them in the next chapter.

61. See above, p. 83.
62. See, e.g., *Kerem Hemed*, IV, Letter 10.
63. *Ibid.*, pp. 46–48.
64. *Kerem Hemed*, VI, 45: "Surely you know that there are *Mithasedim* in the land and in the city. The frogs swarm in every house and in every room. These fiery serpents who burn with the breath of their mouth . . . the name of every *maskil* . . . and, at most times, even if his heart is like the heart of a lion, it melts, and therefore to this very day the upright *maskilim* there are few."

CHAPTER FIVE

Joseph Perl, Isaac Erter, and Abraham Kohn

Joseph Perl's disappointment—His satire *Boḥen Tzaddik*—Perl's criticism of the various strata in Jewish society—Upright men can be
found only among farmers—The poet Aryeh Leib Kinderfreund—
The idyll on the Jewish colonies in South Russia—Isaac Erter, the
"watchman of the house of Israel"—The *maskil* Joseph Tarler—Erter's
poetic style—His "visions"—Erter's battle against the Hasidim and
the rabbis—Erter's tract *Tashlich;* the significance of his satire *Gilgul
Nefesh*—The revolution of 1848 and its echoes in Galicia—The battle
between the orthodox and the "Germans"—The Reform rabbi
Abraham Kohn and his *Briefe aus Galizien*—The Polish nationalist
movement and the struggle in the community of Lemberg—The social
bases of this struggle—The anonymous author and his *Sendschreiben*—
Abraham Kohn's tragic death—Erter's programmatic article "Toledot
He-Ḥalutz"—Erter's sudden death.

FTER THE
publication of
his *Megalleh
Temirin,*[1] Jo-
seph Perl ex-
perienced a not
inconsiderable
disappointment.
The *Aufklärer* of
the eighteenth
century were
firmly con-
vinced that in
the course of
world history an
enormous error
had taken place:
men did not un-
derstand, al-

1. See the preceding volume, pp. 240ff.

lowed themselves to be led astray by swindlers and frauds, and were therefore mired in superstition and barbaric ignorance, following crooked and false paths. Hence, it is necessary to enlighten them, to disclose the truth, to illuminate eyes through the light of knowledge—and then the sun of justice and righteousness will shine over the whole of mankind. Joseph Perl saw in Hasidism the greatest threat, the chief cause of the abnormal life of the Jews. In the founders of the Hasidic movement he perceived only swindlers and avaricious frauds, and he believed that as soon as one "opens the eyes" of the deceived people and gives them to understand that the Hasidic world of ideas is nothing but superstition and idolatry, there will be an end to the *rebbes* and *tzaddikim* and the whole movement, and the bright rays of enlightenment will shine over the Jewish quarter. To this end he produced his *Megalleh Temirin* and issued forth against the dangerous enemy with the whip of satire and the destroying arrows of ridicule and laughter.

But Joseph Perl was forced to see with deep pain that precisely in the first decade after the publication of his satire, the strength of Hasidism waxed powerfully in Galicia. [2] However, with his militant nature, he did not lose courage. "Even if our words are now in vain," Perl declared, "we must still fulfill our duty—be it for future generations. And also in the present generation, if even one out of a thousand will, as a result of our work, be saved and not let himself be led astray by the swindlers and frauds, we are obliged to do everything we can for this single one. As the sages say: 'Whoever saves a single soul of Israel, it is as if he saved the whole world.' "[3] And approximately ten years after the publication of *Megalleh Temirin*, Joseph Perl wrote his second satirical work, *Bohen Tzaddik*.[4]

Bohen Tzaddik is composed in the form of a letter. It is of even broader scope than *Megalleh Temirin* and yet incomparably weaker. The style is not consistently maintained; at the beginning it is written in the same satirical fashion as *Megalleh Temirin*, but in the middle it passes over into the emotive, *maskil*-like style. The story is also excessively artificial. The keeper of the Baal Shem Tov's writings transmits to Obadiah ben Petahiah, the pseudonymous author of *Megalleh Temirin*, a special document with great mysteries. Thanks to this document, Obadiah

2. Rapoport also notes this in his review of *Bohen Tzaddik* (*Kerem Hemed*, I).
3. *Bohen Tzaddik*, 112.
4. *Bohen Tzaddik* was first published in 1838, but in a letter of 1838 to Isaac Baer Levinsohn, Perl writes that *Bohen Tzaddik* has long since been completed by him and that it is two years since he has obtained authorization from the censor (*Be'er Yitzhak*, 41).

can make himself invisible and fly on a cloud. Also through the keeper's aid, he obtains a marvelous writing-tablet from a hidden cave; on its pages all the words heard around it are written down of themselves. Thus, Obadiah wanders about, with the writing-tablet in his pocket, through the marketplaces, study-houses, and various homes as one who sees and is not seen, listens to what is said about his *Megalleh Temirin,* and everything is immediately and automatically noted down in the tablet. Perl attempts to transmit in Hebrew translation the unique Yiddish speech of his characters and deliberately renders it in caricatured form.[5]

The words noted down of themselves in marvelous fashion on the pages of the writing-tablet can be erased by only one thing in the world: the breath of a truly honest person. As soon as one who is free of falsehood and sin blows on the pages that have been written up, the inscriptions will disappear and the pages become clean again. When the pages of the tablet have become written up on all sides through the overheard conversations, Obadiah begins to seek the suitable person who, through his pure breath, will again be able to make the tablet clean. This, however, is not so easy to attain. He turns first of all to the *tzaddik* of the generation, to the Hasidic *rebbe,* tells him the whole story, and begs him to blow with his holy breath on the writing-tablet. The latter, however, absolutely refuses to do this —"obviously out of great modesty," Obadiah declares with irony.

He goes to another *rebbe* but does not tell this one that, to make the pages clean, what is required is precisely the breath of a person free of sin. For a good fee the *rebbe* blew with all his might on the writing-tablet, but his blast was of no avail and the letters did not move from their place. This, Obadiah explains with a pious mien, is probably because the *rebbe* in his youth sinned through having studied the *Gemara* in the Mitnagdic fashion. He went from one *rebbe* to another, and the writing-tablet always remained inscribed on all sides. Then Obadiah proceeded to the great scholars of the generation, the rabbis, but their breath, too, had no power over the inscriptions on the writing tablet. In this connection the following characteristic point is worth noting. The anonymous "Peli"[6] of *Kerem Ḥemed*

---

5. It is beyond doubt that Levinsohn's satire *Divrei Tzaddikim,* which originally bore the title *Megalleh Sod,* served Perl as a model in this connection. This satire was sent by Levinsohn to Perl as early as 1820, and it appeared in print, thanks to Perl (together with Levinsohn's other satire *Emek Refa'im*), in 1830 (see *Be'er Yitzḥak,* ii, 41–43).
6. See above, p. 82.

attacks the rabbis for their rigorous interpretations of the law and the innumerable fences they create around the Torah. The more temperate Joseph Perl, however assails the Galician rabbis mainly because they have not the courage to take a stand against the power of the *rebbes*, humble themselves before them, and pretend that they, too, supposedly are their disciples and believe in their holiness.[7] Obadiah then attempts to turn to other strata of the Jewish community in Galicia, first of all, the mercantile circles. For this purpose he goes to the typical commercial town of Brody (disguised as Abderi).

"In Abderi," Obadiah relates,

the whole populace is greatly absorbed in matters of trade . . . I was there among many rich men and saw how they do not even have a definite hour for eating, and on the Sabbath and festivals they do not know what they eat and drink, for all their thoughts are engrossed in the market-days that take place in the German and Russian lands. Four weeks before the market-days they are all absorbed with the preparations: the lender prepares to lend money, the borrower to make loans, the seller to sell the merchandise left over from the previous market-days, the purchaser to buy this merchandise at a cheap price, the banker to carry through all the business deals that must be completed before the market-days. The wagon drivers, messengers, servants—all are greatly absorbed in preparing for the market-day that is approaching. Even the teacher and the children's nurses in the home of the merchant are engrossed in business. They give their employer a certain sum to buy some item of merchandise for them, so that it should not cost them any wagon-shipping-charges. The journey to the market-day together with the return trip takes some six weeks. In the course of this whole period the men and women who remain at home are busy with preparing betimes the shipping charges for bringing home the merchandise bought on the market-day and also the sum required to cover the loans made in the course of the market-days, to pay them off as soon as the merchandise is brought home. When the merchants return home, they are again greatly involved with buying and selling, lending, paying out, giving and taking gifts, distributing the merchandise in the various territories, buying products, exchanging unsuitable merchandise for better, etc. And as soon as these matters come to an end, the time of another period of market-days approaches. Thus, the people of Abderi are always harried, to the extent that they literally do not know in what kind of world they go about.[8]

7. In this connection Perl utilizes the opportunity to settle accounts with the rabbi of Lemberg, Jacob Ornstein, for his persecution of the *maskilim* with the punishment of the ban (*Bohen Tzaddik*, 49–54).

8. *Bohen Tzaddik*, 62–66.

So Obadiah wanders with his writing-tablet among the most
varied strata of the Jewish populace. He observes the conduct of
the merchants, bankers, brokers, shopkeepers, dealers—everywhere falsehood, swindlery, and thievery. They take usury, they
falsify, they cheat one another. "And all these characters consider themselves the finest householders in town, stand at the
eastern wall of the synagogue, are honored in being called to the
Torah, and our rabbis gladly enter into marriages with them."
Even among the workers and artisans it is no better. There also
laziness and demoralization are prevalent. They do not properly
know their craft. They greatly abuse their apprentices, employ
them mainly for work in the house, forcing them to look after
the children; and the craft itself they teach them most superficially. When the apprentices grow up, they do not know the
work as they should, and so they must falsify, cheat, and rob
their clients.

Joseph Perl sees the only salvation in agriculture. The honest
man from whose breath the written-up pages of his writing-
tablet at once became completely clean is found by Obadiah in
the first Jewish colonist with whom he became acquainted in
southern Russia.

We had occasion to indicate earlier[9] how village and shep-
herd idylls belonged to the favorite genre of the generation
of the Meassefim and their followers. At the same time that
Perl composed his *Boḥen Tzaddik* in Lemberg the talented
Aryeh Leib Kinderfreund[10] published (1834) his collection of
poems *Shirim Shonim* in which the most prominent place is
occupied by the cycle of poems "Ha-Meshorer Ba-Kefarim"
(The Poet in the Villages) in which village life on the bosom
of nature is portrayed in mild and gentle tones. The last
poem "Ba-Erev" (In the Evening) concludes with the pious
wish:

> O Thou who dwellest on high
> And seest their labor,
> I pray Thee, O God,
> Make sweet their sleep.

Joseph Perl's satire *Boḥen Tzaddik* also concludes with a village
idyll. In radiant, naively tender colors the first Jewish colonies
that the government of Nicholas I established in southern

9. Vol. VIII.
10. Born in Zamosc in 1797, died in Lemberg in 1837.

Russia are portrayed.[11] The childishly blind belief in the good will of "beneficent, enlightened absolutism," so characteristic of the *maskilim* of that era, contributed to the fact that Perl, the talented satirist and capable merchant and communal leader, allowed himself to be misled by two enthusiastic ladies of Brody. These ladies had occasion at the beginning of the 1820s to visit the colonies settled by the first group of Jews who came in 1806–1807 from the region of Moghilev, led by the energetic Nahum Finkelstein. The women were superficial observers; they had no notion of the frightful hardships and sufferings which the hundreds of Jewish families had to endure in the clumsy and cruel colonization that was carried through under the supervision of the czarist bureaucrats.[12] The great tragedy was transformed by them into an idyll which they described in a special correspondence published in 1823 in the Warsaw journal "Der Beobachter an der Weichsel."[13] This correspondence was employed almost verbatim by Perl in his *Bohen Tzaddik*, and with this saccharine-sweet, feminine portrait his satirical battling activity ends.

Of a quite different style was the other satirist of Galician Haskalah, Isaac Erter.

Isaac Erter was born in 1792 in a village near Przemysl. As was the fashion in those times, he was married off at the age of thirteen. However, a misfortune took place and half a year later his wife died. His father did not wait long and soon married off the young widower for a second time. The fourteen-year-old groom went to live with his father-in-law who resided in the village of Wielkia-Otchi. Like Joseph Perl in his youth, the young Erter was also an ardent Hasid, immersed himself daily in the ritual bath, danced with the Hasidim, and listened to wonder tales about *rebbes* and *tzaddikim*. "My understanding did not light up in this darkness," Erter later tells of his youthful years (in *Hasidut Ve-Hochmah*); "one could touch the pitch blackness all around with one's hands."

Unexpectedly a crisis occurred in his life. From a neighboring town a young *maskil* arrived in Wielkia-Otchi and settled in the very house in which Erter lived. The name of this *maskil* was Joseph Tarler. In his review of Perl's *Bohen Tzaddik*, Rapoport relates (*Kerem Hemed*, IV, 50) how a certain Hasid reproached a

11. *Bohen Tzaddik*, 97–102.
12. For precise documentary information about this, see Nikitin, *Yevrei-Zemledeltzi*, 8–92; S. Borovoi, *Yevr. Zemledelch. Kolonizatziya*, 1928, 41–71.
13. Reprinted in *Literarishe Bleter*, 1934.

prominent *maskil:* "To be sure, among us Hasidim there are enough gypsies (i.e., swindlers); among you, however, there are much greater ones." Another time (*Kerem Ḥemed,* VI, 42) Rapoport complains of the kind of *maskilim* who make of their education a "destructive instrument to do harm" and employ their knowledge of languages to send denunciations and informers' letters to the government. To this category of *maskilim,* whose education and knowledge was associated with immoral deeds, belonged Joseph Tarler.

Along with his thirst for knowledge, Tarler distinguished himself with a no lesser drive for wealth. He soon realized that through education alone he would not manage to achieve a prominent position in society; for this purpose extensive material resources were a prerequisite. If it is not possible to obtain these honestly, one ought not to recoil before fraud and crime. Tarler had a skillful hand and was ingenious in calligraphy, and so hit on the following scheme: when one of the wealthy estate-owners in the neighborhood died, he would forge fraudulent notes for a certain sum with the signature of the deceased landowner. In this way he made a considerable fortune for himself. Finally, Tarler's falsifications were discovered and, to save himself from the grievous punishment hanging over him, he converted to Christianity. Thereafter for many years he served as censor of Hebrew books in Lemberg, was extremely harsh toward Hasidic literature, and supported the *maskilim.* It is told that at the end of his days he became a penitent and used to appear frequently in the synagogue and worship with great devotion.[14]

Tarler became acquainted with Isaac Erter when he was still a youthful *maskil.* He "opened the eyes" of the fanatical young Hasid and familiarized him with the Haskalah literature and, above all, with the works of "both Moseses," i.e., Moses ben Maimon's *Guide for the Perplexed,* and the works of Moses Mendelssohn. Isaac Erter traversed the same stages as Joseph Perl in his day. From a Hasid he was transformed into a bitter opponent of Hasidism. He left Wielkia-Otchi and settled in Lemberg, where he earned a living by giving private lessons. He soon occupied a prominent place in the Haskalah circles in Lemberg, and this, indeed, brought it about that he was one of the first against whom Rabbi Jacob Ornstein's excommunication in 1815 was directed. Erter had to leave Lemberg and moved to Brody. The excommunication made an enormous impression on him.

14. *Ha-Kol,* V, Nos. 24 and 25; M. Weissberg, *MGWJ,* 1928, 185.

He came to the conclusion that not only Hasidism but the orthodox rabbinate as well was a pernicious and inimical power
which must be fought against, and he decided to fight with the
only weapon he had—the power of the word, the lash of satire.
And as the object of his first satire he selected the rabbi of
Lemberg, Jacob Ornstein, so popular in scholarly rabbinic circles, who had hurled the thunders of excommunication at his
head.

We mentioned earlier that Rapoport attempted to show that
Rabbi Ornstein, the great scholar, in his composition *Yeshuot
Yaakov*, which was so greatly admired in the rabbinic world, had
committed plagiarism; he was alleged to have employed a great
many other books and nowhere noted the sources. This charge
is utilized by Erter in his satire *Moznei Mishkal.*[15] "A Vision of
the Night," is the subtitle of this satire. At night, in a dream, a
golden scale appears before the satirist. In this scale a marvelous
power is hidden. It transvalues all values. What in ordinary life
is highly esteemed and considered among the most precious
treasures is, on this marvelous scale, suddenly shrunken, loses
its weight, and all its vanity and pettiness are at once disclosed.
Also innumerable books, whole mountains of volumes produced
in the course of generations, appear before the author; and the
scale is to determine their value. Now again marvels occur.
Many gigantic books that were renowned throughout the dispersions of Israel do not pass the criterion.

Here I saw such a thick-bellied composition on the scale, and suddenly
a hand appeared and swiftly began to tear one page after another from
the book—everything the author had snatched and stolen from other
sources. All at once the thick volume shriveled; only the title-page and
the introduction remained. I cast a glance at the title-page and saw that
its author is a man who "was established for the salvation of Jacob
(Yeshuat Yaakov) in a city and mother in Israel," sat on the rabbinic
chair in a large Jewish community.

In this first work Erter's satirical talent does not yet manifest
itself in all its brilliance; nevertheless, even here the gentle
beauty of his poetic style is discernible. Erter remains loyal to
the traditions of the Meassefim and utilizes only the relatively
limited treasury of words preserved in the Bible. With the sensitivity of the true artist, however, he knows how to overcome the
magic of the Biblical sentence, the enchanting and, at the same

15. First printed in *Bikkurei Ha-Ittim*, III, 1823.

time, enslaving power of the classical style. Erter does not write rhetorical flourishes. He does not employ verses or fragments of verses from the Bible, but re-forges the treasury of Biblical words in his artistic laboratory and creates his own poetic style —a rich style, with Oriental images and colors.

Before the poetically-souled village youth raised on Talmudic-rabbinic literature, on arid *pilpul* and on Hasidic tales which later, as a *maskil,* he regarded with contempt and a rationalist smile, the world of poetry and loveliness in the Bible and in its classical language first disclosed itself. Erter by no means regarded the language of the Bible as withered and obsolete. It was his first love, the incarnation of marvelous beauty, filled with vitality and youth. The biblical world of images and the tribunes of the biblical era, the prophets, ruled his imagination. His task also was to be a national tribune, and ceaselessly the commanding words resounded in his ears: Son of man, I have appointed you a watchman for the house of Israel; you are designated to reveal before their eyes everything false and base, everything leading to degradation and enslavement. And it is not the poet's fault that his world-view, his concepts of good and evil, of liberation and enslavement, were bounded by the limitations of the ideals of Haskalah.

After *Moznei Mishkal* Isaac Erter was silent for many years. His Muse in general was not a very fertile one. Moreover, he set for himself extremely rigorous standards in regard to the printed word. He used to file and polish each word and struggle laboriously over every line. "You must maintain the following principle," Erter teaches his young friend Fabius Mieses:

If you compose poetry or a scientific monograph, let it lie in your desk drawer ten years and be in no hurry to print it. If it still pleases you at that time, and you find no error in it, only then may you publish it. This has always been my custom, and I hold constantly to the principle to polish everything that goes forth from my pen innumerable times, and this in the course of many years.[16]

At this time an important change took place in Erter's private life. At the age of thirty-two he decided to learn a profession and set out for Budapest to study medicine. During his years of

16. *Otzar Ha-Safrut,* III, "Toledot Anshei Shem," 17. See also, Erter's letter to Isaac Baer Levinsohn (*Be'er Yitzhak,* 62). That he was a man who practiced what he preached is demonstrated by the following fact. As early as 1841 the satire *Gilgul Nefesh* was virtually finished, but it was handed over to the printer by Erter only in 1845 (See his letters to S. Sachs in *He-Avar,* I, 150–158).

study he and his family were supported by his friend and first teacher Joseph Tarler. After completing his studies (in 1829), he spent some time in Rava and in 1831, when the cholera epidemic broke out, settled as a practicing physician in Brody. Indeed, on the very day of his arrival in Brody, his friend, the author of *Kinat Ha-Emet,* Jehudah Leib Miesis, died in his arms from the epidemic. Erter remained in Brody all his life and achieved great popularity among the poor because of his sacrificial devotion as a doctor and as a man.

Only in 1834, eleven years after *Moznei Mishkal,* did Erter's second satire *Ḥasidut Ve-Ḥochmah* appear (in *Kerem Ḥemed,* II). In this satire, also written in the form of a vision of the night, are certain autobiographical features. Erter relates how, in his youth, he groped in the darkness of ignorance until an enlightened man who lived in the house of his father-in-law had pity on him, opened his eyes, and familiarized him with the work of "the two Moseses," and he suddenly perceived how ignorant he was. An inner struggle begins in him. In a dream two women, each of whom wishes to win him over as her devoted servant, appear to him. The appearance of these women is completely different. One is yellow, crazy, with long, protruding ears and a large knob on her throat. She has a voice like a trundle-bed, speaks in wild gibberish, repeats the same words many times, throws her hands about, and shakes with her whole body. The second woman is calm, sedate, with a bright, shining face. A radiant diadem of stars encircles her head. Her voice is gentle like the tones of a violin. She speaks beautifully and sedately. Her clothing is clean and modest.

The first woman is Hasidism; the second, Wisdom or Science *(Ḥochmah).* The speech of Hasidism, with which she wishes to persuade him, is naturally transformed into an act of accusation intended to demonstrate clearly that the entire Hasidic movement is a skein of folly, wild superstition, falsehood, and vileness, and that its leaders are nothing but frauds and cheats. Then Wisdom comes forth with her sedate, rational words:

Hasidism wishes to dazzle you with wealth through falsehood and baseness. You must know, my son, that prophets and priests stained with sin have always been the plague of our people. In the years of homelessness and times of exile they also degraded it to the ground and made it a shame and a derision among the other peoples. Do you also wish to rob your people, along with those swindlers? Do you want to trample its glory in the dust, so that your honor may be great among fools? Do you desire to tread on your people like mud in the streets in order to fill your treasuries with gold?

Wisdom displays before him all her countless treasures, lists all the sciences which man must explore and attain. The author is enchanted by Wisdom's marvelous words.

I fell before her on my knee. Without words I declared to her very joyously that I desire her alone and no other. And as the shadows of night flee before the bright rays of the rising sun, so Hasidism disappeared before Wisdom's light which became ever brighter and stronger in the course of her speech. The room became filled with radiant light, and I awakened . . .

Three years later appeared (*Kerem Ḥemed,* III) Erter's little satire *Telunat Sani Ve-Sansani Ve-Samangaluf.* This work, too, is directed against Hasidism, against its fantastic world of ideas, with its belief that from every *rebbe's* saying an angel is born, and with its superstitious dread before Lilith, who supposedly lurks for Jewish children and wishes to destroy them.

Of far broader compass is the satire entitled *Tashlich,* which appeared in 1840. This, in fact, is not a satire but a tract written with great talent and in masterly language. At the bank of a river, when Jews go piously to perform the ceremony of *tashlich* and cast their sins into the water, Satan stands with his retinue, and they immediately catch all the sins thrown into the water. With diabolical laughter Satan addresses the "watchman of the house of Israel" and says: "See what is going on." So, the "watchman" relates, I looked around and saw: Here the most prominent people of the community, its rabbis, its *rebbes,* all its holy ones, Hasidim, pietists, each zealous for God and His Torah, had assembled: they came, babbled with their lips, tossed their heads, and shook out their skirts. Satan pointed out to him all the sins cast into the water, and the "watchman" became terrified by what his eyes saw. The sins of the holy community obtained form and structure—disgusting, terrible forms of vileness, criminality, arrogance, and benighted ignorance.

Erter portrays the rabbis in the blackest colors, reproaches them for their moral pettiness, assails them for their countless severities and prohibitions that they cast like a heavy burden on the masses and are not to be borne. He also reproaches them for their mountains of writings filled with foolish conceits and barbaric notions that poison minds. Erter can still not forget the rabbi of Lemberg and his fanatical son Mordecai Ze'ev Ornstein, with their excommunication and persecutions of the *maskilim.* When Erter wrote his *Tashlich,* the rabbi's son had already been in his grave for three years. Nevertheless, the author's anger was not yet assuaged, and he deems it necessary to cover him with his mockery and to expose him in all his moral corruption as Satan's most devoted servant.[17] Erter issues forth no less sharply against the *rebbes*, Hasidim, and fanatical pietists. There is no sin, the satirist asserts, that has not leapt forth from under their skirts: "the sin of thievery, the sin of lying to one's neighbor, the sin of deceit and extortion, the sin of defrauding one's brother, the sin of lending money at usury, the sin of hating one's neighbor, the sin of putting him to shame, the sin of persecuting him with hatred."

In his *Bohen Tzaddik* Joseph Perl touches the *maskilim*, too, with his criticism and notes that among them are also a considerable number of ignoramuses whose whole education consists of a bit of superficial information that they have snatched up. Isaac Erter also confesses that his camp, too, is not free of sin. Some of its members become penitents in their old age. Many of the *maskilim* remove themselves from the people and view their requirements and needs with the coldness of ice. On witnessing the sufferings of the people, their hearts are not warmed. They are not concerned that the people are so foolish and benighted. They do not wish to come to their aid, to lift them from their lowly condition. They think only of themselves, of their own welfare.[18]

Five years later (1845) Erter's most popular satire, *Gilgul Nefesh*, appeared. For decades the powerful influence of this satire was discernible in Hebrew as well as in Yiddish literature. Young *maskilim* used to learn Erter's masterpiece by heart, and it was printed in special editions. Isaac Meir Dick translated it into Yiddish, and Abraham Baer Gottlober reworked it in a new fashion *(Der Gilgul)*.

The story of *Gilgul Nefesh* is as follows. Erter was a physician. One of his patients died, and the soul of the corpse relates the numerous metempsychoses it went through in the sinful world. This soul lived through seventeen transmigrations: from a human being it was transformed into a beast and from a beast again into a person. From each transmigration a double image is derived. The beast into which the soul is transformed is the symbol and reflection of the person's character. The Hasid who drinks whiskey like water is transmigrated into a frog. From the croaking frog comes a cantor, from the cantor a fish (a pike), from the pike a lessee of meat-taxes and candles "who swallows up his brethren like a pike." The meat-tax official is transformed

17. *Ha-Tzofeh Le-Veit Yisrael*, 54–56.
18. *Ibid.*, 67.

into an owl that hovers in the darkness, the owl into a Kabbalist. From the Kabbalist comes a mole, from the mole a gravedigger, from the gravedigger a dog, from the dog a fanatic who "attacks everyone like a barking dog." From the fanatic a fox is created. The soul of the fox is transformed into a Hasidic *rebbe*. The *rebbe* is changed into a donkey. The donkey becomes an ignorant doctor, a charlatan. The ignorant doctor becomes a turkey, the turkey an arrogant creature proud of his pedigree "who puffs itself up like a turkey."

On this canvas Erter portrays with an ingenious hand a whole panorama of contemporary Jewish life. The threads he utilizes in this connection are of one color—pitch black. Erter sees only the negative sides of life. He knows of only a single motif— "There is no rest in Jacob." Everything is rotten and corroded. The stifling air is poisoned, filled with noxious miasma, because the shutters are firmly locked. It is darkest night in the Jewish quarter. Barbaric superstition and false, base watchers do not permit the least ray of light to penetrate. In this monotonousness lies Erter's power, but also his limitation. He mercilessly exposes the negative aspects of Jewish life. He uncovers them with all the power of his great satirical talent, but he is not in a position to reveal the true causes of the negative phenomena against which he battles with such profound hatred and virulent contempt. That is why he becomes so naively awkward when he attempts, in portraying the Kabbalist, to give a description of the "sages of truth" and to expound the essence of Jewish mysticism.

The same thing recurs in his portrait of the meat-tax official. The scope of Erter's satire is certainly considerably broader than Perl's *Megalleh Temirin*. In the "world of confusion" of *Gilgul Nefesh* figure not only *tzaddikim* and Hasidim but the whole "band of town fathers and householders"—rabbis, meat-tax officials, burial society people, men of distinguished pedigree and "refined" Jews who rob the poor masses. When, however, Erter speaks with caustic irony about the tax on meat and candles "to which a Jew of our land gave birth, devised in his thought, and transformed into a firmly established law," he dwells at length only on Solomon Koppler, the initiator of the candle-tax ("wiser than Solomon was this man, for King Solomon spoke about trees and beasts, about birds, worms, and fish, and made a thousand and five poems about them; the present Solomon, however, thought only about candles and meat and obtained a hundred thousand *thaler*"). But Erter overlooks the fact that the candle tax was "devised" not only by one Solomon

Koppler. As is known, the *Aufklärer* Herz Homberg also participated in this and obtained a certain percentage of the "hundred thousand *thaler.*" Erter also forgets that the tax itself was closely associated with the Edict of Toleration of the "gracious king, Joseph II" and with the "normal schools" that were to have enlightened the Jewish populace and freed them by force from "benighted superstition."

However, to perceive the causes of the abnormal Jewish mode of life not only in the rabbis and *rebbes,* but also in the external power and the oppressive social-political circumstances—this the *maskilim* of that era did not undertake to do. And it was not only Metternich's strict censorship that was responsible therefor. Characteristic in this respect is the work begun by Erter and entitled *Megillat Damesek.* The blood libel, or ritual murder charge, which took place in 1840 in Damascus agitated the whole Jewish world. Apparently it made a powerful impression on Erter. He projected a work of art in which this bloody drama that the Jews of Damascus lived through would be portrayed in a purely epic tone. But the reign of the dark shadows hanging over the Jewish quarter was extremely powerful. The *maskil-*satirist, the militant battler against obscurantism and superstition, overcame the artist-epic writer. *Megillat Damesek* remained a fragment, and the satire *Gilgul Nefesh* was published and appeared in the world.

Three years after Erter's *Gilgul Nefesh* appeared, the revolution broke out and put an end to Metternich's despotic rule. The stormy events of 1848 naturally made an enormous impression in the Haskalah circles of Galicia, too. The *maskilim* were excited by the proclamation of freedom, equality, and brotherhood, and they were certain that the constitution born in the storms of the revolution would also bring liberation and equal rights for them. The seventeen-year-old poet Menahem König celebrates in poetic verses "the freedom that arises over Austria."[19] There was also a considerable impression in the orthodox circles, but there the events of March evoked quite different sentiments and hopes. A very unique web of antitheti-

---

19. In the poem "He-Hofshut" which begins with the following stanza:

> What is this in me like a hammer strike?
> The light of the world has broken through in our days!
> A hidden thing has been revealed from thunder—
> Liberty has now come to Austria.

cal interests and demands was formed, and all this on the banner of the Polish nationalist movement which emerged in strength after the March Revolution. These contradictions manifested themselves most clearly in the largest Jewish community of Galicia, Lemberg.[20] There the battle, in which the chief role was played by social motives, assumed especially bitter forms. Men were no longer content with the weaponry of the word, with writing petitions, tracts, and proclamations. They did not recoil even before bloodshed, and attempted to remove their hated opponents with poison.

After the fanatical Rabbi Jacob Ornstein died in 1839, a stubborn battle broke out in the Lemberg community between the two camps—the orthodox and the "Germans," i.e., the "enlightened" persons raised on the Berlin Haskalah. Each faction wished to have the rabbinic office occupied by its candidate. The orthodox, in fact, constituted the most considerable majority of the community, but the "Germans" found strong support in the local officials. In consequence of this support, only "Germans," all of them with European education, were appointed in 1842 as leaders of the community: Doctor Emanuel Blumenfeld, Doctor Leo Kalischer, Doctor Oswald Menkes, Doctor Baruch Rapoport, and Marcus Dubs. They managed to bring it about that, a year later, the European-educated Abraham Kohn was appointed a preacher in Lemberg and, sometime thereafter, district rabbi.[21]

Abraham Kohn was a highly energetic and gifted man. Born in Bohemia at the end of 1806 into the family of a poor peddler who used to wander around through the villages with a pack of merchandise on his back, he obtained the knowledge required to pass the gymnasium examination without any outside help. Later he studied philosophy in Prague and for more than ten years occupied a rabbinic post in Hohenems. In Lemberg Kohn proved that he was not only a skillful speaker but that he also possessed the keen eye of a good observer. Testimony to this is provided by his "Briefe aus Galizien"[22] published in Isidor Bush's *Kalendar und Jahrbuch für Israeliten* (1847 and 1848). These letters have still not lost their cultural-historical value. Kohn

20. In 1848 the Jewish community of Lemberg numbered some 30,000 persons.
21. On Kohn's life and tragic death, see Jacob Kohn: *Leben und Wirken Abram Kohns*, 1865. There is also a Hebrew translation by A. Zupnik (1869). See also Gothilf Kohn, *Abram Kohn in Lichte der Geschichtsforshung*, 1898.
22. Kohn's "Briefe Aus Galizien" (in Bush's *Jahrbücher* they were signed only with the closing letters of his name: -m -n) were reprinted *in toto* in Gothilf Kohn's abovementioned monograph on Abraham Kohn.

was the first among the *Aufklärer* who attempted to present a more or less objective picture of the Hasidic movement.

The German-Jewish historians Isaac Marcus Jost and Peter Beer relied, in their portrayal of Hasidism, exclusively on the one-sided polemical brochure produced in Joseph Perl's circles.[23] We noted in the previous chapters the colors with which the Galician *maskilim* portrayed the *Beshtnim* in Hebrew literature. But the *Rabbiner* who came from abroad concluded that the enlightened picture this "folk-movement" in overly black colors. Abraham Kohn publicly declared that "to our friends of light" Hasidism seems "more fearful then it really is." He had the courage to state that he also finds "good sides" in the movement. "In any case," he declares, "I am not afraid of being branded by you as an obscurantist if I defend this 'monster,' abused and verbally impotent, against the overly violent attacks of impatient enlightenment, in fulfillment of the injunction: 'Open your mouth for the dumb.'" Kohn perceives in Hasidism a justified protest against the "swindlerish, mind-breaking *pilpul* and *ḥillukim,*" a protest on the part of the masses of the people "who were increasingly rebuffed by the proud Talmud scholars and despised and neglected by the rabbis."

Among the "avaricious, swindlerish *rebbes,*" who were so deeply hated and fought against by the *maskilim,* Abraham Kohn also observes "honest people" who "distribute the largest part of the offerings given to them among their poor." He further concludes that the *maskilim* ridicule without good reason the lack of worry and blind confidence which Hasidism implants in its followers, since, "given the great poverty and helplessness and manifold limitations of sources of livelihood, this unworried trust in God is the only thing that makes the existence of the miserable people bearable." Kohn also does not understand why the *maskilim* speak with such mockery and contempt about the behavior of the Hasidim in prayer. "Their worship," he notes, "as little as it can appeal to a refined taste, is nevertheless full of vitality, corresponding to their level of education, and it works an indubitable magic on the masses, who love strong excitement." Hence, Kohn asserts quite definitely that "in moral respects the Hasidim truly stand no lower than their non-Hasidic brethren." "Hasidism," he asserts, "is a return to childhood, but also to childlikeness, which, in certain respects, has more value and certainly offers more hope than worn-out and life-weary adult cleaverness." He even concludes

23. See our *History,* Vol. IX, p. 238.

that Hasidism itself "is a popular reform and has paved the way for a rational reform." "In any case," Kohn adds at the end, "I believe more is to be expected from an education that retains Hasidic elements, namely, heart and soul, than from one stuffed full of coquettish wit and cold criticism."

Abraham Kohn also acutely indicates in his "Briefe aus Galizien" how difficult and abnormal is the situation of the European-educated rabbi and religious teacher in a pious, orthodox community. Such a community, he declares, will in no case "entrust to a young man who has attended a university, even if he be a second Moses, the care of souls" (i.e., ministerial duties). He understands quite well that no community "can recognize a man as its teacher, leader, and keeper of souls in whom, for whatever reasons, it has no confidence, and of whose religiosity it has doubts, inasmuch as it does not consider him one of its own." Hence, for such a rabbi, Kohn notes, it is extremely difficult to accomplish anything if he thinks only of himself and the welfare of his family. After all, he does not wish to quarrel with the community, and takes care not to intensify suspicion of himself.

Abraham Kohn, however, was of too energetic and aggressive a nature to be content with a passive role. He deliberately set out on the path of intense struggle, and the stormy conditions of those years contributed to the fact that the preacher and rabbi of Lemberg grew into a tragic figure. Kohn laid major weight on reforming education and the schools. As a result of his energy, in 1845 in Lemberg a German-Jewish public school for boys and girls, following the model of Joseph Perl's school in Tarnopol,[24] opened. Kohn was not only leader and director of the school; he was also instructor in religion and composed special textbooks on Jewish history and the Hebrew language.

The school was extremely popular; the crowd around it was so large that even in its first year 580 children studied there, and many had to be turned away for lack of space. Kohn also projected the establishment of a special seminary for teachers that would prepare suitable instructors for the Jewish schools. In 1845 the new temple which the progressive leaders of the community built with the aid of the energetic preacher was completed. Kohn, however, used his new pulpit not merely for religious and moral homilies. Like all the enlighteners, he was an ardent champion of productive labor and a convinced opponent of usury and petty trade. Hence, he made the pulpit a platform

24. See the preceding volume, p. 239.

from which he would frequently launch attacks on the usurers who grow rich through the sweat and blood of the needy. He would even publicly name the particularly noxious usurers and openly censure them.[25]

This especially intensified the hatred felt for the disagreeable preacher by the leaders of the orthodox elements. These consisted of a compact group of rich men ("in fur hats and caftans," as a Haskalah tract stresses)—usurers, estate lessees, tax farmers, and farmers of the candle-tax. Leading these men were the wealthy Jacob Naftali Herz Bernstein; Hirsh Orenstein, who sat for a while on the rabbinic chair and still laid claim to the rabbinic office; and his secretary Meir Mintz, who was regarded by his associates as an expert in languages and used to write all their petitions and denunciations to the government.

The quarrel of this group with the "enlightened" was by no means a religious one, but an obdurate struggle for power. They despised the preacher and district rabbi Abraham Kohn not because they considered him a heretic and a man of slight knowledge in Talmudic literature, but mainly because he intruded into their territory and occupied the rabbinic chair against their will as the choice of the opposing party which commanded power in consequence of its influence among the officials. And now the hated preacher dared to cast dirt at them from the pulpit of the temple and attack their social and economic interests. All this, however, was still too little; the despised preacher refused to be content with words and soon passed over to actual deeds.

In 1847 there was a very poor harvest in Galicia, and not only in the villages but in the towns a great famine broke out. In this time of trouble the Jewish masses felt the burden of the meat and candle-taxes with special painfulness.[26] The energetic Abraham Kohn thereupon decided that the government must be prevailed upon to abolish these heavy taxes. For this purpose he made a special trip to Vienna with a petition. This enraged the wealthy orthodox clique enormously. After all, they were the lessees of the meat and candle-taxes and had grown rich from them. Hence they began to propagandize with special force among the Jewish masses against the "heretical" preacher. They disclosed

25. See Gothilf Kohn's abovementioned work.
26. On how heavily the candle-tax pressed on the poor masses of the people a picture in bold relief is provided us by the *maskil*-writer Hirsh Reitmann who was the director of the Jewish school in Brody in his poem "Der Kitl" (a paraphrase of Schiller's "Die Glocke").

such grievous sins on his part as that he permitted himself to carry a handkerchief in his pocket on the Sabbath and on festivals walked with an umbrella in hand; his wife wore her own hair instead of a wig; etc. They also promptly sent a petition to Vienna with "iron" proofs that, without the meat and candle-tax, Judaism can have no existence and cannot survive. Abraham Kohn returned from Vienna with nothing accomplished. But he did not abandon the struggle. At the beginning of 1848 he traveled again to the capital, and in the first half of March finally managed to bring it about that the government ordered the abolition of both taxes.[27] Several days later the revolution broke out.

In the first stormy days following the revolution, when the flag of liberation waved so proudly on high and the words of redemption—liberty, equality, fraternity—resounded so joyously, every group of the urban populace in Galicia endeavored to adapt itself to the new conditions as quickly as possible.

This appeared most prominently in the major city of eastern Galicia, Lemberg. Among the Polish populace the nationalist movement that strove for self-government and cultural-political hegemony over all of Galicia was strengthened. The Polish *Rada Narodowa* soon turned with a summons "to our Israelite brethren," in which it declared that it has "accepted them with open arms in the common bond of brotherhood and greets in them the children of the common mother Poland, and as our brethren they have equal rights with us in our dear home." For the "equality with us in rights and freedom which humanity demands," *Rada*, in return, sets forth the categorical demand: "Unity of language must absolutely prevail among us." Since we accept you also with equal brother-love in the fraternal bond of the Polish nation, the Polish nationalist representatives declared, you must be "perfectly and forever incorporated into it through the acceptance of our language." Naturally, in the schools "the major weight must be placed on the Polish lan-

---

27. In a tract by a *maskil* of Lemberg on the Hasidim and their leader Orenstein, when "Kohn the preacher" is mentioned, it is at once noted:

> All the favors which he did for the Jews;
> He did not sleep, could not rest,
> He worked day and night
> Until the candle- and meat-tax were abolished.
> (*Historishe Shriftn*, I, 751)

guage, and German must be assigned merely a subordinate position."[28]

The "Germans," i.e., all the *maskilim* who had been raised on the Berlin Haskalah, gladly agreed to purchase equal rights through linguistic assimilation. We noted previously[29] how, as early as the 1820s, Solomon Jehudah Rapoport raised the question: Why the Judeo-German, or Yiddish, language in the land of Poland? And we observed that he at once gave a categorical answer: "Either Hebrew or Polish." Abraham Kohn, who took a very active part in the social life of Lemberg in the spring days of 1848, frequently touched on the question of language in his public appearances. For him Rapoport's dilemma—either Hebrew or Polish—did not exist, for he had little respect for Hebrew,[30] and "Judeo-German" he regarded with no lesser contempt than Rapoport.[31] Already in his "Briefe aus Galizien" he declared that "Polish should be zealously cultivated (before all foreign languages) and learned thoroughly and grammatically by the children of the land." In this connection he immediately adds: "Our naturalization, our existence, depends on this." However, he is still so much a "German" that he recognizes German as the "model language" and stresses that "the German mother tongue alone is, nevertheless, that on whose ground we can acquire true culture." He even concludes that this is also valid for the Jews who live in Russia. For, Kohn asks, "what Slavic dialect will here soon become the mother tongue of so many, and especially of the intellectually alert and cultured, of our co-religionists, and therefore be able to accomplish so much for us as the German language?"[32]

The leaders of the orthodox party were not at all passive toward the revolutionary events. They immediately made their own interpretation of the freedom slogans. They, the majority of the community, had lost the battle with the enlightened, who were merely a small minority, simply because the latter had influence with the government; as a result of this, the enlighteners became the leaders of the community and also managed to bring it about that their candidate for the rabbinate was confirmed by the government. Now, however, that the "people"

---

28. The summons is reprinted in German translation in Gothilf Kohn, *op. cit.*, 183–187.

29. See above.

30. On this see Bernfeld's *Toledot Ha-Reformatzyon Ha-Datit*, 148, 193, 194.

31. Abraham Kohn's son and biographer, Gothilf, characterizes the Yiddish folk-tongue as follows: "The infamous dialect, the thieves' Latin of the seventeenth century" (*op. cit.*, 202).

32. *Ibid.*, 144–145.

had obtained power, the pious leaders, the spiritual guides of the "people," hoped that they would, first of all, manage to remove the disagreeable rabbi who interferes in communal matters and causes great harm to their business. They also attempted to exploit Polish national politics and argued before the *Rada Narodowa* that they do not wish a "foreign" rabbi: *My chcemy polskiego Rabina.* They undertook a strong propaganda campaign among the Hasidim and the backward masses to the effect that it is a true "desecration of God's name" to have over them a "heretical" rabbi who is literally close to apostasy.

Through their well-paid agents they collected signatures to the public petition which they submitted to the praesidium of the district. In this quite lengthy petition the orthodox complain that the Lemberg community "has been sobbing for many years" under the yoke of the oppressions and despotic behavior which the leadership that was "provisionally forced on the Jewish community" permits itself. This leadership, it is further noted, represents only the interests of a small "party that is a protegé of the government and stands at the helm." This leadership "imposed" on the community a district rabbi who has no Talmudic knowledge and displays such great ignorance in this realm that he has become a mockery in the entire community. The whole community is very suspicious of his religious behavior. He does not inspire any confidence, and because of his unfriendliness and "rude behavior" is hated by everyone. Hence, the community begs that its ardent desire be fulfilled and that it be freed from the despotic district rabbi.

To this petition the enlighteners immediately responded with a special appeal. A particular impression was made, however, by a German brochure which appeared anonymously in the summer of 1848 under the title: "Offenem Sendschreiben an die Petitionäre und sogenannten Verfechter des orthodoxen Judenthums gegen den Herrn Kreizrabbiner Abraham Kohn in Lemberg."[33]

The author of this polemical brochure was undoubtedly a gifted publicist. With biting sarcasm he tears away the masks of the pious "petitioners" and discloses them in their true form. He shows that what is involved here is not at all a matter of religion, a question of the heresy and impiety of the district rabbi. With this the framers of the petition merely wish to deceive, to dazzle the eyes of the ignorant masses. What goes on here is a struggle for power and involving petty financial interests. Are these

33. The "Sendschreiben" is reprinted *in toto* in Gothilf Kohn's monograph, pp. 208–246.

petitioners—mockingly asks the anonymous author of the *Send-schreiben*—these pietists, these money-aristocrats arrayed in fur hats and long caftans, concerned for the general welfare, for the interests of the impoverished masses? Do they, the authors of the "rejoinder" who begged the government not to abolish "the disgraceful candle-tax that demoralizes the people," who have waxed rich from the blood and sweat of the poor masses—do they wish to be the shepherds of Israel, the guardians and protectors of the poor people?

The anonymous battler obtained his goal. The petition of the orthodox was unsuccessful. The district rabbi whom they so despised continued to take part in communal life with great energy. He projected issuing a newspaper ("Der israelitischer Volksfreund") which would defend Jewish interests, and on September 6 even prepared the editorial for the first number. This his opponents could not bear. The pietistic Bernstein-Orenstein clique decided not to recoil even from murder. They dispatched an individual named Berl Pilpul who stole into Kohn's kitchen and, unnoticed, poured arsenic into the food. The whole family was poisoned. Abraham Kohn and his youngest child died of poisoning on September 7, but the other members of the family survived.[34]

At that time the post-revolutionary reaction had already become markedly strengthened. Two months after Abraham Kohn's tragic death, Austrian cannon shattered the barricades on the streets of Lemberg. The reaction sustained one victory after another. The Jews had to wait another twenty years for equal rights. Freedom of the word, however, remained. Metternich's censorship was not revived, and what Abraham Kohn was not fated to carry through, the establishment of a Jewish newspaper, Isaac Erter wished to accomplish—not, however, in "High German" but in his beloved Hebrew. Together with his young friend Joshua Heschel Schorr, Erter in 1851 decided to establish a journal called *He-Halutz*. The founders of the journal proceeded from the view that now, after the achievements of the revolution, all forces must be applied to struggle against the internal foe,[35] and the battle of knowledge against ignorance, of wisdom against folly, must be sharpened. The program of the journal ("Toledot He-Halutz") was written by Erter in the form of a "night vision" that he so loved. At night the language of the

---

34. A German eulogy on Kohn's tragic death by Joseph Blumenfeld was published by M. Balaban in *Historishe Shriftn*, I, 742–749.
35. *Ha-Tzofeh Le-Veit Yisrael*, 6.

Bible appeared to him in the form of an old woman. "She was old, her face filled with wrinkles, and her hair white as snow. But wondrously gentle was her voice; it sounded like the golden bells on the hem of the High Priest's robe when he entered the sanctuary."[36]

Into the mouth of this old woman with her magical voice the poet places his wishes and demands. She dictates the program of the proposed journal. First of all, Erter pours out his wrath on the rabbis, who refuse to take account of the needs of the time, cling tenaciously to the old, long withered customs, and base themselves on the principle that "no rabbinic court can nullify the words of another rabbinic court unless it be greater in wisdom and numbers." All the peoples of the world, Erter argues, know and understand that wisdom is the chief thing and that numbers are secondary. All, too, realize quite well that the later generations have much more knowledge than the earlier ones. Ancient times, after all, were the childhood of mankind, and the later times are the era of ripeness and maturity. The long gone generations can be compared, in the realm of knowledge, to the present ones as a child to an adult. Only the "shepherds of Israel" refuse to acknowledge this. They cling with utter firmness to every custom. They have no pity on the money of Jews, and make the most essential products more expensive for the poor Jewish masses. The impoverished Jews hunger, and no one comes to their aid—and all this for the sake of the ancient authorities' honor! Is this not genuine idolatry? Our rabbis have to do only with the dead. They do not look at the living, unless it be the rich; these do interest them, so that they may marry into their families. They are stuck entirely in the erstwhile, long dead times. The people of the present generation remain unknown to them. They do not understand their distress and desires. Everything in the world is dynamic, changes its form, but our rabbis do not budge and cling firmly to the old ordinances and severities, proceeding from the principle: "Let the people perish, but let the Torah not perish." And Torah, to them, means every mildewed custom, every ordinance of ancient times.[37]

The "old woman" of Erter's vision further lists all the points of the program which the *maskilim* of that time set forth: to study languages, to devote oneself to productive labor, to learn artisanries and crafts. The "old woman" further underscores

36. *Ibid.*, 7.
37. *Ibid.*, 18.

the point that, besides Jewish public elementary schools, also Jewish high schools, where the students will, along with general knowledge, systematically study the Hebrew language and literature, ought to be established, and thus the students will be properly prepared to study in the rabbinical seminary. Here the following characteristic feature is worth noting: Erter, who himself wrote in a pure biblical style, complains of the Hebrew writers for neglecting the rich treasure of words and concepts assembled in the Talmudic literature, in the Midrashim, and in the philosophical books of the Middle Ages. He, the artist of fine taste, sharply criticizes the "rhetoricians" *(melitzim)* of his time who endeavor slavishly to copy, in the Oriental language, the forms borrowed from the outside world, so that one gets the impression that "they speak German with Hebrew words."[38]

Like Naḥman Krochmal, Isaac Erter was persuaded that national survival would be enjoyed only by those works written in the language of the Bible. He refers in this connection to the significant Jewish works that were written in Greek or Arabic; only those that were translated into Hebrew betimes were not swallowed up in the sea of oblivion and were preserved for the national culture.

Like Abraham Kohn, however, Isaac Erter was not privileged to bring his projected journal into the world. Even before he completed his "Toledot He-Ḥalutz," sudden death wrested the pen from his hand. On April 20, 1851, Erter died of a heart attack. The platform provided by *He-Ḥalutz* was utilized by his friend Schorr who, for decades, carried on his bitter struggle against the rabbis and Talmudic scholars. This, however, already belongs to the later era.

38. *Ibid.*, 23.

CHAPTER SIX

Samuel David Luzzatto
and His Generation

Compromising *maskilim*—The rhetorician Samson Bloch and his
Shevilei Olam—The poet Meir Halevi Letteris and his *Divrei Shir*—The
sentimental-romantic motif in the Haskalah movement—*Faust* and
Elisha ben Abuyah—Letteris as prose writer—The Austrian-Italians;
Isaac Samuel Reggio—The spiritual and intellectual condition of the
Italian communities—Reggio's *Ha-Torah Veha-Pilosofyah*—Franz Delitzsch and his *Zur Geschichte der jüdischen Poesie*—Slavery in the midst
of freedom—Samuel David Luzzatto as a personality—The reactionary elements in Luzzatto's philosophy—Luzzatto against the dogmas
of Haskalah—Luzzatto's criticism of the Science of Judaism—Luzzatto
the romantic—Luzzatto's teaching about Atticism and Judaism—His
battle against Maimonides and Abraham Ibn Ezra—Luzzatto's teaching on life-illusions—*Ḥelek ke-ḥelek* (equal portions).

HE   *MAS-
KILIM*   were
not   all   as
aggressive
toward   the
rabbis as Isaac
Erter   and
Joshua Hesch-
el Schorr. Sev-
eral members
of the same
circle of *mas-
kilim* played
the role of
peace-seekers.
Closely   as-
sociated with
the battlers for
enlightenment, they were also in friendly relationships with the
"shepherds of Israel," the rabbis and orthodox leaders. The most
colorful among these "bearers of peace" were the "rhetorician"
Samson Bloch and the poet Meir Halevi Letteris.

Samson ben Isaac Bloch, born in 1784 in Kulikow,[1] was associated with the Galician Haskalah by lineage and descent. He was in close relationship with the author of *Netzaḥ Yisrael* and with Solomon Rapoport. The above mentioned head teacher of the normal school in Zolkiew, Baruch Ney, was his uncle and it was in his house that he became acquainted with Naḥman Krochmal and even declared himself his disciple. Under Krochmal's influence he interested himself for a time in philosophy and considered himself a Kantian. However, he remained all his life the typical compiler and dilettantish eclectic. Without a philosophy of his own, without a firm character, he made pretensions merely to the role of compromiser.

Typical in this respect is his first appearance in literature. He published in a separate brochure Rabbi Solomon ben Adret's well-known proclamation concerning the prohibition of the study of Greek philosophy in one's youth, together with Yedaiah Ha-Penini's well-known letter of protest against this proscription.[2] The preface preceding this brochure is highly characteristic of Bloch's style or, more correctly, lack of style. He imitates the manner of the Meassefim. His rhetoric is filled to overflowing with Biblical verses and fragments of verses to such an extent that, at times, it is difficult to understand what he really wishes to say. In addition, he has an enormous weakness for quotations. Whether they fit or not, he constantly spews quotations from the old Hebrew literature and thereby shows his learning in parentheses, noting the passage where each statement is to be found.[3]

The most characteristic thing in this connection is that Bloch in his day was regarded as a model rhetorician *(melitz)*. Both *maskilim* and rabbis wrote of the "splendor and beauty" of his rhetoric. The then still quite young Ḥayyim Tzevi Lerner assured Bloch that he was a "teacher in the ways of elegance." Isaac Samuel Reggio declares with enchantment that Bloch has no peer "in the finest honey of rhetoric," that he deserves the laurel wreath "among the speakers of elegance" and the crown among all the "rhetoricians" *(melitzim)* of "the congregation of

---

1. Kulikow is noted as Bloch's birthplace by all his biographers (Letteris, Weissberg, Bader). Bloch himself, however, calls Brody "the city of my birth."
2. See our *History*, Vol. III, p. 93.
3. A quite successful parody of Bloch's style is given by Isaac Baer Levinsohn in a letter of his to Rapoport (*Be'er Yitzḥak*, 27–29). Also known is Bick's witty paraphrase of the well-known Biblical verse "And they shall make for them fringes *(tzitzit)* on the corners of their garments so that you may remember:" "And they shall make on the corners of their writings citations (in Yiddish: *tsitatsies*) and they shall be for them for citations in order that men may see and remember that they are erudite."

Jeshurun."⁴ The rabbi of Nikolsburg, Mordecai Banet, for his part asserts that Samson Bloch "raised the crown of our holy language and demonstrated its splendor and beauty."⁵

Bloch acquired a reputation with his *Shevilei Olam,* a popularly written geography and ethnography in three parts. The first part, which deals with Asia, appeared in 1821; the second, on Africa, in 1827; and the third, on Europe, remained fragmentary⁶ and was published only after the author's death, together with the rest of Bloch's literary remains (*Zehav Shebah,* 1855). The two published parts of *Shevilei Olam* are dedicated to the two great pillars of Galician Haskalah—the first to Naḥman Krochmal, the second to Solomon Rapoport. The work itself, however, is written in so genteel, irenic, and pious a tone that even such orthodox rabbis as Mordecai Banet and Moses Sofer gave their *haskamot* to Bloch's composition. *Shevilei Olam* was highly popular for two or three generations in a wide circle of readers. Jews refreshed themselves with it as with *Josippon* and *Tzemaḥ David.* From it they became aware of what transpires in the larger world. The book, therefore, played a certain cultural role because, with its respectable, half-secular, half-pious style, it penetrated without hindrance into circles wherein other Haskalah books had no access.

More significant and more talented than Samson Bloch was the poet Meir Halevi Letteris. Letteris was born August 10, 1804, in Zolkiew. His father Gershon ben Ze'ev, the proprietor of a Hebrew press, was a knowledgeable man and something of a "rhetorician." He wrote commentaries to difficult passages in Abraham Ibn Ezra's commentary to the Torah and also published (in 1817) a *Perush Maspik* ("Adequate Commentary") to the *Seliḥot.* Gershon Letteris also attempted to write poems. Hence, it is not suprising that he took care that his only son Meir should study Scripture thoroughly and be proficient in grammar. The greatest influence, however, on the young Letteris was exercised by Naḥman Krochmal, to whom he first came as an eleven-year-

---

4. *Otzar Ḥochmah,* I, 4, 33.

5. In regard to the literary taste of that age, the following is worth noting: When Solomon Rapoport ceased to write rhetorical pieces and poems and began to publish his famous scholarly monographs for which he worked out a purely scientific style, many of his readers and admirers took it amiss and came to him with arguments: "You were struck speechless and refrained from further taking up parable and rhetorical language in pleasant words that draw the heart as were usually found in your compositions hitherto and now your words are chatter, and if they are comprehensible to their readers, they lack spice to give them taste sweet to palate and soul" (see Rapoport's preface to *Toledot Rabbenu Hananel* in *Bikkurei Ha-Ittim,* XII).

6. On the reasons why Bloch did not complete the third part, see Meir Letteris, *Zikkaron Ba-Sefer,* 109.

old boy thirsting for knowledge. Krochmal strengthened his interest in secular poetry, pointed out as the best model Moses Ḥayyim Luzzatto's *La-Yesharim Tehillah*,[7] and also familiarized him with German poetry.

Letteris devoted himself intensively to self-education and studied French and Latin with great industry. Later he also received higher education at the university in Lemberg, and from a *yeshivah*-student was transformed into Doctor Max Letteris. He edited a whole series of German journals (*Wiener Blätter, Wiener Monatsblätter, Wiener Mitteilungen*, etc.). He himself also wrote German poems, and for his collection *Sagen aus dem Orient* (1847) received a gold medal from the Austrian emperor Franz Joseph. Nevertheless, throughout his life he remained loyal to the command of his spiritual and intellectual mentor Naḥman Krochmal—to write in Hebrew.

The language of the Bible remained Letteris' only love; he was her most devoted knight and also her excellent master. With the greatest ease he transported various European poetic forms and rhythms into the Hebrew poetic art. However, he lacked two major qualities that prevented him from rising to the level of a significant national poet with a clear individuality: rich imagination and temperament. His verses are distinguished by sound and rhythm, but they lack the most important thing—the innermost fire of a deeply sensitive personality. The motifs of his poem are old-fashioned, bearing the stamp of the firmly established, standard style. Typical in this respect is his first collection of poems, *Divrei Shir*, which he published in 1822, thanks to Krochmal's financial support, and which two years later already appeared in a new edition. The collection of the young poet begins with a poem "Masa'at Nafshi" (My Ideal), in which the old, elegiac, sentimental motif about the vanity of earthly life, with all its trouble and sorrow, which are in no way to be compared with the marvelous light and splendid beauty of the heavenly world, resound. The poem ends with the old-fashioned chord so well known from the medieval religious *seliḥot*-poetry:

The world for the righteous is like a wayfarer's lodging;
Only in the loftiest heights does the tent of the just
flourish.[8]

7. Letteris always remained Luzzatto's ardent admirer and first published the work of the Italian scholar's youth, *Migdal Oz*.
8.   *Tevel hi la-tzaddik ki-melon ore'aḥ*
        Ach bi-meromei ad ohel yesharim pore'aḥ.

Also in Letteris' most popular poem "Yonah Homiyyah,"[9] which for generations was sung in Galicia and Lithuania, the ancient motif employed by virtually all the Hebrew religious poets—the motif in which the congregation of Israel is compared to a dove that has been exiled from her nest for her sins —sounds forth. The author of these lines still remembers the sad melody to which young *yeshivah*-students and *maskilim* used to sing the elegiac, sentimental verses:

> Oh, I am sad,
> I do nothing but wander about,
> From the habitation of the cleft of my rock
> Oh, I have descended . . .
>
> My Beloved abandoned me
> When His wrath waxed hot against me,
> Because I was
> Led astray by a seductive spirit.

This sentimental mood is characteristic not only of the young poet Letteris. It is a typical feature of the entire Haskalah movement of that era. The *maskilim* with militant natures—Wolfsohn-Halle, Jehudah Miesis, Joseph Perl—were consistent rationalists. They knew of no doubts. Everything for them was clear and comprehensible, everything divided into two quite separate worlds: one, ruled by reason, is covered and irradiated with light and beauty; the other—the world of benighted superstition and fanaticism, of "rebels against the light" and folly—must be fought against. Among the *maskilim*, however, there were also men who were, indeed, attracted to the new world with its broad scope, but had not the courage or the firm conviction to break in enmity with the old world. These were more passive, meditative natures. They lacked partisan, aggressive force, and so felt helpless and weak. From this derived their sentimental, romantic mood.

One seeks in vain poems of battle in Letteris. Fighting motifs were absolutely alien to him. The *maskil*, the *Aufklärer*, makes himself noticeable in Letteris in only a single poem—his "Siftei Renanot," a poem of praise to the community of Brody in which the city is lauded because it "spreads light among the people of Israel," "bestows the light of life among those who grope in the dark," and "endows the erring and lost with knowledge and

9. First published in the collection *Ha-Tzefirah*, issued by Letteris (1824).

understanding."[10] Letteris carries on no battles and lives in
peace both with the rabbis and the Hasidim. Whereas Krochmal, Rapoport, and Erter saw in Rabbi Jacob Ornstein of Lemberg the "Grand Inquisitor" who issued forth against them with
the harsh punishment of the ban, Letteris was a familiar guest
in Ornstein's home and, as a "rhetorician" and "linguist,"
would, on suitable occasions, provide the rabbi with official
letters or elegies.[11] For this reason Ornstein, for his part, gave
the constantly needy Letteris the financial possibility of publishing his collection of poems *Palgei Mayyim* (1828).

One other detail is worth noting. We pointed out earlier how
popular the German poet Friedrich Schiller was among the
Galician *maskilim*. One of the first, if not the first, who familiarized the Hebrew reader with Schiller's poems was Letteris. Out
of fourteen translated poems published in his *Divrei Shir*, seven
are from Schiller. To this, one should also add the dramatic
scene "Mot Aḥitofel," which is listed in the collection among
the original poems but is merely a re-working in rhymed lines
of the first scene of the third act of Schiller's *Fiesco.*[12] Among the
seven poems of Schiller here translated the poem "An die
Freude," so loved by the Galician *maskilim*, is included. The
translation, however, appeared with a characteristic alteration
in the text. Schiller's mood when he sang his hymn "An die
Freude" was quite different than when he wrote the drama *Die
Räuber* in his youth. With the passing of time the poet's stormy
social protest cooled off, and in his poem Schiller comforts the
poor masses:

> Endure courageously, O millions!
> Endure for the better world!
> Above, over the starry sky,
> A great God will recompense.

But there still resounds quite bravely in Schiller's poem the
joyous motto of the *Aufklärer* of the eighteenth century: Man is
born for happiness! The poet sings a passionate song of praise
to "joy." He asserts that only joy "drives the wheels in the great

10. *Divrei Shir*, 1832, 94–98. It is interesting that the anonymous author of the above-
mentioned polemical *Sendschreiben*, when speaking of the educated and enlightened in
the community of Lemberg, also deems it necessary to stress: "These few also are
indebted for their education to Brody and the late Herr Perl in Tarnopol (G. Kohn,
op. cit., 243).
11. See *Zikkaron Ba-Sefer*, 141.
12. M. Weissberg noted this in *MGWJ*, 1928, 199.

world-clock." Happily he hails joy: "All men become brothers where your gentle wing flutters!" And the choir emotively sings: "Embrace, O millions! This kiss for the whole world!"

All these lines are also rendered in Letteris' translation. At the end, however, in Schiller the choir permits itself to utter the following "heretical" wish:

> Truth against friend and foe,
> Manly pride before the thrones of kings!

To display "manly pride" against the throne of kings—this was completely inconsistent with the program of the *maskilim* of that era. We have noted previously,[13] and will have occasion to repeat, the reasons why the *maskilim* had such great respect for "enlightened" absolutism and perceived in it the bearer of light and culture.[14] Schiller's "revolutionary" line is therefore transformed in Letteris into a pious moral maxim: "Do no evil and practice no deceit."[15]

Letteris translated not only lyric songs of European poets but also long poems and dramas, such as Ludwig August Frankl's *Rachel* and *Primator*, and Racine's plays *Esther* and *Athalie*. A particular impression in its day was made by Letteris' translation of Goethe's *Faust*, Part One; a whole polemic even took place on the significance of the Galician poet's achievement. The young Peretz Smolenskin made his debut in Hebrew literature with a sharp critique of Letteris' translation, and the Galician Langbank came forth with a defense entitled *Mishpat Emet*. Certainly a translation in rhymed lines of such a masterpiece as Goethe's *Faust* is a significant achievement, and Letteris did, indeed, demonstrate in it his mastery of the art of Hebrew versification.

13. Above, p. 28.
14. Highly characteristic, incidentally, is the simple question that Letteris asks when he mentions, in his memoirs, the great success that Perl's private synagogue in Tarnopol enjoyed: "A remarkable thing; I cannot understand it at all. All the synagogues which were established in Galicia following the command of the king and his officers and counselors on the basis of the edict which the justice-loving emperor Joseph II issued —virtually all these were closed and had no effect. And precisely a synagogue which one of the people built without any command from any ruler or officer but out of the good will of his heart exists to this day and enjoys great success" (*Zikkaron Ba-Sefer*, 126).
15. That one need not here take into consideration the strict conditions of censorship under Metternich's regime is attested by another translation of the same poem by Schiller that Baruch Schönfeld published in *Bikkurei Ha-Ittim*, VII, 100–104. There the verse in question is rendered more or less correctly: "An upright spirit before great men."

Nevertheless, Smolenskin was not entirely unjustified, for Letteris refused to content himself with a simple translation. He undertook to rewrite in poetic form the German poet's immortal work, to clothe it in a national Jewish vestment. However, he carried this through in an extremely mechanical fashion. *Faust* in him bears the name of the famous *Tanna* of Rabbi Akiva's times who became a heretic and was changed from Elisha ben Abuyah into *"Aḥer"* (the other one), an apostate.[16] The passages in the text where purely Christian motifs occur are "Judaized." When, for instance, in Goethe the choir sings on Easter night "Christ has risen," Letteris' choir sings "The children of Israel have been redeemed from the burdens of Egypt." Gretchen obtains the name Na'amah, and Letteris naively believes that thereby Goethe's remarkably beautiful figure is actually transformed into a Hebrew Shulamith of ancient times. The whole medieval environment with its unique coloration that is so masterfully portrayed by Goethe is transported without hesitation to anterior Asia in the times of the emperor Hadrian.

A particularly comical form is obtained in Letteris by the scene, in its "national" vestment, where Faust's disciple Wagner appears. Since Faust in Letteris is transformed into Elisha ben Abuyah, or Aḥer, and Aḥer's disciple—as is known—was the renowned *Tanna* Rabbi Meir, Wagner in Letteris carries the name Nehorai. Letteris explains in a note that by Nehorai he means the *Tanna*, the "light of Israel," Rabbi Meir, "who is also called in the Talmud by the name Rabbi Mesha and Rabbi Nehorai, as is known."[17] The naive poet who desires absolutely to clothe Goethe's *Faust* in Jewish national garments forgets in this connection that Goethe portrays Wagner as a dull, pedantic idler with petty notions who "is happy when he finds earthworms," and that Faust regards him with greatest contempt as "the poorest of all sons of earth." And it is in this role that Letteris places Rabbi Meir, who was called Nehorai, meaning "the illuminator," because he was renowned as one of the keenest minds of his time and created clever fables and sharply pointed parables by the hundreds.

Letteris was active not only as a poet; he also wrote a great deal of prose. His collections of letters (*Michtavim*, 1827; *Michtevei Ivrit*, 1847; *Michtevei Kedem*, 1866) have a definite cultural importance, because in them a considerable number of letters by his

16. Letteris' translation bears the name *Ben Abuyah.*
17. *Ben Abuyah,* 227.

contemporaries—Krochmal, Rapoport, Bick, Bloch, and many others—are published. Of no lesser significance are his memoirs (*Zikkaron Ba-Sefer*, 1869) which embrace the years 1800–1831.[18] In it are presented important biographical details about Naḥman Krochmal (37–75), Solomon Rapoport (114–135), Samson Bloch (97–112), Isaac Euchel (90–97), and Ludwig August Frankl (145–168).

Meir Letteris was the epigone of the Galician Haskalah. With the death of Isaac Erter, the brilliant period of Haskalah in Galicia actually comes to an end. The Galician *maskilim* whom we have introduced to the reader in these last chapters also had a great influence on the Haskalah movement in Russia, but before leaving Galicia we must dwell on two diligent contributors to *Bikkurei Ha-Ittim* and *Kerem Ḥemed*. In close friendship with the chief leaders of the Galician Haskalah, they nevertheless stood aside, "isolated from the major stream," because they grew up in a quite different cultural environment. These men were Samuel David Luzzatto and Isaac Samuel Reggio, born in the Italian-Austrian provinces.

Isaac Reggio (also known by the acronym IaShaR) was born in Gorizia in 1784 into an affluent and prestigious family. His father Abraham Vite, a wealthy proprietor of estates with his own fields and vineyards, was also a scholarly man and in his last years served as rabbi in Gorizia. This, however, did not hinder the rabbi's only son from studying, besides Talmudic literature, several European languages. No one also prevented the young Isaac from devoting himself to painting and music. The old traditions of Italy still had not died out completely. The youthful Reggio manifested particularly brilliant capacities in the field of mathematics. It is related that the well-known French mathematician Baron Augustin Cauchy is supposed to have given high praise to the new proof of Pythagoras' theorem devised independently by Reggio. In 1810, when Gorizia and the whole region passed over to France, the French governor appointed Reggio as rector and professor in the local lyseum.[19] After Napoleon's downfall, however, the province was restored to Austria, and Reggio, as a Jew, had to surrender his position. Soon after this, his literary activity began.

Properly to evaluate this activity, one must first of all bear in mind the environment in which Isaac Samuel Reggio was fated

18. The promised second volume did not appear because two years later (in 1871) Letteris died.
19. See Reggio's autobiographical notice in *Otzar Neḥmad*, I, 33.

to live and work. Cultural life in the numerically small Jewish communities of the Italian provinces that were under Austrian sovereignty was monotonous and congealed. The Jews were isolated from both sides. In the urban Italian populace there was a whole network of secret societies which dreamed of national liberation from the heavy yoke of Austria; the Jewish populace remained alien to this movement and was loyal and subject to the "gracious king," the Austrian "emperor, may his glory rise." In Galicia and other Jewish communities a powerful Hasidic movement spread and became strengthened, and against it the *maskilim*, the "enlighteners," undertook a bitter struggle. In the German communities at that time, a battle was carried on over religious reform.

In the communities of Italy, however, all this found a very slight resonance.[20] The external vestment was gentile: the Jews spoke Italian, they wore European dress, their beards were shaven. But they conducted themselves in the old orthodox fashion; and when, for instance, someone had the impudence to publish in Leghorn, or Livorno, in 1810 a project on reforming cultural-religious life among the Jews,[21] the leaders of the community promptly confiscated the whole edition and burned it.[22] Not without reason does Reggio complain in a letter to the *maskil* of Brody, Ignatz Blumenfeld (the later publisher of *Otzar Neḥmad*):

How well it is with you! You have friends such as your heart desires, and can converse with them. But I am solitary and forsaken in my native land. There is no one in the whole region to whom I can unburden my heart, carry on a conversation on learned matters, and not be afraid of the zealots who trample everything precious with their feet and declare every seeker after truth a thoroughgoing heretic.[23]

Reggio himself displays sufficiently the backwardness of his environment. He, the "perfected man," who for years, according to his own report, was a professor of humanities, still operated in the 1820s with the four basic elements of medieval science, and he speculates on how, after the Deluge, the "elemental

---

20. Samuel David Luzzatto notes with satisfaction in a letter of his to Rapoport: "Of the sect of the foolish Hasidim in your land there is no trace in the land of Italy" (*Iggerot Shadal*, 323).

21. *Prospetto filosofico di una completa riforma del culto et dell' educazione politico-morale del popolo Ebreo.*

22. See *Ha-Torah Veha-Pilosofyah*, 149.

23. *Otzar Neḥmad*, I, 14.

fire" collected in excessive amounts in certain mountains, and thus the volcanoes, the fire-spewing mountains, were produced.[24] Reggio was well acquainted with German and diligently studied Mendelssohn, in whom he saw the greatest thinker of modern times. However, when Ignatz Blumenfeld of Brody inquired of him in 1833 concerning his views on Heine and Börne, Reggio asks a simple question. I have never read or heard of Heine and Börne, he says, and do not know what they write about in their works. "Do they treat scientific questions or write about Jewish matters?"[25]

Reggio's literary debut occurred with *Maamar Torah Min Ha-Shamayim* (1818), an introduction to his Italian translation of the Pentateuch, which he provided with a special Hebrew commentary (1821). After the imperial decree of 1822 to the effect that the rabbinic office could be occupied only by a candidate who also possesses secular and philosophic education, Reggio published at Venice in Italian a statement regarding the establishment of a rabbinical seminary in which, besides religious-rabbinic subjects, the students would also study philosophy, history, philology, and exegesis. Through his initiative, in fact, such a seminary was soon established in Padua. Reggio worked out the necessary statutes and a complete program for the seminary. In order that the orthodox rabbis might not be suspicious of the new school in which students concerned themselves with such a "heretical" study as philosophy, Reggio wrote his chief work *Ha-Torah Veha-Pilosofyah* (Vienna, 1827).

The full title of the work, *Ha-Torah Veha-Pilosofyah Hoverot Ishah El Ahotah* (Torah and Philosophy United With Each Other), already provides some notion of the apologetic content of Reggio's work. "Torah and philosophy are connected with a strong bond."[26] "There are two lights—the light of our Torah and the light of our science or wisdom."[27] Such sentences are already well known to the reader; we have encountered them at every turn in many older philosophical books which treated the same themes. It must, however, be conceded that, of all of the Hebrew apologetic works which attempt to show that critical investigative thought is in no way inconsistent with faith, the work of the European-educated Reggio is precisely the weakest.

24. *Ha-Torah Veha-Pilosofyah*, 166.
25. *Otzar Nehmad*, I, 34: "I have not seen or heard anything of the books of the authors Heine and Börne. The subject of their writings—whether it is science or pertaining to the conditions of our faith and matters connected with it—is also hidden from me."
26. *Ha-Torah Veha-Pilosofyah*, 211.
27. *Ibid.*, 118.

To be sure, *Ha-Torah Veha-Pilosofyah* does have one virtue; it is written in a lovely and simple style. Reggio himself was greatly enchanted by Bloch's artificial rhetorical style.[28] However, he had too much innate good taste to imitate Bloch. He is by no means a strict puritan and very successfully employs not only the verbal treasures of the Bible but also those of the Talmud and the *Midrashim*.

Unfortunately, however, the content is of considerably lower quality than the language of the book. To obtain some notion of the scholarly level of *Ha-Torah Veha-Pilosofyah*, it suffices to note that, for Reggio, a supreme scholarly authority is Naftali Herz Wessely. The latter's *Divrei Shalom Ve-Emet* and his commentary *Ruah Hen* to *The Wisdom of Solomon* serve Reggio, the Italian scholar himself notes,[29] as the surest guide in the most serious religious-philosophical problems. From them he draws generously, and rewrites whole pages.[30] With such a dilettante and clumsy architect as Wessely in the role of teacher and guide, it is not surprising that Reggio's work contains so much confusion that it is frequently difficult to determine what he really means or intends to say. Reggio himself stresses, for instance, that by philosophy was formerly understood generally "the external wisdoms," i.e., all the disciplines of secular knowledge.[31] His theme, however, is only the question of the discipline of "what comes after nature," i.e., metaphysics. But he himself quickly forgets this and speaks of the "*Geonim* and rabbis" who wished "to destroy among us all the external wisdoms based on human speculation, and forbade Jews to occupy themselves with philosophy through the most rigorous prohibitions."

Setting forth the motto "To join faith and philosophy" or "To forge together the Torah and speculative thought," Reggio asks a simple question: Why should not "the great light, Rabbi Moses ben Maimon," serve us as an example and guide in this matter? The author considers it superfluous to discuss the factors that brought about the long and obdurate struggle against the ideas and tendencies of Maimonides' *Guide for the Perplexed* and *Sefer Ha-Madda*. He merely asserts with a pious mien: It is, after all, clear that even if, among all our sages of former times, only our great scholar Rabbi Moses ben Maimon, may his memory be for blessing, had occupied himself with philosophy, he alone, with

28. See above, p. 112.
29. *Ha-Torah Veha-Pilosofyah*, 90, 163, 166.
30. Isaac Baer Levinsohn, *Yehoshafat*, 28, 33, 36.
31. *Ha-Torah Veha-Pilosofyah*, 18, 24, 26.

his great piety and holiness, could serve as sufficient proof that there is nothing to fear in engaging in philosophy. And, indeed, we see—Reggio adds—that from the time his compositions were circulated throughout the world, the number of thinkers and philosophers, e.g., the renowned Abraham Ibn Ezra and others, grew greatly among us.[32] Reggio forgets that Ibn Ezra was considerably older than Maimonides, and that the young Maimonides first began his scholarly work only shortly before Ibn Ezra died.

In general, Reggio is not very meticulous about chronology and systematic order. For example, he makes of the author of *Or Ha-Hayyim*, Joseph Yaabetz,[33] who lived in the fifteenth century, and of Jacob Emden (known by the acronym Yavetz) of the eighteenth century, one person. To prove how strongly the great Jewish scholars favored philosophy, Reggio presents torn-out, frequently quite accidental quotations from the most varied authors. In this way Gersonides and Isaac Arama, Hasdai Crescas and Menasseh ben Israel, Jehudah Halevi and Rabbi Moses Isserles, are fraternally related by the author of *Ha-Torah Veha-Pilosofyah*.[34] Mendelssohn and Naftali Herz Wessely are also joined together by Reggio. He passes over in complete silence the struggle which these two "great lights, marvels of the generation," so admired by him, provoked in rabbinic and orthodox circles. For him it is clear that, by virtue of the fact that a certain rabbi gave a *haskamah* to Mendelssohn's *Biur* or Wessely's *Gan Na'ul*, it is proven in the most brilliant fashion that the way these authors pointed out found favor in the eyes of the rabbis, and that the Torah scholar may proceed calmly "in the footsteps of speculation and inquiry, to explain through them the principles of the faith."[35]

The reader learns still other interesting things from Reggio. The Italian author assures us that even Rabbi Solomon ben Adret, Abba Mari, and Rabbi Asher ben Yehiel, the last of whom proudly declared, "Your worldly sciences are unknown to me, and I thank and praise God that He has preserved me from them because they may, God forbid, lead a man away from piety and from the holy Torah"[36]—all these were by no means opposed to philosophy in general. What, then? They fought

32. *Ibid.*, 20.
33. See our *History*, Vol. III, pp. 282–83.
34. *Ha-Torah Veha-Pilosofyah*. 17.
35. *Ibid.*, 23.
36. *Ibid.*, 34–41.

only against Greek philosophy, because the wisdom of the Greeks, according to Reggio, is, indeed, noxious. It considers even Epicurus, the very symbol of heresy, a philosopher. The most important Greek thinker, Aristotle, taught the eternity of the universe, denied divine providence, and expressed many other false and strange theories that are inconsistent with the foundations of our sacred Torah. But "true philosophy" is in full consonance with the Torah. It was, in fact, only against the "false wisdom of Aristotle" and against his pernicious ideas that all the great Jewish scholars issued forth. Not only Rabbi Solomon ben Adret and Asher ben Yehiel, Joseph Albo and Abravanel—Reggio asserts—but Rabbi Moses ben Maimon and Rabbi Levi ben Gershon (Gersonides) also "despised and mocked Aristotle."[37] Our author even adds triumphantly: It is "clearly proven" that the celebrated Jewish Aristotelians, Maimonides and Gersonides, regarded their own teacher and guide, the foremost Greek thinker, on whose fundamental ideas they constructed their own systems, with mockery and contempt.

No less characteristic of the backwardness of the rabbis of Italy in that time is Reggio's further account[38] of how an orthodox Italian rabbi who regarded philosophical speculation with great suspicion came to visit him. Reggio managed to calm the rabbi and demonstrate to him with his "iron" arguments that his fears are vain, and that between Torah and philosophy there is complete agreement and peace.

Reggio's numerous smaller works[39] also had a rather slight significance for their time. But his *Behinat Ha-Kabbalah* (1852), in which Leo de Modena's anti-Talmudic tract *Kol Sachal*[40] was published for the first time, has a definite cultural-historical interest.

De Modena, the well-known free thinker of the seventeenth century, had in general a large influence on Reggio. The latter himself[41] relates how strongly the Kabbalist books with their mystical secrets impressed him in his youth. However, de Modena's *Ari Nohem*, which, at that time, still circulated only in handwritten copies, opened his eyes and he became a convinced

---

37. *Ibid.*
38. *Ibid.*, 131–142.
39. In part collected in *Iggerot Yashar* (1834–36) and *Yalkut Yashar* (1854). The rest appeared in *Bikkurei Ha-Ittim*, *Kerem Hemed*, and *Otzar Nehmad*, For a complete list of Reggio's works, see M. Schwab, *Repertoire*, 1900, 311–12; *Die hebräische Publizistik in Wien*, 1930, 179–188.
40. See our *History*, Vol. IV.
41. *Kerem Hemed*, I, 79.

opponent of Kabbalah. A strong influence was also exercised on him in his later years by *Kol Sachal,* which he issued with numerous comments and explanations. Already in his *Ha-Torah Veha-Pilosofyah* Reggio sharply assails David Friedländer and his followers who set forth the demand that Jews be freed of the positive, practical commandments, since these are in conflict with the demands of modern times. In this connection Reggio invokes Mendelssohn, who observes in his *Jerusalem* that the children of Israel cannot disavow the fulfillment of the commandments.[42] Later, however, Reggio himself declared that once the Jews battle for emancipation and equal civic rights, they must adapt their religious life thereto and introduce certain changes into Jewish ritual.[43] Even more radical thoughts are expressed by the Italian scholar in his comments to *Kol Sachal,* where he proceeds from the view that the ordinances of the sages of the Talmud have only a temporary character and the Talmud itself is to be considered not a religious code but only a "protocol" in which various views were noted down.

Considerably more interesting and colorful is the other Italian scholar who was also a steady contributor to the Galician journals—Samuel David Luzzatto (known by the acronym SHaDaL). In order properly to appreciate this unique figure, it is useful first to dwell on the literary debut of a Protestant theologian who, when still very young, associated his name with the history of Hebrew literature. This theologian was named Franz Delitzsch. Born in 1813, Delitzsch, while still in his student years, devoted himself with great love and diligence to Hebrew literature, and in 1836 published his work *Zur Geschichte der jüdischen Poesie* (from after the Biblical period to modern times), which has not lost its cultural-historical value even to the present day.

This twenty-three-year-old Christian theologian refused to agree with the representatives of the Berlin Haskalah that the "Israelites" are by no means a nation but merely a religious sect. He declares simply, without any subtleties, that "the Jewish people is still today a nationality without a fatherland."[44] The young German scholar concludes that the poetic productions of the Meassefim and the poets of *Bikkurei Ha-Ittim* are colorless and unoriginal because these poets wish to imitate alien models and remove themselves from the traditional national motifs.[45]

---

42. See our *History,* Vol. VIII, p. 56.
43. See *Otzar Neḥmad,* I, 33–34, 47–51.
44. *Zur Geschichte der jüdischen Poesie,* 123.
45. *Ibid.,* 88–89.

"The national poetry of all peoples," Delitzsch declares, "is, in its substance, the legendry of the fathers carried by the consciousness of eternal indestructability." However, the poets of the Meassefim and *Bikkurei Ha-Ittim*, the German scholar points out, refuse to acknowledge this; hence, it is not surprising that their own power of creation is so petty.[46] They have devoted themselves chiefly, Delitzsch further notes, to translations and poetic imitations, endeavored to adapt themselves as much as possible to alien forms, and have not understood what treasures of wealth are collected in the Talmudic and medieval literature. They have no notion that the national past of the Jewish people "furnishes inexhaustable material for dramatic works," that in the rich legends and maxims of both Talmuds a heaven which is perhaps of broader scope than Plato's world of original forms is disclosed, that here one can learn "as in the Pantheon of Athens, as in the Vatican at Rome."[47]

Sixty years before Aḥad Ha-Am, the young German theologian characterized the assimilated Jewish intellegentsia with the bitter sentence: "Slavery in the midst of freedom." "Medieval Jewish poetry," writes Delitzsch, "is a document of the freedom of the people in enslavement; modern Jewish poetry, of the enslavement of the people in freedom."[48] It is interesting that Delitzsch especially excludes from all the contemporary Jewish poets Samuel David Luzzatto. He finds that in Luzzatto's poems, interwoven with national motifs, are hidden seeds from which "an entirely new era of Jewish poetry can blossom."[49]

Samuel David Luzzatto was a scion of the same Italian family to which the poets Moses Ḥayyim and Ephraim Luzzatto and the older authors of the sixteenth century, Simḥah and Jacob ben Isaac Luzzatto, belonged. He was born on August 22, 1800, in Trieste, then under Austrian sovereignty. His father Hezekiah, a poor turner, was a scholarly Jew. The Bible was his favorite book, and he even wrote commentaries on several books of the Prophets and the Hagiographa. Hezekiah was also strongly attracted to Kabbalah. In addition, he had in him a spark of the inventor. He was intensely interested in mechanics and spent much time in attempting to construct a perpetual motion machine. He also devised a model of a steamboat but

46. *Ibid.,* 103–104.
47. *Ibid.,* 120–123.
48. *Zur Geschichte der jüdischen Poesie,* 95. In later years, when the Christian theologian in Delitzsch overcame the historian of culture, he set himself the task of bringing "liberation" to the Jewish people through holy baptism and was active as a missionary.
49. *Zur Geschichte der jüdischen Poesie,* 94.

lacked the financial resources required to realize his inventions. These experiments, however, cost him much time and strength; hence, he lived with his family in dire poverty. The young Samuel David, who later asserted that he owed his father a great deal, obtained his education in the model Jewish school of Trieste which was established in 1782 according to the program that Naftali Herz Wessely proposed in his *Divrei Shalom Ve-Emet.*[50] Besides Hebrew studies, the school also taught Italian, German, and natural sciences. In 1808, when Trieste was occupied by French legions, still other studies were added in the Jewish school: French, Latin, geography.

The early matured, intellectually curious Samuel David refused to be content with the studies that he pursued in school and devoted himself diligently to self-education. His young, still unformed body, however, could not endure such severe strain. At the age of thirteen, the boy became seriously ill. After his illness he ceased to attend school; it could give him very little. Only for an hour a day would he study Talmud with the local rabbi, Abraham Halevi. The Bible he studied with his father. Hezekiah originally thought his son would be an artisan, too, and so attempted to teach him his trade. But he soon realized that Samuel David would not be a craftsman, and therefore allowed him to go his own way—the difficult, arduous way of seeking and struggling.

Already in his early childhood years Samuel David Luzzatto dreamed of literary activity. As an eight-year-old child he celebrated Napoleon's great victories in Hebrew verses. At the age of eleven he conceived a work in two parts on the famous Greek fable poet Aesop, but soon exchanged his interest in the ancient fabulist for love of the Bible and its language. At the age of fourteen Luzzatto had already prepared a program of philological and exegetical investigations, calculated for all of twenty-six years. In the same year he made an exciting discovery which had a definite influence on his later world-view. Studying the Talmud and *Ein Yaakov*, the young Samuel David, with his sharp, critical eye, noticed that in the times of the *Tannaim* and *Amoraim* the books of the Bible still lacked vowel-points. In the *Zohar*, however, the vowel-points and accents are frequently mentioned. Hence, Luzzatto came to the logical conclusion that the *Zohar* was not written, as the devotees of Kabbalah asserted, in the generation of Rabbi Simeon ben Yoḥai and his disciples, but considerably later. His father, the pious Kabbalist, was en-

50. See our *History,* Vol. VIII, pp. 66ff.

raged at his son's heresy. The young Luzzatto, however, already at that time was one who firmly defended his own view. He maintained his position, and at that time conceived his *Vikkuaḥ Al Ḥochmat Ha-Kabbalah,* which he published many years later.[51]

Luzzatto also wrote numerous Hebrew poems, and at the age of fifteen had already completed a whole collection which appeared ten years later under the title *Kinnor Na'im* as a supplement to *Bikkurei Ha-Ittim.* At the same time he studied various languages with great industry. Besides Hebrew, Italian, and French, of which he had a perfect command, he also studied Syriac, Aramaic, Arabic, Latin, German, and Greek. His favorite language, however, was the tongue of the Bible. He became its great, peerless master, its paladin and protector.[52] But while he devoted his finest powers to Hebrew and with great diligence collected the material necessary to disclose and make accessible the literary treasures assembled in it, he considered it necessary to note that Hebrew in general is not a *holy* language but a language like all others, and that Aramaic, for instance, is considerably older.[53] Hebrew is important and precious to him not as a sacred but as a national language, and the Bible is so beloved because it is the chief national monument of culture.

The young Luzzatto was also deeply interested in ethical-religious questions. He studied various ethical and philosophical works assiduously, and at the age of seventeen himself began to write a large theological-philosophical composition in twenty-four chapters.[54] In it he still remains loyal to the rationalistic tendencies of Haskalah and endeavors to show that man is obliged to employ the light of understanding with which God has endowed him; with the aid of reason and profound speculation, he ought to elucidate and evaluate religion and his deeds. Luzzatto also sets forth the maxim that was so ardently accepted by the *maskilim:* "For the Torah of God has no dread of light and is not afraid of true criticism." This work, however, remained unfinished, for the author soon broke the rationalist tablets and became the decisive opponent of the *Aufklärer* and their credo. Many years later when Luzzatto attempted, in his old age, to

---

51. Luzzatto expressed his sharp hostility to Kabbalah as early as 1820 in his letter to S.H. Luli(?) (*Iggerot Shadal,* 78–80) in which he declares: "Innumerable are the fallen, cast down by the Kabbalah when it darkened the splendid beauty of our Torah." See also *ibid,* 233, as well as his poem "El Ha-Mekubbalim."
52. On this, see *Iggerot Shadal,* 425, 553, 629ff.
53. *Ibid.,* 632, 1360.
54. Some details about this work are given by Luzzatto in *Otzar Neḥmad,* IV, iii–114.

explain[55] the reasons why he did not set out on the trodden path and did not become a "heretic" like others, he notes:

I did not become a heretic . . . because I never felt the pain of exile in myself . . . I was always one who rejoiced in my portion and always felt that it was the Bible, the Mishnah and the Talmud that made me so, a man who relies calmly on God's care . . . My love for the sages of the Mishnah and the Talmud was so great because their words, deeds, and whole conception were so tenderly permeated with truth and compassion, without false brilliance, without superfluous phrases and dazzling of the eye . . . And later, when I had given much study to the works of the sages of Greece and Rome and become familiar with their words and deeds, I did not encounter in any scholar and philosopher in the world such childlike simplicity, such righteousness, such selfless devotion to the welfare of another as in the sages of the Mishnah and the Talmud . . . And when I observed the most complete inconsistencies among the scholars of the heretical camp and read how Rousseau complained of the sages of his time, the Encyclopedists, I obtained even more love for the sages of the Talmud, and this saved me from falling into heresy and atheism.

We have deliberately presented this long quotation because it demonstrates quite clearly that the backward atmosphere of the Italian Jewish community had its influence on Luzzatto also. We wish, too, at once to remark here that in Luzzatto's philosophy reactionary elements are strongly represented. For this reason some historians of culture have even considered it justifiable to dismiss Luzzatto with the brief verdict—"a petty bourgeois reactionary." From a certain standpoint, Luzzatto, who, as we shall see further, wished to see everything good only in Judaism and everything negative in European culture, was, indeed, a reactionary, a kind of Jewish version of the Russian Slavophiles. But he was a quite unique reactionary. While firm as steel in defense of theism and the divinely revealed character of the Torah and believing in the miracles related in the Bible, he was also one of the first to show that the Biblical text is erroneous in places and himself, with his fine philological sense, made some highly successful emendations.[56] Luzzatto, who was so in love with the sages of the Talmud, also speaks enthusiastically of Leo de Modena's anti-Talmudic tract *Kol Sachal* and declares that he would very much wish to see the work printed.[57] How-

55. *Ha-Maggid*, 1858, 118–119.
56. On this, see *Iggerot Shadal*, 168, 706–707, 1203.
57. *Ibid.*, 993: "I desire that this book be known . . . I would rejoice if the book were widespread."

ever, this is not the main thing. The most important point is that the Italian scholar, with all his reactionary tendencies and maxims, was, nevertheless, one of the most interesting and original personalities of Jewry in the first half of the nineteenth century.

Luzzatto's chief significance does not lie in the fact that he was an indefatigable scholar and acquired a reputation as a philologist and remarkable Bible exegete. His importance consists, above all, in the fact that he is a *personality*, a whole man of one mold who knew of no compromises. He was organically unsuited to be silent about the truth that he accepted; he could not but cry aloud what others considered it more convenient to conceal and be silent about.[58] This impacted power of harmonious personality impressed men, had to impress them. Even such a cold and sedate scholar as Simḥah Pinsker becomes emotive when he speaks of Luzzatto:

He (Luzzatto) is the one who most deserves the greatest and highest praise; he is a *man*, in the loveliest meaning of the word. Well it is with them and happy are they—among them, myself—who have had the privelege of being friends with him for many years. On numerous occasions I learned from him and always endeavored to adapt my qualities to his, but I never attained this. He is the lion who calmly strides on his way and is not frightened by the cries of the numerous antagonists who attack him and wish to overcome him. They had no success because the banner of truth waves over him.[59]

Also Luzzatto's disciple Samson Gentiluomo, who became a free thinker and removed himself from Luzzatto's world-view, cannot sufficiently praise his teacher's remarkable personality: "I have not sufficient words to laud his ways . . . Go through all the streets and markets of the city, and everywhere you will hear only that to him belong the titles: father of the poor, speaker of truth, judge of righteousness, confessor of truth, hater of ill-gotten gains."[60]

Only when one becomes more closely familiar, through Luzzatto's enormous collections of letters, with his life and work, does the enthusiasm that he evoked among his intimate friends as a moral personality become comprehensible. Then it becomes

58. For this reason the two monumental collections of letters by Samuel David Luzzatto, published after his death, are so extraordinarily interesting. These are *Iggerot Shadal*, 1882–1892, 1426 pp., and *Epistolario*, 1890 (Luzzatto's Italian, French and Latin letters), 1072 pp.

59. *Likkutei Kadmoniyyot*, Supplements, 114.

60. *Otzar Neḥmad*, I, 63.

clear that these emotive expressions—"speaker of truth," "judge of righteousness," "the banner of truth waves over him"—are by no means mere phrases. It also becomes clear that Luzzatto himself is fully justified in repeating frequently in his letters: "My mouth speaks what my heart thinks;" "Since my earliest youth I have loved only the truth and sought it with all my powers;"[61] "I have always spoken and written only what I considered pure truth;"[62] and "A little kernel of truth is far more important to me than the love and hatred of all the children of men."[63]

In this rigorous, learned, and ardent battler there inhered in very remarkable fashion the simplicity of the child of Andersen's tale who utters the secret about which all are silent—that the king is naked. The "banner of truth" waved over him constantly because, in private affairs and in questions of practical life, he was "not a cultured person." In the quotation from his autobiography, which he wrote in his old age, he stresses several times that he is a man who "rejoiced in his portion!" And this contented man lived an extremely hard life, filled with poverty and affliction. At the age of nineteen, when Luzzatto already entertained various scholarly plans, the economic situation of his family was so critical that he, along with his father and his sister, worked in a noodle factory, and all three of them together earned only from fifteen to twenty *Kreuzer* a day.[64] Hence, it is not surprising that when he conceives scholarly investigations, the comment immediately follows: "If hunger will not prevent me."[65]

"Had not the Torah been my delight, I should have perished in my affliction" he notes several times.[66] Even when, in 1829, he was fortunate enough to obtain a permanent appointment as a professor in the rabbinical seminary that had been established in Padua,[67] his economic situation was not significantly improved. The seminary was very poorly supported financially, and Luzzatto's wages were therefore constantly reduced.[68] For

---

61. *Iggerot Shadal*, 1273.
62. *Pardes*, III, 101.
63. *Iggerot Shadal*, 1331. Another time he expresses his firm conviction that a false person cannot become a valuable and meritorious scholar (*ibid.*, 701).
64. *Iggerot Shadal*, 393.
65. *Ibid.*, 11.
66. *Ibid.*, 665, 685, 722.
67. In the Collegio Rabbinico Luzzatto taught the Hebrew language, exegesis, and history.
68. *Iggerot Shadal*, 301, 1130, 1377, 1381.

a certain period he received no pay at all, and had it not been for a patron from Trieste,[69] the great scholar and his family would literally have expired of hunger.

In addition, Luzzatto had a very tragic family life. His first wife was mentally ill for all of eight years.[70] His brilliantly talented oldest son Ohev-Ger (Philoxenus) who began his scientific activity as a scholar of Oriental languages at the age of thirteen, died at twenty-five after a long and painful illness.[71] After him, Luzzatto's only and much-loved eighteen-year-old daughter Miriam died.[72] With all this, Luzzatto remained content and had the courage to declare: "With these terrible troubles, I live in joy."[73] He lived in joy because he, the poor man, was the great bestower, the great spender who endowed everyone with his rich treasures. Living in constant poverty, he saved his last penny and gradually assembled, with great love and devotion, a large collection of the rarest manuscripts. And these treasures, gathered with so much trouble, he did not use for his own purposes only; day and night he sat over the old manuscripts until he, the first-rank expert, managed, after difficult and strenuous labor[74] to arrive at the correct text, and the results obtained were made available for use to anyone who wished them.

Persons known and unknown to Luzzatto, friends and ideological opponents—all applied to him, and he did not refuse anyone. He made whole summaries and extracts for those who requested them, sent improved and corrected texts with all the necessary explanations, arrived at through strenuous toil. And it happened not infrequently that the recipient did not even consider it necessary to indicate the source from which he had obtained all his information. When Zunz reproached Luzzatto for bestowing his treasures even on persons of slight value and importance, the Italian scholar responded: "Even if Satan himself should come to me and say: 'Give me an old manuscript and I will print it on my press in Hell,' I will kiss his hands and grant him whatever he wishes. Is my labor for the sake of my enjoy-

---

69. *Ibid.*, 1056. According to J. Opatoshu who, in his splendid *Poylishe Velder*, provides in the chapter "Der Letster" a masterful portrait of the leaders of the Galician *maskilim*, Luzzatto is supposed to have received support also from Poland.

70. *Iggerot Shadal*, 722, 952.

71. See Luzzatto's moving letter in *Otzar Neḥmad*, I, 76–77.

72. *Iggerot Shadal*, 1390, 1393, 1406.

73. *Pardes*, III, 115.

74. Because of a great deal of strain he lost one eye at the age of fifty-six (*Iggerot Shadal*, 1132).

ment or glory?"[75] And to M. Sachs, Luzzatto writes: "I abide in my foolishness; I am always prepared with the greatest devotion to be of help to anyone seeking wisdom, knowing even that in none of them will I find a dedicated friend."[76]

This remarkable man who was always ready to aid, with so much self-sacrifice, anyone who devoted himself to scholarship and literary problems actually did find few "dedicated friends" on his creative path. Not without reason does S. Pinsker speak of Luzzatto's "numerous antagonists who attack him and wish to overcome him." Luzzatto himself discloses in his many letters the reason for this strange phenomenon: "I have been 'a man of strife and a man of contention to the whole earth' (Jeremiah 15:10)."[77] "My heart feels otherwise than do many others, and therefore it happens so frequently that many things that pass among the majority as good, fine, and right are, in my eyes, the complete opposite, and precisely what for me is clear and firm and beyond doubt is very far from the ideas of the majority of men."[78] Just as I do not believe in anything merely on the basis that it is confirmed by others, I do not deny anything merely because the whole world denies it.[79] Luzzatto feels like a "solitary in the desert" and knows that he has no companion on his life's way. "My world-view," he declares, "is alien to the present generation and no one understands it. To all who hear of me, I am like a dream without an interpretation and like a riddle without an explanation." To Solomon Jehudah Rapoport he writes: "I know that I must carry on a difficult struggle, because the spirit of the present generation is opposed to me."[80] Proudly Luzzatto declares: "I am the man who wishes to live in peace with everyone, but I am not afraid of war with any man." In one of his Italian letters he notes: "I have no fear of anyone and do not rely on anyone. I know that the men of my generation can not or will not understand me. I am content that they let me live and write."[81]

Luzzatto, however, was imbued with the firm belief that his

---

75. *Iggerot Shadal*, 1130. See also *ibid.*, 553, 978, 1378. When Zunz could not obtain a publisher for his scholarly work, Luzzatto was beside himself with anguish (*Iggerot*, 1231). And when he heard that Salomon Munk had become blind, he wrote to him: "If it were possible to give you one of my eyes, I would gladly give it" (*Iggerot Shadal*, 1078).

76. *Iggerot Shadal*, 1029.

77. *Ibid.*, 713.

78. *Ibid.*, 193.

79. *Ibid.*, 698.

80. *Ibid.*, 234.

81. *Pardes*, III, 101.

ideas would not be lost. To the young Joshua Heschel Schorr he writes: "I will write down my thoughts, and if the present generation be not suited for them, I shall leave them for the generation that comes after me, and it will publish them after my death."[82]

If my struggle were merely for my own benefit, I would certainly have suffered great anguish from the fact that so many are against me, and I would have fled from the battle-field. My battle, however, is a battle of ideas, and I hope to God that if my words will not affect many people, they will at least help a few; and if they will have no effect on the present generation, they will on a later one. Hence, I will not be silent as long as I breathe.[83]

"I am certain," Luzzatto writes in another letter, "that in a later generation, when I, too, will be ancient, my words will be the blessed seed that will produce the ripest fruits."

In what did Luzzatto's militancy consist? Whereby was he "alone in his generation," without companions on his life's way, with a philosophy and world-view that was alien to his entire generation? The Italian scholar had, indeed, to be like a "solitary in the wilderness" in the circles of the *maskilim*, for he ruthlessly shattered the gods before whom the battlers for Haskalah bowed, and he covered the ideas for which they fought so impetuously with ridicule and bitter contempt. The young Franz Delitzsch, as we noted previously, in evaluating modern Hebrew literature, spoke of "slavery in the midst of freedom." Luzzatto, however, saw no freedom but only slavery and meanness of spirit. With the fiercest wrath he issues forth against the basic motto of the *maskilim*: "Let us be like all the nations." He angrily rejects their view that Jews ought to imitate all the other peoples. With intense bitterness he speaks of the self-deprecation with which the rationalist *Aufklärer*—the Friedländers, the Wolfsohns, and Miesises (whom he especially despised)—regarded Christian culture. He underscores how much feeling of contempt and hatred for one's people and its historical past is inherent in this self-deprecation.

Luzzatto writes to I.S. Reggio:

Our present-day rationalism is so closely bound up with contempt for our people, for everything that bears the pure national stamp . . . This contempt does not allow them to see in Judaism any original and independent feature—not any good, not any evil. Everything in it,

82. *Iggerot Shadal*, 566.
83. *Ibid.*, 713.

they assert, is learned and copied from others; the ideas, the customs, the social laws, the code of punishment—all are taken from other peoples. The strongest wish of our present-day rationalism is: to see that our co-religionists in every way imitate the civilized population around us, that Jewish studies become precisely such a discipline as Christian theology, that our synagogues and study-houses are transformed into Protestant temples, that education, customs, life, death—everything among the Jews—is copied from the Christians, and the Jews become similar to them in all things.[84]

In another letter Luzzatto complains:

One must have super-human powers to set oneself against an entire generation whose sole desire is to find grace in the eyes of the other peoples. In this consists the whole program. And the pain is very great . . . The innermost pride which gave us the feeling that we ought to exult in being Jews, that we need not lower ourselves to gain favor among others, is lost. We believed joyously in our spiritual powers and were filled with the conviction of our righteousness and the truth of our faith.[85]

Luzzatto also mocks the loveliest dream, the supreme ideal for which the *Aufklärer* strove: emancipation. In emancipation, writes the Italian scholar, they see the greatest happiness of our people. Merely for the shadow of emancipation they are prepared to sacrifice everything, to extinguish the old national pride. And what great agony it is to witness how the old, strong spirit is completely lost, how children of the people appointed to be the model and teacher of the human species slavishly degrade themselves, always imitate their neighbors like apes, and their ideal of perfection is to be similar to others, and gain esteem in their eyes.[86] With wrath and pride Luzzatto hurls at his generation the bitter verses composed in the old-fashioned form:

> Let him be lost who mocks his mother's instruction
> And ridicules his father's age
> And makes emancipation his idol.
> Let my tongue cleave to my palate,
> Let my right eye be dimmed,
> Let my hand be withered,
> If I forget thee, O Zion.

84. *Pardes*, III, 106–107.
85. *Ibid.*, 120.
86. *Pardes*, III, 107; *Iggerot Shadal*, 660.

Not in external emancipation, Luzzatto asserts, ought we to see our highest bliss, but in innermost emancipation, in self-liberation from servile humility and subjection to foreign influences.[87]

With the question of emancipation is also bound up, for Luzzatto, the problem of the Science of Judaism. We noted in the first chapter that the young Leopold Zunz, the founder of the Science of Judaism in Germany, regarded Hebrew literature as a closed, finished object on which one must place an honorable monument, so that the peoples of the world may see that the Jews, too, had a rich culture. We also observed that Zunz believed this would certainly contribute to the speedy recognition of the Jews as citizens with equal rights.

This thought, indeed, is expressed quite clearly in the introduction to Zunz's important work *Zur Geschichte und Literatur,* published in 1845: "The equalization of the Jews in custom and life will proceed from the equalization of the status of the Science of Judaism" (*ibid.,* 21).

It is quite comprehensible that with such a firmly established goal—to show that the Jews also "had a history, a philosophy, a poetry comparable to other literatures,"[88] and that Jewish ethics was filled with humanitarianism and love of mankind—the Science of Judaism had to bear a certain apologetic character. It suffices, for example, to note merely one passage of Zunz's *Zur Geschichte und Literatur.* In the chapter "Sittenlehrer" (122–156), Zunz dwells on the *Sefer Ḥasidim.* He quotes from it many passages intended to show the love which the authors of the *Sefer Ḥasidim* bore for their Christian neighbors. To this purpose he quotes[89] Section 1018 which teaches that "if a Jew sees that another Jew wishes to kill a gentile who bears no evil toward that Jew, then the Jew witnessing it must come to the aid of the gentile." Zunz, however, is silent about the previous statement (No. 1017) which suddenly, like a flash of lightening on a stormy night, throws a blinding light on the terrible, fearfully dark and inhumanly bloody circumstances under which Jews lived at that time.[90] He is deliberately silent about this, because there the *shedding of innocent blood* is spoken of.

Luzzatto writes to Solomon Rapoport:

87. *Pardes,* III, 107.
88. *Zur Geschichte und Literatur,* 21.
89. *Ibid.,* 136.
90. See our *History,* Vol. II, p. 55.

The Science of Judaism with which some scholars of Germany occupy themselves in the present generation can have no endurance, for they themselves engage in it not because it is especially dear to them; in the final analysis Goethe and Schiller are much more important and precious to them than all the prophets, *Tannaim*, and *Amoraim*. They scrabble into Jewish antiquities as other Orientalists explore the antiquities of Egypt, Assyria, Babylonia, and Persia—only out of love of scholarly investigation, or for the sake of glory. They have still another purpose: in order that the Jewish people may find favor and be elevated in the eyes of the nations of the world, they praise the virtues of some of our ancients. This, they hope, may help hasten the great redemption which, for them, is emancipation. This Science of Judaism will, therefore, have no continuance. It will be nullified as soon as the "redemption" is attained or as soon as those who still studied Torah in their youth and still believed in God and in Moses before they went to study Bible criticism with Eichhorn and his disciples will die out.[91]

In another letter Luzzatto points out: "In earlier times Jews used to write Hebrew. Because they wrote for our own sake, for our own people, they wrote what they thought. Now, however, they write in Italian, German, French, English. Hence, they must take account of 'what the gentiles will say'; so they adapt themselves, alter the content, embellish externally, and give it a more Christian appearance."[92]

Luzzatto issued forth with no less sharpness against the Jewish scholars in Germany who speculated fervently about the "mission" that historical Judaism must still carry through. When Luzzatto read Ludwig Philippson's work *Die Entwicklung der religiösen Idee im Judenthum, Christenthum und Islam*, which soon also appeared in English and French translation,[93] he wrote to Eliezer Liebermann: Philippson proceeds from the view that "Judaism must explain to itself and to others why it exists and for the sake of what it wishes to exist." Both the Jew who believes in the divinely revealed Torah and the Christian who believes in the dogmas of his faith, wrote the Italian-Jewish savant, will stand in wonderment before this thesis of Philippson's. What does it mean? they will ask. The Jew will say: Judaism has existed and will exist further because such is God's will, and we are obliged to fulfill and keep it, for God has so commanded us.

The Christian, again, will say: Judaism existed until a definite

91. *Iggerot Shadal,* 1367.
92. *Pardes,* III, 121.
93. On Philippson's work, see the subsequent chapters.

time because such was God's will, and since this terminus, it has
existed merely because the Jews are foolish and do not understand that Judaism has long since been nullified. The thesis that
Judaism must first explain why it exists and for what purpose
it wishes to continue to exist is thoroughly false. Neither for
Jews nor for Christians who believe in divine revelation does
such a question arise. It is clear that Philippson put this thesis
forth not for believers, but for those who have no faith in the
prophecy of Moses. It is for them that the questions sharply
stand: Why does Judaism exist, and why do Jews remain Jews?
It was as a reply to these questions that Philippson wrote his
book, in which he attempts to show that Judaism must endure
until the time comes when the whole world will begin to have
faith in the one and only God. All human beings will become
God-fearing, men of truth, and haters of ill-gotten gain; slaves
and masters, rich and poor, will no longer exist, and falsehood
and robbery, swindleries and crimes, will disappear from the
earth. As long as this goal has not been attained, Judaism still
has its task; its mission has not been completely fulfilled, and it
must continue to exist in order to perfect the bliss of mankind.

Luzzatto, however, concludes that all this is "vain consolation," foolish comfort. After all, Holy Scripture has been spread
abroad for many generations, and more and more so with every
passing day; yet no effect is visible. And if the dissemination of
the sacred writings in the course of all of eighteen centuries has
not brought the human species to perfection, how will the Jews
be of avail here, especially those who do not believe in the
divinely revealed Torah? These are merely empty dreams. Not
with teaching about "mission" will one persuade these unbeliev-
ing Jews in whom the sentiment of linkage with their own
people has already died, and whose heart is empty "of all Jewish
faith," to remain loyal to Judaism, to play the martyr's role, and
to suffer the yoke of exile and hatred.[94]

Yes, Luzzatto declares in a letter to Steinschneider, certainly
divine providence has chosen the children of Abraham faithfully to transmit from generation to generation and to preserve
the useful doctrine that bears the name "the way of the Lord"
and consists in carrying through justice and righteousness. And
the survival of our people, which has outlived many considerably larger and stronger peoples, does, indeed, consist in the
purpose that this doctrine might have being and also be capable
of bringing use "for the benefit of the human species in gen-

94. *Iggerot Shadal*, 1335.

eral." But when Jews forget their uniqueness, always imitate other people like apes in order to find grace in their eyes, set out on the ways of atheism, i.e., the ways of sham civilization—then they descend from the level of a "singular people." The world no longer needs them, and they are not worthy of existing."[95]

Here we touch on the most typical feature of Luzzatto's philosophy. We observed earlier how the well-read and cultured Isaac Samuel Reggio in the 1830s asked the simple question: Who are Börne and Heine? The fact that the Jewish bourgeoisie and intelligentsia remained limited in their rights undoubtedly contributed to the fact that, in regard to ideological tendencies also, they were to a certain degree behind the European intelligentsia of that age.

At the threshold of the nineteenth century in Germany, and somewhat later in France also, romantic tendencies occupied a very important place in literature and society. These tendencies, which were in the most complete opposition to the rationalism of the eighteenth century, were closely bound up with the political and social conditions in which Germany found itself at the time of the Napoleonic wars and France after Napoleon's downfall in the period of the Restoration. The *maskilim*, who carried on their fierce struggle against the "superstition" of the Hasidim and the fanatical Jewish masses and had not yet obtained the human rights for which the *Aufklärer* and humanitarians of the eighteenth century had battled, still remained loyal in the 1820s and 1830s to the rationalist banner of these *Aufklärer*. The only nay-sayer, the only romantic, among the *maskilim*-rationalists was Samuel David Luzzatto. However, he was under the influence not of the romantics of the nineteenth century but of the great nay-sayer of the eighteenth century, Jean Jacques Rousseau, who had already at that time declared a bitter struggle against the militant rationalism of his generation.

Not without reason does Luzzatto mention the philosopher of Geneva so frequently in his letters. In a letter to a good friend he writes: "You will have great pleasure, my dear one, in reading [Rousseau's] *Émile*. You will discover in it very good things and, most importantly, you will find there an ardent and honest heart; this will certainly give you joy."[96]

The heart—this, for Luzzatto, is the chief thing, and in the just quoted letter there is an interesting debate that the Italian scholar carries on with reason, a debate ending with the charac-

95. *Ibid.*, 1030.
96. *Pardes*, III, 114.

teristic conclusion: "You (reason) know only to calculate and weigh, but I do not carry on any reckonings. I have a heart, and this heart is worth far more than you, my dear reason."[97]

Among the leaders of the Berlin Haskalah, as we know, the loftiest ideal was: "Let us be like all the nations." Their goal was to join European civilization as quickly as possible. When Naftali Herz Wessely set forth the motto *Torah im derech eretz*, for him Torah was a synonym for Jewishness, and *derech eretz* the symbol of European civilization. But Luzzatto, the ardent admirer of Rousseau, was highly critical of European civilization. He even composed a sharp satire under the characteristic title *Derech Eretz*.[98] In this work, as well as in many of his letters, he endeavors to show that European civilization has contributed little to making man better, morally nobler. Some wish to persuade us, he writes in an Italian letter, that civilization brings men to true perfection *(perfezionanto)*. But this is merely a dream. He who does not wish to delude himself and others sees that what has been is what will be. There has been progress only in technology. In machines, ships, roads, there have been great advances. Man perfects everything, but not himself, not his own heart. He does not become better, but worse. In place of feeling, the dominant position is taken by thought, strictly calculated egotism.[99]

The most important moral elements for Luzzatto, which, in his view, European civilizations lacks, are—he is convinced— found in Judaism. In this connection he sets forth his theory about two antithetical cultures. Its theses were propounded in 1838 in his French essay, "Atticisme et Judaisme," which he published only many years later.[100]

Here Luzzatto declares:

The civilization of the modern world is a product of two opposite elements: Atticism and Judaism, i.e., Greek culture and Jewish culture. To Athens we are indebted for philosophy, art, science, intellectual development, systematic order, love for the beautiful and noble, the

---

97. *Ibid.*, 115.
98. First published in Jost's journal *Zion*, I, 81–83; reprinted in the second part of *Kinnor Na'im*.
99. *Pardes*, III, 103; *Iggerot Shadal*, 1335. Characteristic also is the passage in his poem "Helek Ke-Helek" in which he declares that science and reason are to be cursed when they displace graciousness and compassion:

> Cursed be science if it teaches us only cunning and guile,
> But does not increase righteousness!
> Let wisdom be lost forever, let reason be lost,
> If it remove lovingkindness and compassion from the heart.

100. *Otzar Nehmad*, IV.

discipline of thought. To Judaism we are indebted for religion, the morality of the heart, altruism, love for the good and the just. Atticism is progressive, for reason can always grow and make ever new discoveries. Judaism, however, stands in one place; its doctrine, its moral maxims, remain unchanged. The heart may be corrupted but not perfected. The good is innate in man, and the evil is acquired in life. Judaism may free itself from certain accretions that it obtained from the outside, it can return to its primordial condition; but it cannot perfect itself further.

Since Greek culture is progressive and always assumes new forms, it pleases everyone and has numerous adherents. But Judaism, remaining unchanged, appears old-fashioned, and graceless to everyone. Hence, it is tiresome, striking one as used-up, useless scrap. It is, therefore, quite understandable that Atticism triumphs and has the upper hand over Judaism. But in man's nature a longing for goodness and justice is still awake and unassuageable. The beautiful and the exalted cannot extinguish this feeling. Human society cannot exist without the sentiment of the good and the just. Reason or Atticism, however, cannot create this sentiment; they can only weaken it or extinguish it entirely. Hence, we see that human nature constantly yearns for the feelings of the heart, for the good, i.e., the spirit of Judaism.

Such is the struggle, according to Luzzatto's conception between the two antithetical powers of civilization in world history: the progressive, the dynamic, which changes its values and forms—Atticism; and the unchangeably static, the bearer of eternally valid moral values—Judaism, which cannot relinquish its external, firmly established forms, because its power over human hearts is strictly bound up with the belief in its divinely revealed nature, in its unchangeableness and eternal validity.

In all the negative aspects of modern civilization—social injustice, hypocrisy, egoism, pursuit of external brilliance—Luzzatto perceives the expression of Atticism. He is convinced that only on the foundations of Judaism can one establish the "society of righteousness," for Judaism appeals not to the mind, to thought, but to the heart, to feeling. The Italian-Jewish scholar is also firmly persuaded that philosophy robs life of happiness. It destroys the joyous simplicity innate in man.[101]

It is characteristic that, like Naḥmanides in his day,[102] Luzzatto also accuses the "sages of Greece," in their great arrogance, of regarding with contempt the bodily desires of human life associated with the passions and yearnings. The Greek thinkers

---

101. *Ibid.*, 116–119.
102. See our *History*, Vol. III, pp. 23–24.

perceived in man's desires and erotic demands the shameful and crudely bestial which degrade man to the level of a common animal and constitute the most serious stumbling-block on the road to perfection. And all this because they saw the chief purpose of man only in knowledge, in abstract inquiry. That is why the unlettered multitude was so despised in their eyes. But the sages of Israel, Luzzatto asserts, were great and exalted in their deeds and not in their speech. They did not deprecate the human body and its pleasures. For them man's purpose did not consist in knowing the Creator but in fulfilling His will. And they perceived the Creator's will not in speculation, not in the sciences, but in "justice, truth, and peace." If study was revered by them, it was study of Torah which leads to action. Our sages intended with their studies only the general good. They do not demand that man rise above his nature; on the contrary, they declare spiritual beings (angels) lower than the truly righteous man. And the person who understands very little of spiritual matters but has all his life eaten, drunk, and rejoiced, but has also been a righteous man and observed the divine commandments, is—for them—superior to the ministering angels, who do not sin because they have no evil inclination. The well-known saying "Greater are the righteous than the ministering angels" in fact expresses the basic distinction between the sages of Israel and the sages of Greece.[103]

Hence, Luzzatto is strongly persuaded that one of the most important, universally human problems of culture is to liberate and isolate historical Judaism from all extraneous additions, from all alien elements that have penetrated into it from other civilizations.[104] He knows very well that this is utterly inconsistent with the motto of the bearers of Haskalah: "Let us be like all the nations." As a challenge, as a declaration of war, he issues forth deliberately[105] with pointed arrows against the idol of the *maskilim*, their incarnate symbol of highest perfection—Maimonides. The thinker and guide so idolized by all the *maskilim* is declared by Luzzatto a "stumbling block;" he asserts that "Rabbi Moses ben Maimon was among our troublers." Maimonides was a misfortune for Jews. He and all his followers, who attempted to bind the Torah together with philosophy, produced great harm. The medieval Jewish thinker and his colleagues, says Luzzatto, wished to force philosophy into the

103. *Iggerot Shadal,* 695.
104. *Pardes,* III, 118.
105. See *Otzar Neḥmad,* IV, 119.

realm of religion; they did not know and understand that these are two utterly different worlds. Philosophy seeks and aims at the truth; religion aims at the good and the just. Man is not pure reason; he is also poetry. And poetry is the major part of man, his life, his soul. Religion was given man to lead the poetry in him to the side of the good and righteousness. But philosophy comes along and undertakes to be the guardian or master of religion. Then both religion and poetry contract and wither.[106]

Luzzatto can also not forgive the author of *A Guide for the Perplexed* his intolerance—the fact that he, a battler for free thought, was a fanatical oppressor of those who believed otherwise than himself (*Iggerot Shadal,* 426–427). This, however, was still too little for the Italian scholar. He also attacked the other "great man in Israel" whom the *maskilim* especially revered—Abraham Ibn Ezra. Luzzatto, the seeker of faith, sees in the great medieval Spanish scholar an ambivalent man ("one way in his mouth and another way in his heart") who plays the ostensibly deeply pious person, whereas in truth he is a freethinker and deliberately veils his free thoughts in allusions and mysteries. As the complete antithesis of Ibn Ezra, Luzzatto sets forth the "perfect and righteous man," the great devotee of the literal meaning of Scripture and modest figure—Rashi.[107]

But Luzzatto's favorite personality—"the beloved of my heart," as he himself puts it—his supreme ideal, was Jehudah Halevi. However, before we dwell on this point, several other details of his world-view must be touched on.

We noted above that, according to our author's philosophy, Judaism is firmly bound up with the dogma of the "divinely revealed Torah." "Judaism without faith in the Torah revealed by God cannot endure," he repeats many times.[108] Not without cause, however, does he say of himself with bitter sarcasm: "I am a fool in the eyes of the new, and an apostate in the eyes of the old."[109] The romantic Luzzatto, with all his reactionary

---

106. *Iggerot Shadal,* 780.
107. *Kerem Neḥmad,* IV, 134–136; *Iggerot Shadal,* 232, 246, 738, 823. Luzzatto's attacks on Maimonides and Ibn Ezra evoked a great deal of irritation in the circles of the *maskilim.* Even the quiet and retiring Naḥman Krochmal came foreward with a special article (*Kerem Ḥemed,* III, 66, IV, 132) in which he fights against, and refutes, Luzzatto's arguments. On this, Luzzatto remarks ironically: "If I were to criticize Moses ben Amram I would be praised, but because I have issued forth against Moses ben Maimon, many attack me. And this is my praise, for I fight the battle of the Lord and I will not fear the myriads of people" (*Iggerot Shadal,* 656).
108. *Iggerot Shadal,* 1031, 1032, 1036ff.
109. *Ibid.* 1405.

tendencies, frequently expressed ideas that had to appear, among the orthodox, as genuine heresy. For instance, the Torah, he declares, is beloved by God not at all for its truth, but for its utility in improving human qualities and virtues. Hence it is by no means necessary that all its words be pure truth, and this in no way diminishes its divinity. For we cannot say for certain that God speaks nothing but words that are absolutely true, since it is impossible to explain to mortal man the power and nature of the work of creation.[110]

In order to make his point of view completely clear, Luzzatto concludes further in his just quoted letter to Marcus Jost: The existence of society and man's happiness are impossible with knowledge of the naked, open truth. Man must live in illusions. Indeed, we see—Luzzatto adds—how nature (and this is certainly done through God's will) frequently deceives us and entices us with dazzling illusions. For example to insure the continuing existence of the human species, nature arouses love in a young man's heart and thereby blinds his eyes so that he forgets the great difficulties that stand before him on his life's path—anxieties about earning a living and the pain of raising children. He sees only his destined mate, and perceives in her nothing but grace and beauty. So it is also with other wishes and desires; man lives solely in illusions. Nature exploits these for its purposes.[111]

Luzzatto goes even further. My God, he declares, is not the God of Kant but the God of *Tnak* (the Bible). My guide is not Kant's "categorical imperative," but the fundamental moral laws of the Torah. The chief principles of all virtues and the "foundation of society's success" are, according to Luzzatto, compassion, love, and—heavenly recompense. Everything is weighed and measured, everything is guided through the ways predetermined by Providence, "all of which are in wisdom and grace, and everything is for good."[112]

However, when our author begins to explain his concept of reward and punishment, one is again reminded unwillingly of his doctrine about the role of illusions in man's life. It is clear, Luzzatto writes in his previously quoted letter to Jost, that the existence of society is inconceivable without reward and punishment and without the belief in the worthiness of certain deeds and the harmfulness of others. In truth, however, all our deeds

110. *Ibid.*, 66; *Yesodei Ha-Torah*, 55.
111. *Iggerot Shadal*, 661.
112. *Ibid.*, 738, 1031, 1093, 1357.

are merely the product of external and internal factors, and what we call the *tzaddik* (righteous man) and the *rasha* (wicked man), are in truth such only from the point of view of the effect that they produce; one brings utility and the other harm, but they are not such from the point of view of the character of the doer, i.e., because one is intrinsically a *tzaddik* and the other intrinsically a *rasha*.[113]

Luzzatto develops this idea further in a letter to Stein-schneider. God, he here explains, gives recompense for everything, but not in the next world. He does so in *this* world. Mendelssohn and his system destroyed morality by assigning reward and punishment to the 'next world.[114]

Not without cause was Luzzatto so strongly interested in Ḥasdai Crescas and did he assert that the author of *Or Adonai* is very beloved and revered by him.[115] It is beyond doubt that the views just mentioned were formulated under the influence of the profound medieval philosopher who recognized the powerful limitations of man's free will and held that, basically, human decisions are not completely free; they are a matter of *necessity*, as definite consequences of certain causes. From this point of view Crescas also considers reward and punishment nothing more than necessary consequences called forth by determinate causes.[116]

"One must accept the world as it is," Luzzatto declares. One must grasp and understand that the order to which we give the name Providence exists in as iron-firm fashion as all other natural phenomena. And it is clear that, even without religion and without a divine Torah, the experience of life teaches us that the problem of the righteous man who suffers and the wicked man who prospers does not in fact exist; it, too, is merely an illusion.[117]

This much-tried man who suffered so much in his life sets forth a unique theory concerning "equal measures." While still young, Luzzatto composed a poem "Ḥelek Ke-Ḥelek Yochelu"[118] in which he develops in some ten octaves the idea, overwhelming even to himself, that the fate of all persons in the world is alike, and that it is ridiculous to believe that "there is a righteous man and he suffers evil, and there is a wicked man

113. *Ibid.*, 661.
114. *Pardes*, III, 123.
115. *Iggerot Shadal*, 1350, 1382.
116. See our *History*, Vol. III, p. 215.
117. *Iggerot Shadal*, 1093.
118. *Kinnor Na'im*, II, 1913, 110–129.

who enjoys good." The author is firmly convinced that every person enjoys in equal measure good and evil, joy and sorrow, tears and laughter, in his life, and that no one obtains "a flower without the accompaniment of thorns."

> One fate awaits all here on earth.
> No man has any superiority over his neighbor.
> Every living being will see good as well as misfortune;
> The fate of each creature will be the same.
> Like the ox, so the lion; like vermin, so man;
> Every person is the same before his Maker.
> All, all are His children, and in proper justice.
> There is no rose, save with a thorn.

Luzzatto underscores the fact that was only later widely treated in European scientific literature: the varied sensitivity with which one receives the same phenomenon under different circumstances. When a person finds himself, for instance, in a room illuminated by bright sunbeams, his eye must be stimulated by a very powerful source of light for him to feel the impression "it grows light." But for one who finds himself in a dark cellar, the tiniest ray of light suffices for his eye to feel that "it has become light." The pleasure that a hungry man feels in assuaging his hunger with a dry piece of bread, declares Luzzatto, is not obtained by the rich and over-sated man when enjoying the finest foods and best liquors. The exquisite delight the laborer experiences in his moments of rest cannot be felt by the rich idler bored with himself. So, again the inconveniences which the poor toiler does not even notice grow into a whole tragedy for the *gevar anog*, the person raised in wealth and comfort. Know, O mortal man, the poet declares, that joy and sorrow are not measured with a clock in hand. One lives forty years in comfort and does not even feel it because he has been accustomed to comfort from birth on, and the face of a poor orphan who knows only anxiety and distress lights up with joy when he spends only one happy hour.[119]

Thus Luzzatto concludes that, all equally, "we shall drink here on earth below both from the cup of poison and the cup of joy."

119. *Kinnor Na'im*, II, 117:
> "Tears of happiness and joy trickle down his cheek,
> If he lives but one hour pleasantly."

Luzzatto remained committed to this theory throughout his life.[120] But the doctrine about the role of illusion in life, which brought more than one thinker to utter pessimism, made the romantic and believing Luzzatto a convinced optimist. One must take the world as it is, he asserts. "This is my faith, this is my doctrine, this is my wisdom," and thanks to it, "I live in joy amidst fearful troubles."

Luzzatto declares that, with all his speculation and critical reflections he remained loyal to religion because "my philosophizing sprang from its depths." He did not take his "philosophy" from outside but from the innermost sources welling out of historic Judaism, and therefore "all the winds in the world cannot move me from my faith" (*Iggerot Shadal*, 633). For he was firmly convinced that the spiritual world of the individual and its normal development are closely bound up with the national community and its culture.

Indeed, that is why Luzzatto found Jehudah Halevi so precious and congenial.[121] The latter saw in the Jewish religion, above all, the disclosure of the national self-consciousness and self-determination, and his whole world-view is permeated with the thought that the Jews are not only a religious society but also a psychologically unique folk-individuality with an enormously rich national-historical, intellectual-cultural heritage. And Luzzatto set as the major task of his life to reveal for his generation, for the assimilated and half-assimilated Jewish intelligentsia, this rich cultural inheritance.

We noted earlier the resentment with which Luzzatto speaks of those who desire to make of the Science of Judaism a means towards emancipation and, at best, a monument for the desiccated Hebrew literature. He sees in Jewry a living, immortal organism and is convinced that the task of the Science of Judaism is "to spread knowledge about the principles of Judaism and to familiarize Jews with the literature of the Jewish people, and thereby the value of Judaism in the eyes of its own members will be raised and the survival of the nation will be strenghtened." This, according to Luzzatto's strong persuasion, ought to be done not in foreign tongues but in the historic national language —Hebrew.

"I shall always," he writes in one of his historical letters, "write in Hebrew, and disclose in it for everyone the old na-

---

120. *Iggerot Shadal*, 661–662, 1093; *Otzar Neḥmad*, I, 91–93.
121. "Rabbi Jehudah Halevi," Luzzatto writes enthusiastically—"the joy of my soul and the friend of my heart, with whose soul my soul is bound up" (*Iggerot Shadal*, 593).

tional feelings that abide in me with all their lifeforce."[122] Hence he does not weary of repeating how precious and dear to him Hebrew is. "The love of the holy tongue burns within me" (*Iggerot Shadal*, 1246). "My entire hope and thought is that all my works shall be published as they were written—in Hebrew," he writes to Adam Ha-Kohen Lebensohn in Vilna.[123] "My only wish and demand," he writes to Leopold Dukes, "is to revive and raise our language from its degradation. For this purpose nothing is too dear for me."[124] "The more my generation removes itself from the Hebrew language, the more sharply do I feel in me the obligation to battle for it."[125] "The only means of keeping alive love for Judaism," he declares, "is to lengthen as much as possible the life of the Hebrew language and its literature."[126]

And the Italian-Jewish scholar was one who practiced what he preached. For decades he devoted himself to studies of Hebrew and its grammar. In the whole of the nineteenth century one can point to very few scholars comparable to Luzzatto in his marvelous sensitivity to all the singularities of the language of the Bible. But all this is, for Luzzatto, only a means. "To make our ancient forebears well known is my chief desire," he declares. To arouse love for the national culture, he set himself the basic task of reviving and disclosing to the world the concealed and half-forgotten treasures of medieval Hebrew culture and poetry. Through extreme self-sacrifice he managed to assemble a splendid collection of manuscripts in which the loveliest works of the foremost medieval Hebrew poets—Solomon Ibn Gabirol, Jehudah Halevi, Moses and Abraham Ibn Ezra, Jehudah Alḥarizi, and others—were hidden. The texts, of course, were in great disorder and numerous errors had been committed by copyists. For Luzzatto, however, no effort was too much. "I have spent many days," he relates, "to obtain the meaning of an erroneous word or expression."[127]

Luzzatto himself wrote many poems, but he created significantly only in the realm of form.[128] He lacked the poetic imagination to become a genuine poet. Moreover, he had a very slight

---

122. *Pardes*, III, 121.
123. *Iggerot Shadal*, 1139.
124. *Ibid.*, 425.
125. *Pardes*, III, 119.
126. *Ibid.*, 107.
127. *Iggerot Shadal*, 629.
128. See, for instance, his beautiful poem "Hevel Yamai" which he composed on the day he attained the age of thirty-seven (equivalent in *gematria* to *hevel*).

grasp of "the secret of condensation," of brevity. His poems are literally drowned in a sea of words and didactic maxims. However, he certainly had a poetic sense, and love, after all, does produce wonders. Hence, it is not surprising that in the field of correcting and improving the erroneous texts of the great Sephardic poets, Luzzatto had no peer among all the Jewish scholars of his time. He himself published many poems by his dearly loved Jehudah Halevi (*Betulat Bat Yehudah*, 1840, and *Diwan Rabbi Jehudah Halevi*, 1864), as well as many compositions and poems by Solomon Ibn Gabirol, Moses and Abraham Ibn Ezra (in *Kerem Ḥemed* and other publications).

He also distributed the texts that he had corrected with so much arduous effort to many of his acquaintances, to everyone who merely promised that he would publish the texts. Indeed, Leopold Dukes and Saul Kämpf are much indebted to him in their editions and translations of the medieval poets. Luzzatto also greatly aided Leopold Zunz in producing his fundamental works on the synagogal poetry of the Middle Ages,[129] and Michael Sachs in publishing his *Die religiöse Poesie der Juden in Spanien* (1845; second edition, 1901) which so inspired Heinrich Heine and gave him the stimulus to create his marvelous poem "Jehudah ben Ha-Levi." Luzzatto was extremely generous not only with his poetic texts but also with purely scholarly and historical documents. What he himself did not manage scientifically to elucidate and work up (and in this realm also he accomplished a great deal) he took care that others should utilize and publish. Rightfully the historian Heinrich Graetz says: "If Krochmal and Rapoport are called the fathers of Jewish historiography, Luzzatto was its mother."[130]

With all his historical and philological inquiries, with all his scrabbling in old texts, Luzzatto, however, never forgot his major purpose—to respond to the demands of the present. In one of his letters to Michael Sachs he even mentions a *ḥiddush*, or novel interpretation, that he gave to a difficult item in the work of Rabbi Samuel Edels. "You will certainly ask," Luzzatto writes, "what do you care about Rabbi Samuel Edels? I shall answer you: *Judaeus sum, judaici nihil a me alienum puto*, 'I am a Jew, and I consider nothing Jewish alien to me' " (*Iggerot Shadal*, 783).

This, however, he says merely in jest. To Abraham Geiger Luzzatto writes: I will not deny to you that, in my view, knowl-

---

129. On these works, see the subsequent volume.
130. *Die Geschichte der Juden*, Vol. VI, 1900, 456.

edge of our past is indeed good and useful; however, the improvement of today and concern for tomorrow is far more essential. And in all my investigations of antiquity I have in mind primarily this goal. But many of the scholars of the generation do not understand me and are opposed to me.[131] Elsewhere he writes: Let the scholars of Israel not be content with giving the people old books and dead men. Let them give them new books with living men, men whose words and deeds awaken love for science and scholarship and honor for civilization and culture.[132]

Luzzatto was certain that in future generations, when he also who now, in his generation, was "like a solitary in the wilderness," would become an ancient, the seeds he had sown would bring blessed fruit. In part his prophecy was fulfilled. Decades after his death many of his ideas found a powerful resonance among the standard-bearers of the nationalist movement. Among them was such a significant writer as Aḥad Ha-Am. Joseph Klausner,[133] Simon Bernfeld in *Dor Ḥacham*, and other Zionist leaders also wrote of him with great enthusiasm.

131. *Iggerot Shadal*, 783.
132. *Ha-Shiloah*, IV, 62. It is worth noting that Luzzatto manifested a lively interest in the political events of his native land. He was personally in favor of the Austrian orientation and says so frequently. But the heroic battle which the Italians waged in 1848 for national liberation inspired him greatly and he then wrote to one of his acquaintances: "Those who now help in Vienna to assemble an army in order to attack us (i.e., the provinces of Lombardy) are enemies of the human species" (*Iggerot Shadal*, 1051–1052).
133. *Ha-Shiloah*, Vol. VII.

CHAPTER SEVEN

Liberation Movements;
RIESSER, MARX, AND PHILIPPSON

The liberation movements in Germany—Young Germany (*Junges Deutschland*)—Echoes in the Jewish quarter—Gabriel Riesser, fighter for self-respect and honor—*Der Jude* as battle-standard—Bruno Bauer on the Jewish question—Karl Marx and his *Zur Judenfrage*—"Vengeance is mine and recompense"—The Jewish intelligentsia and the "rent in the heart"—Ludwig Philippson and his *Allgemeine Zeitung des Judentums*—Philippson's "mission theory."

N THE previous volume we noted with what leaden weight reaction pressed upon the German lands after Napoleon Bonaparte, the brilliant Corsican, was confined on the remote island of Saint Helena and Metternich with his spies and agents ruled without restraint over the free word and thought. But life, the growing powers of the social and cultural evolutionary process, were stronger than the mightiest despots and gendarmes. In the 1830s, after the July Revolution in Paris, the first signs of the growing storm became discernible in the various lands of divided Germany.

From the other side of the Rhine the courageous battlers Börne and Heine hurled their sharply pointed arrows at the fortress of German despotism. In Germany itself there became noticeable in literary and social life symptoms of a progressive, militant movement which soon came to be called *Junges Deutschland* (Young Germany). The standard-bearers of this movement —K. Gutzkow, H. Laube, L. Wienbarg, Th. Mundt, and others —summoned their fellow-Germans to fight for human rights, for freedom of the word and against religious oppression.

In 1835 the two-volume radically critical treatise by David Friedrich Strauss, *Das Leben Jesu*, which evoked a colossal storm in theological and religious circles, appeared. At the end of the 1830s Ludwig Feuerbach's writings on the new philosophy, in which he underscores with special sharpness the complete antithesis between philosophy and religion, were published. Blind subjection to authority and dogma, firm belief in miracles—these are the foundations of every religion. Freedom of thought, bold exploration of the proper course of lawfulness and regularity—such are the fundamental principles of philosophy and science. In 1841 Ludwig Feuerbach's renowned work *Das Wesen des Christentums*, in which he proceeds with his liberal, critical conclusions considerably farther than Strauss, was published. In the same year Georg Herwegh's famous revolutionary collection of poems, *Gedichte eines Lebendigen*, resounded like thunder over all of Germany with a stormy call to battle:

> *Reisst die Kreuze aus der Erden!*
> *Alle sollen Schwerter werden!*

> (Tear the crosses out of the earth!
> Let all of them become swords!)

It is clear that these new tendencies had to find a certain resonance in Jewish intellectual circles as well. After all, the chief leaders of *Junges Deutschland* (Börne and Heine) had come from the Jewish ghetto, and in the program of its battlers a demand for equal rights for the Jewish populace was also set forth. However, in the Jewish milieu the new tendencies assumed rather unique forms. The struggle against religious oppression, the keen critique of religious questions which, in progressive German society, constituted only a part of the program of liberation, were carried on there by free investigators and thinkers. It was otherwise, however, within German Jewry. We shall see further on how the Russian *maskilim*, led by Isaac Baer Levinsohn, dreamed of European-educated rabbis who would lead the communities and conduct them on the way of enlightenment and culture. They had before themselves as a model the German, university-trained rabbis and preachers. As early as the 1830s it was a quite common phenomenon in German Jewry that all, with rare exceptions,[1] who devoted themselves to Jew-

---

1. And this also because of accidental factors. Zunz did not occupy a rabbinic post in Darmstadt only because the rabbi of Berlin, Jacob Joseph Ettinger, asserted that Zunz

ish scholarship and explored the history of Jewish culture, simultaneously occupied positions as rabbis and preachers in various communities. The communities provided them with a living, thus giving them the opportunity to devote their leisure time to scholarly investigation.

Among these European-educated, modern rabbis there were, as we shall observe below, brilliantly talented scholars. However, they were professional theologians, and this necessarily gave their scholarly as well as communal work a definite coloration. Indeed, precisely for this reason does a single figure to whom theological problems were entirely alien, the only "ignoramus" among scholars, a man who occupied himself exclusively with contemporary affairs, distinguish himself so sharply among them. This man was named Gabriel Riesser.

Riesser was born in Hamburg into a prestigious family. His maternal grandfather was the well-known rabbi of Hamburg, Raphael Kohen.[2] His father Lazarus Jacob Riesser, a great scholar who already possessed European education, issued forth in 1818, when the battle over the Hamburg *Reform Tempel-Verein* broke out, with an open *Sendschreiben* in which he battles against the orthodox rabbis of Hamburg and their collaborators because they wished to produce a schism in the Jewish community.[3] His youngest son, Gabriel, received an exclusively German education. He was familiar with Greek and Roman poetry and read the Italian poets in the original, but had only a very superficial knowledge of Jewish history and culture and was barely able to read a section of the Pentateuch in the original.

Riesser considered himself a genuine German and was firmly convinced that the Jews had ceased to exist as a nation since the destruction of Jerusalem and were presently nothing more than a religious community. When one of the deputies to the Frankfurt National Assembly spoke of the Jews as of a *Volksstamm* (race, or tribe), Riesser, who was also a member of the parliament, issued forth very forcefully against "this dream-image of nationality" and asserted with great emotiveness that Jews are only "a part of the German people" on the basis of the fact that they were born in Germany, speak German,[4] and are distinguished merely by their religion, as Catholics are from Protes-

---

was one who ate ritually forbidden food and desecrated the Sabbath publicly. Graetz renounced a rabbinic career because he manifested too little capacity as a pulpit preacher. Steinschneider, at first, also prepared himself for the rabbinate.

2. See our *History*, Vol. VIII, 42, 43, 193ff.
3. See our *History*, Vol. IX, pp. 252ff.
4. Gabriel Riesser's *Gesammelte Schriften*, I, 419–420.

tants. In fact, however, Riesser also thought very little of the Jewish religion. He not only considered the Talmud withered and obsolete; he was also opposed to Jewish ritual in general and concluded that the commandment of circumcision ought to be abolished.[5] He was impressed only by the fundamental principle: "Hear O Israel, the Lord our God, the Lord is One."[6]

Nevertheless, the logic of history leads to remarkable paradoxes. The civic disabilities of the Jews in Germany in the Restoration era brought it about that the calm and sedate Riesser with his philosophy of a moderate, bourgeois liberal, a Jew who denied the national existence of Jewry and considered himself a full German, became a courageous and indefatigable fighter for his brethren, and that *der Jude* became for him a title of honor which he proudly carried as a battle-flag.

On his entrance into practical life, as soon as the twenty-three-year-old Riesser finished his doctoral examination (he studied juridical science), he, the patriotic "German," promptly became convinced that he was a pariah without any rights. He intended to devote himself to scholarly work, and to this end desired an appointment as a *Privatdozent* in his alma mater, the University of Heidelberg. For this a definite condition was set before him: he must convert to Christianity. The same proposal was made to him also in his native city when he wanted to be inscribed in the corporation of advocates, and at the University of Jena, where he wished to lecture on law. A humiliated and angry man, Riesser traveled in the spring of 1830 for a few months to Paris, where signs of the coming storm were already felt. When the July Revolution erupted and electric sparks of the storm-wind also refreshed the stifling atmosphere of the German lands, Riesser was torn along with it. He fulfilled his vocation not as a man of science. He would become not a scholar of the law, but a bold battler on behalf of rights and freedom for his "co-religionists."

We have noted that, in regard to his attitude toward historical Judaism, Riesser was quite close to the view of David Friedländer and others such as he. However, he rejected in the most decisive way the tactics of the Jewish notables of the earlier generation. He refused to know anything of *shtadlanut*, or lobbying, of humble petitions to the government. With contempt and scorn he regards what the orthodox as well as the enlightened permitted themselves even in the *Kulturkampf* that they carried

5. *Allgemeine Zeitung des Judentums*, 1843, 481.
6. Riesser's *Gesammelte Schriften*, I, 539.

on between themselves in their communities, namely, applying for the aid of the government.[7]

In his first public appearance Riesser addressed a proud call *an die Deutschen aller Konfessionen* (to the Germans of all confessions). Riesser's first work, issued at the end of 1830, is called *Über die Stellung der Bekenner des mosaischen Glaubens in Deutschland* (On the Position of the Confessors of the Mosaic Faith in Germany). He refuses to know anything of apologetics, of defending himself against anti-Jewish accusations and reproaches. He demands of his "co-religionists," above all, self-respect and a sense of honor. He wishes to see in them men with straight backs, with proud self-consciousness. Riesser knows very well that even in progressive German society, which was free of anti-Semitism, Jews were not regarded as "equals." The Jews' generations-long servile condition of pariahs without rights unconsciously worked on the psyche of liberal German society, leading it to look down on the Jew, locked up in the ghetto, from a position of superiority with a sympathetic feeling appropriate to "unfortunates."

This offended Riesser's self-respect. He declares the demand that Jews, in order to be endowed with the emancipation they desire, must first demonstrate that they are useful citizens to be ridiculous. We refuse—he addresses the German citizens—to plead for civic rights from you, for human rights are not begged but demanded; they belong to us no less than to you. They are demanded in the name of freedom, in the name of respect for man. Riesser recalls how the proposal that he go through an "innocent ceremony," i.e., outwardly adopt the Christian faith and thereby obtain a position as a *Privatdozent*, was made to him. With mockery and bitter sarcasm he lays bare this petty haggling in which falsehood and vileness are rewarded by special prizes. With fiery emotiveness he denounces the step that such a considerable part of the Jewish intelligentsia had taken: obtaining civic rights through baptism. It is a matter of an elementary sense of honor, he explains, that even when one is inclined in his heart toward the dominant church, he ought not to abandon his own community so long as the sun of freedom has still not risen over the Jews. He also addresses the Christians and expresses his astonishment at how they can regard their faith

7. "Make use," Riesser warns, "of all means of persuasion with which your conscience inspires you. But, above everything in the world, guard yourselves from any association with force that will brand you and your cause for all times, and deliver you and it to deep-felt hatred, and, in case of a shift in circumstances—to vicious reactions."

with respect when they see it used as a means of petty haggling, and that, like purchasers buying the love of women for gold, human rights are bought and sold through petty trade by baptismal water.

The following fact is characteristic of Riesser's tactics. We noted previously that he was critical of Jewish ritual and yet responded very coldly and with reservations to the Frankfurt *Verein der Reformfreunde* which, in 1842, came forward with a radical program consisting of the following three points: (1) we recognize that the Mosaic religion has the possibility of undergoing unlimited development; (2) the collection of all kinds of discussions, investigations, and regulations which bears the name Talmud has for us no authority whatever, neither in a dogmatic nor in a practical sense; and, (3) we do not wait and do not hope for a Messiah who will lead the Jews back to Jerusalem; we recognize no other fatherland than that in which we were born and in which we are citizens.[8]

The Bible—Riesser declares sarcastically—is most courteously spared (by the *Reformfreunde*) because it is in honorable association with Christianity and with "the high police." Riesser suspects that, in the program they proclaim, a servile attempt to beg civic rights through disavowal of the "superstitious Talmud" is concealed. He concludes that it would be proper for the Jewish freethinkers to come forth with such statements only when progressive Christian society will—through practical steps, not merely through scholarly criticism—attempt to remove the inconsistency with the modern worldview in which Christianity finds itself.

The following point is interesting. In the preceding volume we observed how David Friedländer[9] and the journal *Sulamith*[10] attempted to show that the name *Jude* is a crying anachronism and should be exchanged for the more honorable "Israelite." The Jewish merchants and bankers begged the officials to mark their origin in their passports not by the word *Jude* but by such expressions as "of the Old Testament," "of the society of Mosaic believers," and the like. In this, too, Riesser perceived a self-degradation. "If unjust hatred adheres to our name," he asks, "shall we deny it, instead of bringing all our powers to bear to set it in honor?"

8. For a discussion of this program, see Riesser's *Gesammelte Schriften*, I, 355–356; Riesser's public statement in *Allgemeine Zeitung des Judentums*, 1843, 481; S. Bernfeld, *Toledot Ha-Reformatzyon Ha-Datit*, 153–58.
9. See our *History*, Vol. IX, p. 199.
10. *Ibid.*

Riesser himself was one who practiced what he preached. If backward Christian society regarded the name *Jude* with contempt and scorn, he proudly transformed it into a fighting slogan and named the battle-newspaper which he established in 1832 with it. The journal *Der Jude* aroused a feeling of respect not only among Jews but in Christian society as well. *Der Jude* became the recognized standard-bearer of Jewish "Young Germany." In the course of a rather brief period Gabriel Riesser became the most popular personality in German Jewry and was acknowledged as the best Jewish publicist and courageous fighter for the honor and rights of his "co-religionists."

Riesser tirelessly endeavored to make clear to his "brothers in belief" that if they demand equal rights, they must, first of all, feel themselves worthy of equality with all their fellow-citizens, root out from their consciousness every servile feeling, and not consider the Christian world as a superior one to which they must raise themselves. But another writer, a young Hegelian who, in regard to Judaism, was a far greater "ignoramus" than Riesser—for the latter, at least, grew up in the house of a Torah scholar and *maskil*—went much further. This young Hegelian's father, however, was one of the Jewish intellectuals who exploited baptism as a means of advancing their careers. But before discussing him, we must dwell on the great sensation evoked in Jewish circles at the beginning of the 1840s by the well-known radical thinker Bruno Bauer with his two articles "Zur Judenfrage" and "Die Fähigkeit der heutigen Juden und Christen frei zu werden."

Bruno Bauer acquired a reputation with his critical investigations of the Gospels, in which he expressed no less radical ideas regarding Christianity than did Feuerbach. As a professional theologian and atheist by conviction, Bauer saw in religion the prime source and major cause of the enslavement and injustice that dominate society. To destroy it ruthlessly, to battle against this major cause—Bauer was persuaded—is the most appropriate way leading to freedom and justice. From this vantage point, then, Bauer approaches the Jewish question. He sees in it, above all, a religious question. When, Bauer declares in long-winded philosophical-dialectical phrases, the Jews demand of the Christian state that it emancipate them, they are in fact demanding that the state liberate itself from its religious, churchly superstition and make peace with the Jews, the most rabid enemies of the "state religion." But before the Jews free themselves from their own prejudices, how can they demand this of others?

Political emancipation can be expected only from a state that has liberated itself from all religious bonds and is built on philosophical foundations. If the Jews wish to be free, they must battle for the liberation of all humanity from the religious nightmare and, first of all, emancipate themselves from their own religion, forget that they are Jews, and become freethinking, universal men. Whoever wishes to liberate the Jews as Jews, says Bauer sarcastically, sets himself a hopeless, unattainable task. One who tries to whitewash a black man deceives himself. No matter how hostile the radical Bauer is to Christianity, he concludes that the Christian faith is a universal religion and a more advanced stage in the evolutionary process of the "self-conscious spirit;" it stands at a higher level than Judaism, and contemporary Christians therefore possess in significantly greater measure than contemporary Jews the capacity "to become free."

Against Bauer's philosophical anti-Semitic sophisms many writers issued forth—among them also the abovementioned young Hegelian of the extreme left wing, a friend of Bauer's and his erstwhile fellow-battler. At that time this writer was still very little known, but he later inscribed his name with a firm hand on the tablets of world-history as the brilliant creator of a new world-system, as a teacher and leader of the proletarian masses. The young Hegelian was named Karl Marx.

Marx, however, is not content with attacking Bauer. He also makes the bold attempt to consider the Jewish question not as a religious but as, above all, a social-economic one. It must, however, be borne in mind that the future creator of the "historical-materialist" philosophy had not yet completely overcome Hegel's metaphysical, idealistic abstractions at the time he carried on his debate with Bauer. Hence, in his "Zur Judenfrage"[11] echoes of such speculative, idealistic ideas as Marx himself later attacked with all the force of his destructive criticism are still audible.

We noted earlier that historic Judaism was quite foreign to Karl Marx. Even with German Jewry of his own time he had very scant familiarity. Like the German intelligentsia in general, he also knew little of the Jewish artisans and petty traders who lived in poverty in the narrow ghetto alleys of Frankfurt and other cities. Marx was aware only of the Jewish bankers and manufacturers who occupied the foremost ranks of the German bourgeoisie, were the most active and capable leaders of triumphant capitalism, in which he already then perceived the target

---

11. *Deutsch-Französische Jahrbücher* Paris, 1844, pp. 204–244. A subsequent article on the same theme was published by Marx in the collection *Die heilige Familie,* published by him together with Friedrich Engels in 1845.

of his life's battle. Everyone now knows with what keen dialectic Marx later defended the idea that every nation consists of various classes, and each class fights for its own special interests. In his "Zur Judenfrage," however, the young author was still under the influence of Hegel's idealistic abstractions, in which every people or nation is regarded as a definite stage in the "self-consciousness" of the World-Spirit. Hence, he exchanges, in very "anti-Marxist" fashion, the idea of class for a religious-national idea, and sees in the Jewish people the providential bearer of the capitalist spirit. Into the withered, abstract Hegelian form, however, the youthful author places a new "Marxist" content.

The anti-Jewish writers raised a great clamor about the avariciousness, the petty-trade mentality, and the low moral stature of the Jews. Marx is very remote from apologetics. From what we have already written before, it is quite clear how little inclined he was to idealize the "everyday Jew," the Jew of practical, weekday reality. He declares definitely: "The secular basis of Judaism is practical need, self-interest *(Eigennutz)*; the secular cult of the Jews is huckstering; the secular God of the Jews is money." We know how many members of Christian society perceived the source of Jewish "corruption" in the Talmud with its "superstitions." No, declares Marx, "not in the Pentateuch or in the Talmud, but in contemporary society do we find the essence of the present-day Jew—not an abstract essence, but one that is empirical in the highest degree; not as a condition of the Jews' own restrictions but as a condition of the restrictions imposed on Jews by all of civic society."[12]

The capitalist huckstering spirit among Jews, Marx emphasizes, is not a product of its specific national pecularities, but of European capitalist development. "Jewry," he declares, "has preserved itself not in opposition to the course of history but, indeed, thanks to history itself; from its own entrails does civic society constantly give birth to the Jew." The practical spirit of Jewry is, after all, the practical spirit of all the Christian peoples. We see incarnate in Jewry the universal anti-social element of the present, produced by historical development.

An organization of society which would eliminate the possibility of huckstering, i.e., make impossible the existence of hucksters, would, by that very fact, render impossible the existence of the present-day Jew . . . We recognize in the Jews the general anti-social element of the

12. This in fact means, in Marx, capitalistic restrictions or limitations.

present, an element which has, through its historical evolution, with the energetic collaboration of the Jews, presently attained such a high degree that the process of its dissolution must now commence.

For Marx, who stood outside, only the "everyday Jew," only the Jewish capitalist and banker immersed exclusively in secular, monetary interests, existed. The Jewish intellectuals, however, who studied in Jewish seminaries and engaged in Jewish scholarship also knew of "Sabbath and festival Jews" who grew up on the traditions of historical Judaism. We have observed how strong interest in religious problems was among the progressive Christian intelligentsia at that time. This had to occur in considerably larger measure among the Jewish intellectuals, who, after all, perceived in Judaism the only factor that distinguished them from the surrounding European Christian world.

Bruno Bauer could undisturbedly be a convinced atheist and categorical opponent of Christianity, and this in no way weakened his national sentiment. In his later years he was even an ardent adherent of Bismarck's nationalist politics. But the situation was different among the Jewish intelligentsia. They saw in the Jewish community only a religious sect. The Jewish faith alone was recognized as the single connecting link. But the Jew who no longer wished to recognize its authority had, logically, to come to the conclusion that he was "beyond the pale," beyond every bond with the Jewish community. Feeling—more correctly, unconscious national feeling—was, however, completely inconsistent with arid logic. So Jews sought ways out, built various theoretical castles in the air, attempted to resolve the crying contradictions, to cover up the "rent in the heart" with dialectical cobwebs.

Typical in this respect is the distinguished publicist and scholar Ludwig Philippson. Philippson was born (December, 1811) in Dessau into the family of the then well-known *maskil* and pedagogue, Moses ben Uri, who took part in Shalom Cohen's *Ha-Meassef,* published a textbook *Moda Li-Venei Vinah* (1801–1810), and died in the thirty-ninth year of his life (1814). Having become an orphan very early, Ludwig spent his youthful years in poverty and, as a student in the gymnasium, already had to worry about a livelihood. At the age of nineteen Philippson published his study of the two Judeo-Greek writers Ezekiel and Philo, and a year later (1831) completed his dissertation, written in Latin, on Plato's and Aristotle's views regarding the structure of the human body and its capacity for thought. This work created a reputation in the learned world for the young Philippson. In 1833 the community of Marburg invited him to become a preacher and rabbi there.[13]

The energetic and activist Philippson, however, refused to be content merely with communal affairs. In 1837 he founded his weekly[14] *Allgemeine Zeitung des Judentums,* which he edited with indefatigable energy for more than fifty years.[15] This weekly achieved remarkable success. It was read with great interest not only in Germany but "in all the dispersions of Israel," for the editor took pains that his journal be, indeed, a *general* "journal of Judaism." In it were printed correspondence and reports from the major Jewish centers of culture in the whole world. When the Russian government, at the beginning of the 1840's, undertook the reform of Jewish schools, Philippson not only published a whole series of articles and correspondence on the subject but also wrote many letters and proposals on the matter to the czar Nicholas, the minister of education Uvarov, and his agent Max Lilienthal.

As a gifted publicist and social activist, Philippson also took an important part in the battle for emancipation which the German Jews carried on. This created widespread popularity for him in Jewish social circles, and because he also manifested literary talent in the realm of poetry,[16] the Jewish communities entrusted him with the task of issuing a new German translation of the Bible. This literary undertaking also had great success and went through many editions. One of them became especially popular as a result of the well-known Paul Gustave Doré's illustrations for the text. In order to battle against the missionary Bible editions, which, because of their cheapness, penetrated into a considerable number of Jewish homes, Philippson founded an *Israelitische Bibel-Anstalt* and an *Institut zur Förderung der israelitischen Literatur,* and through them created the possibility of spreading tens of thousands of copies, at very low prices, of the text of the Bible along with his German translation.

But this man who devoted so much effort and energy to Jewish communal interests, and with his journal so strongly aroused, as one of his biographers writes, "the feeling of belonging together," the sentiment of fraternity and relatedness among the Jews scattered throughout the world, does not tire of

13. For a discussion of Philippson's Latin works, see Hermann Cohen's article in Philippson's *Gesammelte Abhandlungen,* II, 461–485.
14. At first Philippson's journal appeared three times a week.
15. Philippson died in December 1889.
16. Philippson also wrote dramas and narratives (*Esterka, Joachim, Jakob Tirado,* and others).

repeating that Jews are by no means a nation *(schon längst kein Volk mehr)* but a "religious association" *(Religionsgenossenschaft)*. Philippson himself underscores that the "clear demarcation of nations from each other in various states" would evoke "such a one-sidedness and sharpness" as could produce a genuine obstacle to "the development of the human species."

He knows very well that it has "always" been a quite common phenomenon that one state "embraces several nationalities" and, pointing to England and the United States, confirms the fact that a single state can, along with the chief nation which forms the majority of the population, "include different nationalities with equal civic rights." For, he concludes, if a state consists of various nationalities, they must all have equal civic rights, "and neither from the position nor the size of the nationalities, must any domination of one over the other, any oppression of one by the other, occur."[17] All this is in regard to the "principle of nationality." But Jews, Philippson asserts, are not a nation at all. "We German-Jews," he argues, "are completely German and nothing but German."[18] "We German Jews have been German for more than fifteen hundred years."[19] This period is still too brief for him, and he actually declares on the same page that the Jew "has had his fatherland in Germany for thousands of years." "We," Philippson emotively stresses, "were, are, and will be Germans wherever any members of the German nation are."[20]

Philippson cannot forgive the philosopher Eduard von Hartmann for the fact that the latter, in his anti-Jewish work *Das Judentum in Gegenwart und Zukunft*, allows himself to note that "the Jews lack only a Jewish state and Jewish territory in order to represent a nationality in the same sense as the French or the Italians." This, Philippson asserts, is a tremendous error. "Do not Jews lack what is decisive for a nationality—a common language?"[21] What binds the Jews together, he declares, is not "racial feeling," as Hartmann thinks, but "commonality of belief," and this "commonality" which is "not of a national but of a religious kind" clearly does not diminish among the Jews their German nationality, just as "no one has denied German national feeling to the Catholics and Protestants."[22]

17. See Philippson's article "Das Nationalitäts-Princip" *(Gesammelte Abhandlungen*, I, 89–95).
18. *Gesammelte Abhandlungen*, I, 166.
19. *Ibid.*, 162. See also *ibid.*, 149.
20. *Ibid.*, 168.
21. *Ibid.*, II, 273.
22. *Ibid.*, 281–287, 336.

However, in the 1840s, as we have already noted, the radical German intelligentsia devoted a great deal of attention to religious questions, because they were firmly convinced that in tearing away the aura of sacredness from the religious worldview consists the first stage in the political liberation of the fatherland. The Jewish intelligentsia always endeavored to demonstrate that Jewry is only a religious community. But the German radicals, led by Feuerbach and Bauer, perceived in religion the enslavement of the human spirit and human thought. Thus, the question was aroused among many of the half-assimilated Jewish intelligentsia who strove for emancipation and political liberation: Why should they hold fast to the religion they had inherited from previous generations? Why are they Jews? What purpose do they serve in being Jews? For the sake of what, in general, should Judaism exist? These questions became ever more urgent the stronger the approaching revolutionary storm was felt. Philippson attempted to give a reply to these questions in 1847 in a series of lectures that were later published in a book under the title *Die Entwicklung der religiösen Idee im Judenthum, Christenthum und Islam.* This work was soon translated into English and French.[23]

Philippson was a preacher and a rabbi, but a Reform rabbi who agreed with those who urged that the modern age demands that Jews should be "beyond Talmudic law."[24]

"What wishes to exist," Philippson declares, "will be asked [to specify] its grounds, its content, the justification for its continuance." Since Judaism also exists and wishes to exist, it must make clear "to its confessors and others" why it exists and to what purpose it wishes to survive. Phillipson poses the question: "What, then, is Judaism?" In his response he sets forth the well-known "mission theory" which later played such a prominent role among the Reform rabbis of western Jewry.

As we know, the "mission theory" is not at all new. The "holy Ari" (Rabbi Isaac Luria),[25] the well-known rabbi of Prague, *der hohe* Rabbi Loew,[26] and many others spoke of the universal mission of the Jewish people with great enthusiasm. Among these pious mystics, however, the mission doctrine was the logical consequence of an organically complete world-view. The Jewish people was considered "My son, My firstborn Israel," stood at the center of the universe, and every commandment,

23. On Luzzatto's sharp critique, see above, pp. 137–39.
24. *Die Entwicklung der religiösen Idee*, 10–11, 165.
25. See our *History*, Vol. V.
26. See our *History*, Vol. VI, pp. 76–92.

every act of will, that a Jew fulfilled had a vast cosmic significance. But the "mission doctrine" of the European-educated Philippson, who keeps arguing that we were, are now, and will be true Germans "wherever any members of the German nation are," appears quite extraordinary. But in this "complete and total German," the theologian and rabbi overcame the scientific scholar. Philippson explicitly distinguishes *Judenthum* (Judaism) as a religious system and world-view from *Judenheit,* or Jewishness—from the Jewish collective, the Jewish *ethnos.* The Jewish race, the Jewish people, is, according to Philippson, not the creator of Judaism with its unique world-view; it is merely a previously appointed vessel for the religious idea that disclosed itself through divine revelation in the form of Mosaism.[27] Therewith, he explains, is associated the peculiarity of the Jewish *ethnos,* which is distinguished from all other peoples. Among the latter, consciousness of their vocation develops only in stages, following the course of their history. But the Jewish *ethnos* knew from the beginning "what it should be and for what purpose it is here." It recognized itself "from the first moment on" as a God-people, i.e., as a bearer of the religious idea.[28]

But wherein does the religious idea which disclosed itself through divine revelation in the form of Mosaism, and stood in complete opposition to the external pagan world, consist? Philippson explains that the religious idea as Mosaism brought it into the world consists in the following: "The unity of God, the unity of the world, the unity of mankind, the mediacy of God to the world through the laws of nature, and the unmediated relationship of God to man" who is created in His image and endowed with free will.[29] Mosaism, he repeats a number of times, does not know of any distinction between idea and reality. It proclaims the complete unity of teaching and life, of religious man and social man.[30]

The pagan world proceeded from the idea: The world *is;* therefore, God is. It proceeded, first of all, from man, from the concept of the "I," and this led to two independent concepts concerning good and evil with the logical conclusion that there must be a third power which smoothes out the oppositions. Thus the pagan world arrived at polytheism, at multiplicity of values.[31] Mosaism, however, says: "God is; therefore, the world

---

27. *Die Entwicklung der religiösen Idee,* 7, 24, 34, 55ff (we quote according to the second edition, 1874).
28. *Ibid.,* 57.
29. *Ibid.,* 33.
30. *Ibid.,* 8ff.
31. *Ibid.,* 174–175.

is."[32] In this statement "the great content of Mosaism" is embraced. God is the absolute being, the absolute unity. The world is His creation. But God and the world are not identical. God is beyond the world, which is merely His work.[33] The world is a complex of separate entities and cannot be compared to God, who is "the absolute, unified, unique, omnipresent, and omnipotent." This leads to the fundamental idea of Mosaism—the holiness of man.

Mosaism sees in man "the unity of the physical and the spiritual." Man is similar to God in spirit," and therefore his destiny is "to become ever more like God, free and self-determining." He must be permeated with the consciousness "of elevating the moral over everything sensible and worldly." And the moral element must disclose itself "as love for God and love for neighbor, as justice and compassion before the One."[34]

Mosaism, Philippson stresses, perceives in revelation the complete "immediacy of God in relation to man."[35] One can pose the question, however, why all humanity was not endowed equally with revelation, why only a single "thereto educated little people" was chosen? So that mankind, explains Philippson, should independently go through all the stages of its evolution, "attain what it can attain for itself," and—chiefly—that it freely, through its own will, develop itself to the stage where accepting the truths of revelation would be a natural need.[36] For this reason was the Jewish race predestined "by divine Providence": that in its womb the religious idea should overcome the antithetical pagan world-view, and that it then transmit the idea to all mankind.[37]

This process, this exchange among the Jewish people of the heathen world-view for the religious idea, did not succeed in the initial period, in the age of the First Temple. The Jewish people "lost the Mosaic idea" and surrendered to paganism. "Life broke with the idea." The Mosaic world-view did not dominate the life of the Jewish people. From the womb of the Jewish community, however, grew unterrified battlers for the religious idea—the Hebrew prophets. They were unable to make the full unity of the Mosaic idea triumph over life, but they managed not only to save the idea itself but to develop and ripen the consciousness

32. *Ibid.*, 24.
33. *Ibid.*, 347.
34. *Ibid.*, 34, 51, 54.
35. *Ibid.*, 33.
36. *Ibid.*
37. *Ibid.*, 56.

that the religious idea is destined not merely for the people of Israel but for all mankind. Indeed, in the fact that the Mosaic idea split away from life, Philippson perceives divine Providence, for thereby the transference of the religious idea to all of humanity became easier, since at that stage of human development "only the idea itself could conquer mankind."[38]

The Judean kingdom was destroyed by the armies of Nebuchadnezzar. The Jewish people however, could not succumb, as was the case with other peoples, for—Phillipson emphasizes—beyond its "peoplehood," i.e., its special national peculiarities, this people had a quite different "life-content"—the religious; and this content saved its bearer from going under. Because the permeation of the religious idea throughout all mankind had to be a product of free, independent development, this idea, under the cultural conditions of that time, could penetrate not in its entire scope but only partially.[39] Hence, divine Providence ordained that the Jewish people should, for the second time, lead an independent political life, so that the religious idea might obtain the necessary means of defense to remain preserved in its completeness within the Jewish community for future generations.

In this, Philippson notes, consists the importance of Talmudism, which wove the religious idea into an "all-embracing law of life," produced a solid husk which preserved the seed and maintained the religious idea in its integrity for many generations.[40] One who understands, he declares, that the history of mankind is not a chain of accidents, but a planned process of evolution guided by divine Providence, will at once realize that it is by no means accidental that at the very time Christianity appeared on the world-arena, the dispersion of the Jews over the whole earth took place.[41] "This dispersion was, and will be even more so in the future, the blessing of all mankind, because the Jews as bearers of the religious idea are everywhere the most convincing testimony that this idea exists in the world."[42]

Mankind was not yet suited to accept the religious idea in its full scope, and so this occurred only in part: the peoples of the West accepted it in the form of Christianity, and the peoples of the East in the form of Islam. Christianity did not carry the

38. *Ibid.*, 62, 67, 69, 71, 72, 74, 87.
39. *Ibid.*, 91, 92.
40. *Ibid.*, 91, 92, 148.
41. *Ibid.*, 92.
42. *Ibid.*, 93.

principle of unity through in all its consistency. In it remained the pagan notion of the two independent factors, good and evil, which require a third as mediator. Thus, the concept of unity became diffuse in the idea of the Trinity.[43] In this connection one must further take into account, Philippson stresses, that "all the specific dogmas of Christianity contradict reason;" hence they must deny reason in order to confirm themselves.[44] In Islam also the religious idea is only partially incorporated. Islam, indeed, accepted the principle of unity; on the other hand, however, it denied freedom of action in the choices of men. "The likeness to the form of God" of man's spirit and the freedom of man's will and action, conditioned through this "likeness of form," are exchanged in Islam for the pagan notion of "necessity."[45]

Hence, Christianity, like Islam, forged the religious idea together with pagan elements.[46] Thus, Judaism still remained the sole bearer "of the full religious idea," which is woven into the "Talmudic form of law" and was preserved in the long generations of exile "for the future."[47] Hence, it is clear, Philippson explains, that "the continued existence of Judaism alongside Christianity was a matter of necessity."[48] The Jewish people was not allowed to succumb "for the sake of its higher purpose," so that it might fulfill its mission, maintain the religious idea for the future of mankind, and carry it to its ultimate triumph.[49]

We have observed that Philippson recognized the historical value of Talmudism which, with its "legal form," created a protective husk for the vital kernel—the religious idea. On the other hand, however, the rabbi does not tire of repeating that the modern era is "entirely outside the Talmudic realm."[50] He perceives the "goal of mankind" in the fact that the "unity of the idea and of life in the ideal setting of Mosaism creates itself anew."[51] In life, Philippson notes, "mankind, for the most part, is still sunk in paganism."[52] Hence, so important is the task "of making the ideas of Mosaism always purer, of understanding

43. *Ibid.*, 106.
44. *Ibid.*, 157.
45. *Ibid.*, 120, 128.
46. *Ibid.*, 145.
47. *Ibid.*, 125.
48. *Ibid.*, 111.
49. *Ibid.*, 112, 128, 170.
50. *Ibid.*, 165, 168, 170.
51. *Ibid.*, 150, 187.
52. *Ibid.*, 181.

them ever more definitely . . . of realizing institutionally the great social ideas of Mosaism."[53]

It is clear, Philippson concludes, that Judaism still has a high vocation in the future—in fact, the same that it has always had, and in even greater scope. And when Christianity, after setting aside its specifically Christian elements, will have a firm basis for the full religious idea—then Judaism is there to provide it. The destiny of Judaism *(die Bestimmung des Judenthums)*—to take up the religious idea and bear it for mankind until the idea "permeates it thoroughly"—appears before us in its historic goal. This mission was carried through "in the face of paganism;" it was also carried through "in the face of Christianity and Islam." The struggle the Jewish people first waged with its pagan neighbors and then with the Syrians, Greeks, and Romans, and in the last millenium and a half had to wage with the Christian world—in this consisted its destiny, its essence. This was the exalted battle of the religious idea "against its opposites."[54]

It is not at all difficult to perceive how shaky the whole theological structure of the mission theory is. Judaism endured the struggle of a millenium and a half which it had to wage with the Christian world thanks to the "Talmudic form of law" which kept Jewish society apart from the external world, thanks to the strictly maintained world of ideas that produced for the Jew the spiritual powers absolutely necessary for him to be able successfully to carry on the bloody, obdurate struggle. The masses, the lower strata of Christian society in the Middle Ages did, indeed, set forth in their fight against their rulers and oppressors, like a banner in the battle-program, "the great social ideas of Mosaism." In the "Old Testament" they sought a confirmation of their social demands, discovered the spiritual armor required in their struggle for freedom and justice. And most of the democratic and communist groups of the Middle Ages—the Albigenses, Cathari, the Brothers of Lyons, and the like did, indeed, have a certain closeness to the Jews as representatives and preservers of the "Old Testament."[55] But even these "heretical" groups of the Middle Ages by no means needed to have the Jews instruct them or familiarize them with the social truths inherent in the Bible, even though the printing press did not yet exist. The book was still an overly expensive luxury item for the poor

53. *Ibid.,* 186.
54. *Ibid.,* 179–180.
55. See our *History,* Vol. III.

masses, and the Christian clergy still took special pains to keep the masses as far away from the biblical text, with its overly democratic tendencies, as possible.

Hence, it is especially difficult to grasp in what the "mission" of the German Jews, who so emotively asserted that they are thoroughly Germans "wherever any members of the German nation are," could consist? To be sure, the Jews at that time were still distinguished from the German Christian citizens by their lack of rights, but the preachers of the mission theory fought for emancipation, rightly demanded that they, equally with all, take an active part in the political and social life of the country. In what, then, could the mission of the Germans of "the Mosaic confession" consist?—That the "Old Testamental" assimilated and half-assimilated bankers, lawyers, doctors, and preachers should familiarize Christian society with the truths of Judaism, with the "unity of the religious idea and of life" proclaimed in it? Does the Christian world not know, without this, the truths inscribed on the pages of the Bible? For familiarizing people with the text of the Bible, for the spreading of the Bible throughout the world, the missionary Bible societies, which disseminated the "book of books" in an enormous number of copies, already took sufficient care at that time.

Nevertheless, no matter how abstract, how weakly grounded this "mission theory" was, it played a certain role among German Jewry because it helped, so to speak, to lull them to sleep, to cover over the crying inconsistencies of life, to make a certain compromise between the national feeling that had not yet died out completely and the ever more triumphantly rising assimilationist tendencies.

To be sure, not all were satisfied by the "mission theory." We have already noted[56] the sharp critique with which the Italian Samuel David Luzzatto attacked the theory from his cultural-national point of view. But in Germany itself, attempts were made to respond in quite different fashion to the contradictions and inconsistencies which modern life had called forth. A quite unique response was given by Philippson's contemporary and colleague, the rabbi of Frankfurt-am-Main, Samson Raphael Hirsch.

56. See above, pp. 137–39.

CHAPTER EIGHT

Hirsch, Geiger, Holdheim, and Frankel

[The orthodox Rabbi Samson Raphael Hirsch—The significance of his *Neunzehn Briefe* (Nineteen Letters)—The Jews as a "spiritual people or nation"—Hirsch's attitude toward emancipation and Reform—Back to the ancient sources—Abraham Geiger as battler for reform and freethinker—His *Wissenschaftliche Zeitschrift für jüdische Theologie*—The free moral consciousness—The renewed battle against the Reformers of Hamburg—Isaac Bernays and his attack on the Reform prayerbook—Abraham Geiger and his radical demands—The Reformers of Frankfurt and Berlin—The rabbinic conference in Brunswick—Samuel Holdheim as battler for Reform—*Torat Ha-Kena'ot* as an echo of *Eleh Divrei Ha-Berit*—Zacharias Frankel and his world-view—The controversy-literature after the second rabbinic conference—The revolution of 1848.]

AMSON RAPHAEL Hirsch was born in Hamburg in 1808[1] into a wealthy merchant family. His father Raphael wished to make a merchant of his son. However, the young, romantically-minded Samson manifested very little interest in business. From his childhood on he was under the enormous impression produced by the books of the Bible. More than in anything else,

1. Died in Frankfurt-am-Main, where he served as rabbi for thirty-seven years, in 1888.

he was interested in religious-ethical problems, and already at that time the idea of becoming a rabbi in Israel, a religious leader and educator of his brethren, had matured in him. For several years he studied the Talmud and rabbinic literature with the well-known rabbi of Hamburg Isaac Bernays. At the same time he also studied in the local gymnasium, and later obtained higher education at the University of Bonn. The dreamy student and candidate for the rabbinate was greatly admired by his colleagues for his noble character and the remarkable moral beauty of his whole being. His comrade at the university and later his categorical ideological antagonist, Abraham Geiger, is forced to acknowledge in his older years: "I respected his [Hirsch's] choice spiritual gifts, his strict virtue, and loved his good heart."[2]

In 1830 the twenty-two year old Hirsch was appointed *Landrabbiner*, or chief district rabbi, of the principality of Oldenburg. We already know that precisely in the 1830s liberation tendencies were markedly strengthened in Germany. This aroused in Jewish circles hope for speedy emancipation. Along with this, the question of reform, of adapting the Jewish religion, with its laws and prohibitions, to modern life, was placed on the agenda. It was then (1836) that the district rabbi of Oldenburg (under the pseudonym Ben Uzziel) came forth with his *Neunzehn Briefe über Judenthum (Nineteen Letters on Judaism)*, which made an enormous impression.[3] Only now, less than twenty years after the publication of *Eleh Divrei Ha-Berit*,[4] did the orthodox camp obtain a richly endowed, European-educated, and enthusiastic champion. Whereas *Eleh Divrei Ha-Berit* had evoked dissatisfaction even in certain orthodox circles, *Neunzehn Briefe* aroused respect even among the most categorical opponents. The district rabbi of Oldenburg, with his gentle preachment, managed to win many adherents among the maturing young people and to become the spiritual creator and founder of the Neo-Orthodox movement in German Judaism.

In what did Hirsch's persuasive power consist? In his sympathies and tendencies, the rabbi was a typical romantic. While the German romantics of the school of Novalis dreamed of the

---

2. *Nachgelassene Schriften*, V, 18.

3. More than fifty years later, when the editor of the *Jüdische Presse* mentions the appearance of Hirsch's *Neunzehn Briefe*, he exclaims enthusiastically: "Here the youthful *Landrabbiner* of Oldenburg appeared on the scene with his composition . . . This rang out like a redeeming, shattering word to the listening world which had not yet received such tones."

4. See our *History*, Vol. IX, pp. 253ff.

medieval order of life which shimmered before their eyes in the loveliest of poetic and miraculous colors, Samson Raphael Hirsch, with his entire world-view, with all his hopes and strivings, lived in the ancient world of the Bible. In the laws of the Torah of Moses, in the visions of the Hebrew prophets, in the outpouring of the soul of the singers of the Psalms, he saw the loveliest and most exalted thing that mankind had produced— the peerless doctrine of love and justice.

One senses a strong spiritual affinity between the European-educated German rabbi and the founders of the Hasidic movement. Like the Baal Shem Tov and Levi Yitzḥak of Berdichev, the author of *Neunzehn Briefe* also perceives in love the foundation of the world. "God is love," he repeats many times. "The perfection of life is love,"[5] "love for all, all beings."[6] In the whole world, in nature, everywhere, he sees nothing but a revelation of God's love. "Giving and receiving love"—this is the essence of creation! "Love—everything whispers this to you."[7]

Like the Baal Shem Tov, Samson Raphael Hirsch also regarded God's world with joyous, optimistic eyes. "Oh, if we would carry the fullness of blessing in our hands!" he exclaims ecstatically. According to the Torah of Moses, Hirsch asserts, the supreme service of God consists in "beholding with joy the countenance of the Lord," exulting in beatitude before God's face. "Joyous cheerfulness of life through consciousness: to live under God's eye, to think, to feel, to speak and to work, to enjoy and to suffer. In this highest fulfillment, happiness and pain are forged together."[8]

As a result of this joyous, enthusiastic world-view, all of the *Neunzehn Briefe* are written in an elevated, emotive tone which necessarily exercised a powerful influence on the young and on the feminine soul.

"In this world," Hirsch declares, "we tread on holy ground. We live in God's world and are each servants all around . . . everything is God's servant, everything in its place, in its time . . . All are servants around God's throne." And in this God-filled world, in this "choir of servants of God," the major role is to be played by man, who is created in God's image. "Man must exult in the great choir of servants." He must be "the first servant in the servants' choir." And he can serve God only through love

5. Twelfth Letter.
6. Fourteenth Letter.
7. Third Letter, end.
8. Fifteenth Letter.

and justice. It is not the world that is bestowed on you, but you are bestowed on the world—"so that you may esteem it as God's ground and every one of its creatures as God's creation, as your brother, to esteem it as such, to love it as such, and actively to further its goal—according to God's will."[9]

The obligations of men as "God's servants," Hirsch stresses, "are taught to us by Judaism." As certain German romantics saw their most beautiful dreams realized in the Middle Ages, the Jewish romantic Samson Raphael Hirsch perceived the loveliest and most exalted in Judaism and its history. "Israel," he notes, "is a historical phenomenon among others," but this phenomenon is, in his view, the most brilliant and instructive page in world-history. From the Torah we know the position of man in creation: "Neither as god nor as slave should he stand in his earth-world, but as brother, fellow-serving brother, occupying, however, the position of first-born because of the nature and scope of his service."[10] The Torah teaches that he deserves to bear the name man "who has fulfilled righteousness and love in his existence; his whole life, his thinking and feeling, his speaking and acting, his business affairs and enjoyments—all are service of God."[11]

It is a great error, Hirsch declares, that many understand by the term *hasid*, or pious man, one who isolates himself from the world and spends his days only in prayer and fasting. "Merely contemplative and prayerful life is not Judaism." According to Judaism, the name *hasid* is merited only by him who "devotes himself entirely in love, who surrenders his claims on the world only in order to live more actively for the world in works of love, who does not withdraw from it but lives in it and for it."[12] As a result of this, Hirsch asserts, the uniqueness of the Jewish people was created. Others perceive the ground of life in possession and enjoyment. The people of Israel sees, however, "in the one and only God the sole ground of life, Him alone as founder, leader, and lever (or dynamic power) of its thoughts, sentiments, words and deeds."[13] This, the author concludes, the people of Israel clearly manifested in its long exile and wandering. "Its whole history of exile is an altar on which the people, in God's name and teaching, sacrificed everything that men yearn for and

9. Third and Fourth Letters.
10. Fifth Letter.
11. Fourth Letter.
12. Fifteenth Letter.
13. Seventh Letter.

love. And among all peoples and lands such altars smoked for Jews."[14]

In total opposition to Ludwig Philippson and many other enlighteners, Hirsch does not at all distinguish the Bible from the Talmud and Midrash. All these, in his view, form an integral whole; one complements the other. Not without reason, says the author of *Neunzehn Briefe*, did the generation of Israelites in the wilderness declare "We will do and we will hear." One is required not only to grasp and understand the ethical principles of the Torah but also to fulfill them, not merely "as beliefs or propositions of knowledge, but as principles of life to be acknowledged and to be taken up with the mind and heart."[15]

With great emotiveness Hirsch speaks of the vast psychological significance of symbols and emblems, how necessary it is to inscribe in the human soul "fundamental ideas" through "action-symbols, through signs and deeds." Precisely this is intended by the commandments of the Torah and the Talmud. With intense enthusiasm the romantic Hirsch speaks of the mystical beauty of the Sabbath which hallows and elevates man, and he cannot understand how one can desecrate the Sabbath for the sake of earnings and enjoyment. To be sure, he knows very well how many "Germans of the Mosaic confession" do not fulfill the commandments of the Sabbath not so much for economic reasons as because of their intercourse with non-Jews. They are afraid: "If one distinguishes himself thus, he will at once be recognized as a Jew." "You, son of my time," Hirsch exclaims, "who tells you that you should deny being a Jew?" Be a Jew truly, strive to realize the ideal of a genuine Jew who fulfills the commandments of the Torah concerning righteousness and love. Then you will be respected *because* you are a Jew, not "despite the fact that you are a Jew." Understand yourself as a Jew and spread this understanding among your non-Jewish brethren through your word—even more, through the acts of your life.[16]

To the argument that the prohibition against eating ritually forbidden food isolates the Jew from the neighboring populace, Hirsch responds: "Be just in action, be truthful in word, bear love in your heart towards your non-Jewish brother, as your Torah teaches you. Feed his hungry, clothe his naked, heal his sick, comfort his suffering. . . . Unfold the whole noble fullness

14. Ninth Letter.
15. Tenth Letter.
16. Fifteenth Letter.

of your Israeldom—and will he not love you?"[17] Hirsch does not grow weary of fighting the charge that Judaism strives for isolation. He endeavors to show that the supreme goal of Judaism consists in the "universal brotherhood of mankind."[18] Here he comes into touch with the two most urgent problems of his day, emancipation and reform.

As is known, in the orthodox camp there were men who had a negative attitude towards emancipation out of fear that, through coming closer to the alien milieu, the singularity of the Jewish people might be erased.[19] Hirsch considers this absolutely ungrounded. He endeavors to show that "land and soil" were never the "bond of unity" for the people of Israel. Even in the ancient era of its political independence, the Jewish people was united not by the state, by the power of government, but by the ethical-religious teaching of the Torah. Always, Hirsch asserts, the people of Israel was, and has remained to the present day, a *spiritual* people *(rein geistige Natur der Volkstümlichkeit Israels)*, what is called in Hebrew *am* and *goy*, not what is denoted by the German term *Volk*, which is closely bound up with the notion of a common soil. Indeed, for this reason the Jewish people managed to maintain its unity in exile and at the same time also manifest the capacity to make itself at home in every land where it settled, as the prophet Jeremiah had already commanded in the times of Nebuchadnezzar: "Build houses and live in them; plant gardens and eat the fruit of them . . . And seek the peace of the city where I have sent you into exile, and pray to the Lord for it, for in its peace you will have peace" (Jeremiah 29:5,7).

Hirsch cannot understand why the Reformers are so shocked by the hope for the "advent of the Messiah" and endeavor to demonstrate that they in no way think of any fatherland other than the land in which they were born. Not *we*, the deeply religious Hirsch asserts, will provide the "future that is to come." Not through *our* active power of will is it be attained. We merely hope for this future as for God's grace and favor, which will occur "hand in hand with the elevation of all mankind to universal brotherhood under almighty God,"[20] i.e., when all humanity will be redeemed.

Because the Jewish people is a spiritual people, it believed even in the homelessness of exile that all civic rights which the

17. *Ibid.*
18. *Ibid.*
19. Sixteenth Letter.
20. *Ibid.*

state can grant in order to secure material possession and enjoyment are merely instrumentalities to fulfill the highest vocation of man. His civic disabilities and the persecutions he suffered, however, made the life-struggle of the Jew extremely difficult in the "dark as night days of the Middle Ages." Hence, Hirsch welcomes emancipation, because, as a result of it, the spirit will no longer be crippled. I bless emancipation, he exclaims emotively, because in it is proclaimed

respect for right, for human right: for a man to be a man among men, and the view that the earth is God's and whoever bears the human stamp as His child will be joyously respected by all as a brother . . . I welcome it exultingly as a dawn of the reawakening humanity in mankind, a preliminary stage for the recognition of God as the sole Lord and Father of all men, who are His children and thereby brethren.

However, Hirsch stresses, I bless emancipation only "if Israel accepts it not as the end of its vocation but as a new side of its task, as a new test, and as one much more difficult than oppression." How sad it would be, he concludes, if Israel should have such a slight notion of itself and its significance that it welcomed emancipation as the end of its exile, as the supreme goal of its vocation. How greatly I would mourn if Israel would have so little grasp of its own task that it would purchase emancipation —the possibilities "for acquiring possessions and enjoyment" through liberation from unjust oppression—at too high a price: "through capricious curtailment of the Torah, through wanton surrender of the soul of our life."[21]

"Jews must we become," Hirsch exclaims,—"in the true sense, Jews permeated by the spirit of the Torah, accepting it as the source of life."

The romantic rabbi was not satisfied with the capitalist world of his time, with its pursuit of "possession and enjoyment." However, in Judaism, wherein the youthful Karl Marx saw the incarnation of the egotistical capitalist spirit, he perceives the bearer of the most splendid ideals of man—love and social justice. "And imagine once," the dreamy Hirsch addresses his readers,

the portrait of such an Israel, living in freedom among the peoples, striving to attain its ideal—every son of Israel esteemed and a widely

21. End of Sixteenth Letter.

influential exemplar-priest of righteousness and love, spreading not Israeldom [i.e., specific Judaism]—which is forbidden to him—but pure humanitarianism among the peoples.[22]

Emancipation in and of itself, Hirsch concludes, neither diminishes us nor aggrandizes us. Another goal stands before us, and to achieve this is entirely in our hands: the ennobling of ourselves, the realization of Judaism through the Jew himself.[23] "We have not for a long time been what we should be." And this, the author insists, leads us to the question: What is denoted by the term "reform?" The goal of reform cannot be anything other than "the realization of Judaism through Jews in our time." It is not the religion that needs reforming, but we ourselves. Education, the elevation of our age to the Torah—not the levelling of the Torah according to the time, not the lowering of the lofty mountain peaks to the flat plain of our life. "We Jews need to be reformed through Judaism, newly comprehended and grasped by the spirit, realized with all the power of our action," but not by wishing to modify the eternal precepts and laws given by God for all time and adapting these to our temporary requirements and strivings. God's Torah ought to elevate us. But we? We desire to drag it down to ourselves.[24]

The profoundly religious author of *Neunzehn Briefe* is firmly persuaded that traditional Judaism has been and will remain the radiant star of mankind. Two revelations, he declares, were given to us: nature and the Torah. And for both "there is only one method of investigation." In nature the phenomena stand before man as solidly given facts; man endeavors to explore the laws that bring them into dynamic activity. However, when he does not manage to achieve everything and all is not clear and comprehensible to him, the phenomena still remain as given facts which cannot be denied. So also is "the investigation of the Torah." It is for us a fact, like heaven and earth; its regulations lie before us as actual facts. In the Torah, as in nature, the ultimate ground is—God. As in nature, so in the Torah "no fact is to be denied," even if its reason and connection are not explained, "but as in nature, so in the Torah the traces of God's wisdom are to be sought."[25]

Not with anger, not with sarcasm—these were alien to the inspired romantic Hirsch—but with deep pain does he speak of

22. Sixteenth Letter.
23. Beginning of Seventeenth Letter.
24. Seventeenth Letter.
25. Note 4 to the Eighteenth Letter.

the religious Reform movement of his time and of the rational-
ist-critical attitude toward traditional Judaism on the part of
those Jews who declare themselves Mendelssohn's followers.[26]
These who proclaim themselves Mendelssohn's "disciples" have
rejected the Talmud. They see in it "nothing but nitpicking
subtleties and petty shopkeeping." The multi-volume inquiries
and speculations about these laws and ordinances, which, from
their rationalist point of view, are obsolete, are nothing more in
their eyes than "spiritually deadening clericalism, and Judaism
as generally practiced-nothing other than spiritless drudgery."[27]
They think that by adorning the garment "through the reform
of worship, following alien models," they will renew Judaism
after they have stifled the spirit and life-content. With arid cate-
chisms, with abstract moral concepts, they wish to win the
youth. "For Heaven's sake," Hirsch exclaims, "where are Jews
to come from, Jews with a living spirit of knowledge of God and
vocation, and armed with strength for the battle against sensual-
ity and error, against the burden of the times and against mis-
conception?"[28]

Hirsch sees the only solution in forgetting as quickly as possible all rationalist speculations and false notions about Judaism
and returning to its primary sources—the Bible, Talmud, and
Midrash. "Read, study, and understand them in order to live
them. Draw out of them Judaism's teachings concerning God,
world, mankind . . . Know Judaism out of itself, out of its own
concepts, rise out of it to a science of wisdom of life."[29]

Hirsch is optimistic. He is certain that "it will become different in Israel." There will come a generation of "self-liberating
Judaism," a generation which, in regard to the questions,
"What, then, am I as a Jew? What is Judaism?," will apply not
to alien authorities who frequently have a false notion of Judaism and some of whom think of how to destroy it, nor to the
writings of our "Reformers" who have in mind ulterior motives,
but to the primordial sources of Judaism—the Bible and the
Talmud. And this with the single aim: "to understand life out
of Judaism, and Judaism as an institution for grasping the meaning of life." This single aim will lead to the ardently desired
goal: "to produce what is true and life-giving as truth and life;

26. Toward Mendelssohn himself Hirsch has an attitude of great respect. He regards him
as a very brilliant personality.
27. Eighteenth Letter.
28. Seventeenth Letter.
29. Eighteenth Letter.

according to the ancient but, regrettably, neglected rule: to learn and to teach, to observe and to do."[30]

The extreme antithesis of the battler for traditional orthodox Judaism is represented by Hirsch's university comrade and friend of his youth, Abraham Geiger. Born in Frankfurt-am-Main in 1810 into a poor family, Geiger in his childhood already evoked astonishment with his extraordinary capacities. At the age of four he studied the Bible and Mishnah. At the age of eight he was renowned as an *ilui*, or "prodigy," and at twelve manifested great learning in the vast Talmudic literature. Soon his father died, and he was without means of livelihood. However, the Frankfurt Rothschild interested himself in the young, richly talented orphan and gave him the resources required to study German, Latin, and Greek with special tutors.

Geiger's own family, however, wished that he should prepare himself for a rabbinical career in time; hence, he continued to devote much time to Talmudic-rabbinic literature. However, he was already attracted to secular knowledge, to the sources of European culture, and as early as those youthful years there awakened in the future champion of Reform a feeling of hostility toward the Talmud, which he had to study contrary to his will. In 1829 he went to Heidelberg where he studied Semitic languages—Syriac, Aramaic, and Arabic at the university. Then he went to Bonn where he obtained a prize (1832) from the university for his first scholarly work, *Was hat Mohammed aus dem Judenthume aufgenommen?*

The richly gifted young scholar, blessed with a keenly analytic mind, iron energy, and a gigantic thirst for scholarship and knowledge, knew very well that for him, the Jew without rights, all paths in Germany were closed, and only one career was open —the rabbinate. He, the free thinker, who already in the early years of youth had a sharply critical attitude toward Talmudic-rabbinic Judaism and declared with contempt that "the fire of enlightenment has made an end to these moldy scraps of pages" had to become a "pastor of souls" and official representative of the rabbinate. As early as 1831 he wrote in one of his letters that

the most correct way is, according to my firm persuasion, splitting or separation . . . As soon as Jews of a certain province have arrived at

---

30. Eighteenth Letter. Hirsch's *Neunzehn Briefe* was translated by Moses Aronson into Hebrew (1890) under the title *Iggerot Tzafon*. Aronson also published in Hebrew Hirsch's work *Choreb, oder Versuche uber Jissroel's Pflichten in der Zerststreuung* (1839), which must be considered as a supplement to *Neunzehn Briefe*.

the conviction that the yoke of the Talmud must be cast off, they should combine into a separate group and publicly declare that they do not recognize the authority of the Talmud. They should also demand of the government permission to form separate communities distinguished from the Talmud Jews.[31]

Five years later (1836) he wrote in another letter:

We must reject the Talmud, reject the Bible as a *sacred* book, notwithstanding the fact that the latter is precious to us as a highly valuable poetic work of art. To be sure, this cannot be done in one day, but we must *strive toward this goal.* We must put an end to the lie that we offer people in the synagogue by presenting biblical legends as actual historical facts.[32]

It was this free thinker who immediately after completing his university course had to accept the rabbinic office in the small Jewish community of Wiesbaden. One must, in this connection, bear in mind that even the community members who already thought very little of Jewishness and, in their own homes, conducted themselves quite freely and without restraint demanded of their "pastor of souls" that he behave piously, as befits a rabbi. We noted that the community of Darmstadt rejected the candidacy of Leopold Zunz only because a rumor was bruited about that he did not have a *kasher* kitchen in his home. In this fashion, a quite unique situation was produced in the German communities of that time: not the people, but the rabbis themselves, were chiefly interested in religious "reform," in adapting the religion to the requirements of modern life.

In 1835, the same year that David Friedrich Strauss came forth with his two-volume, radically critical treatise *Das Leben Jesu,*[33] Geiger established his *Wissenschaftliche Zeitschrift für jüdische Theologie* which became the platform for all battlers in the cause of Reform. The title of Geiger's journal is characteristic. All of Judaism is considered nothing but "theology," and this theology must obtain a purely scientific elucidation. The religion must be adapted to life, to the spiritual and intellectual requirements of the people.

The essence of Judaism, Geiger declares, is "free development

31. Geiger's *Nachgelassene Schriften*, Vol. V, 55.
32. Bernfeld, *Toledot Ha-Reformatzyon Ha-Datit*, 134.
33. As soon as Geiger read this work he wrote with enthusiasm to Jacob Auerbach: "A work that is excellent and must be read by everyone who does not wish to remain behind the times; a work that is of the highest significance in scholarly respects but also of no lesser influence on Christian theology" (*Nachgelassene Schriften*, V, 96).

of inner moral power, the recognition of man and his worth." The striving and activity of Judaism must therefore stream out of purely moral conviction, and in the battle to which it is called actually lies the consciousness of its importance and value. However, in the course of history, Geiger laments, there gathered around the kernel of Judaism "a formal belief and formal cult" in whose fulfillment one no longer sees a product of "free moral conviction" but *"obligatory observances of laws"* (italics Geiger's). In these [the laws connected with the "formal cult"] are placed an independent content of magical power which influences the whole order of the world. With such an *association,* Geiger concludes, a truly free human morality is impossible. Genuine reverence of God, the striving for self-sanctification, must unconditionally presuppose the consciousness that only "in spiritual—moral independence does man's bliss lie." As soon as the "must," the firmly established, untouchable forms, are represented as the chief principle, the free moral consciousness of man is thereby obscured; "then, the full development of the inner moral kernel is, in general, quite impossible."

The program set forth by Abraham Geiger was not very clearly formulated. In what the "free development of inner moral power" actually consists is not altogether comprehensible. One merely senses the courageous call to battle for the liberation of the human personality from the congealed forms hallowed by tradition. Moreover, in this connection, two tendencies are quite clearly marked: (1) the adaptation of the Jewish religion to the ardently anticipated emancipation and, (2) the idea that the religious reformation must erase from Judaism the slightest national symbols and signs, since Jews are not a separate nation but true Germans. Still another characteristic feature must be noted: the Friedländers and Wolfsohns regarded Christianity and its morality with a certain amount of self-deprecation, but Geiger was very hostile toward Christianity, and there is a bit of truth in Bernfeld's remark regarding Geiger that "his Judaism was only a vigorous opposition to the dominant religion."

The militant tone and radical tendencies of Geiger's journal evoked strong displeasure in orthodox circles, and when the rabbinic office in Breslau was open and Geiger submitted his candidacy, a stubborn battle which lasted for more than two years broke out. Geiger finally managed (in 1840) to obtain the desired post.

We noted previously that at the beginning of the 1840s, under the influence of Ludwig Feuerbach, Bruno Bauer, and other radical scholars, anti-religious tendencies were strengthened in Christian intellectual circles in Germany. This naturally found a sharp resonance in Jewish intellectual circles as well. The beginning of the renewed campaign for religious reform broke out in Hamburg, where the fire of controversy had flared up twenty years earlier on account of the "Reform Tempel" established there.[34] The leaders of the Hamburg *Reform-Tempel-Verein* in 1841 decided to issue a new edition (under the title *Seder Ha-Avodah: Gebetbuch für die öffentliche und hausliche Andacht der Israeliten*) of the Reform prayerbook which Meir Bresselau and Zekil Frankl had published in 1818.[35] The new editors were quite irenically minded[36] and did not allow themselves to carry through further reform changes in the text. This time they even reprinted in the Hebrew original several prayers which were printed only in German translation in the first edition. Nevertheless, a storm erupted. Samson Raphael Hirsch's master, the European-educated but orthodox-minded Rabbi Isaac Bernays of Hamburg, had a proclamation read in three of the synagogues of Hamburg to the effect that the prohibition which the president of the rabbinic court of that city had issued in his day in regard to the Reform prayerbook[37] also applies, with all its rigor, to the new edition, and that no right-believing son of Israel may pray from this heretical prayerbook. The enraged leaders of the *Tempel-Verein* promptly addressed a call to numerous rabbis to express their views in regard to the controversy which Bernays evoked with his proclamation.

Times had changed considerably. Whereas in the beginning of the reactionary era of the Restoration there were only four rabbis who supported the Reformers of Hamburg with their approbations,[38] now the leaders of the *Reform-Tempel-Verein* had on their side a host of young rabbis who issued forth with charges against Rabbi Bernays. The controversy in regard to the new edition of the Hamburg Reform prayerbook called forth a whole literature of pamphlets, declarations, and proclamations.[39]

On the side of the Reformers, Abraham Geiger issued forth

---

34. See the preceding volume, pp. 244ff.
35. Ibid., p. 244, Note 25.
36. Their mood of compromise is stressed by the editors and publishers themselves in the introduction.
37. Vol. IX, p. 253.
38. Ibid., pp. 246ff.
39. For some bibliographical details, see Bernfeld's *Toledot Ha-Reformatzyon Ha-Datit*, 148–149.

most decisively.[40] Naturally, he sharply attacked Bernays, but he was also not satisfied with the leaders of the Hamburg *Reform-Verein* and with the editors of the new edition of the prayerbook, because he found that they went only half way, were compromisers, and lacked the courage to follow to the end all the necessary logical conclusions entailed by the firmly established thesis that Judaism is not a national but a religious institution. In order not to run afoul of the orthodox, the Reformers of Hamburg did not strictly erase from their prayerbook all the prayers bearing a national character, everything that has some relationship to the hope for redemption and the ingathering of the exiles.

Geiger was convinced that there must remain in the Reform prayerbook no memory of the prayers in which the offering of sacrifices in the Temple is mentioned. On the contrary, we ought not to lament the fact that sacrifices are no longer offered at present, but thank and praise God who has illuminated our minds and we now understand that we must not serve Him with sacrifices, for this is a custom of idolaters. In the Reform prayerbook, however, in the service of the Day of Atonement, there remained the order of the *Avodah* [the account of the sacrificial ritual performed by the priests in the ancient Temple], even if in considerably abbreviated form. Geiger even concluded that many beautiful liturgical hymns of the Sephardic poets ought to be discarded because in them, too, sacrifices are mentioned. Hence, he cannot forgive the editors of the Reform prayerbook for not having removed the poem "Atta Konaneta," since it contains a phrase such as the following: "Out of love for the sweet odor [of the incense] Thou didst bless his [i.e., Noah's] children."[41]

Geiger, who himself wrote excellent Hebrew and published many scholarly articles in Hebrew journals,[42] could also not forgive the Reformers of Hamburg for exchanging the German translation of some of the prayers for the Hebrew original in the new edition. The Hebrew language, he declares, is not comprehensible to us, and it is not the language of our fatherland. One ought to pray in the language that we all understand. Furthermore, the weekly portion of the Torah should be read in the vernacular.[43]

40. In a special brochure "Der Tempelstreit, eine Zeitfrage," reprinted in *Nachgelassene Schriften*, I, 113–196.

41. *Nachgelassene Schriften*, I, 171–172.

42. The full list of Geiger's 313 works, which he published in Hebrew and German journals, is given by Moïse Schwab in his *Répertoire*.

43. Characteristic are Geiger's critical remarks in a letter of his of August 4, 1853 in regard

The controversy between the Reformers and the orthodox of Hamburg was suddenly interrupted in quite unexpected fashion. In May of 1842 a terrible conflagration broke out in Hamburg which destroyed a considerable part of the great commercial city. The catastrophe for a time caused party interests and Reform projects to be forgotten.

However, Reform ideas remained in the air. If not in Hamburg, they were placed on the agenda in other centers of culture. In the same year (October 1842) the Reformers of Frankfurt, led by Theodor Creizenach, founded a society of *Reformfreunde*. The members of the society addressed the Jewish community with a long proclamation in which they formulated their program in three points which we previously quoted when discussing Gabriel Riesser.[44] The program, in fact, intended publicly to state that the *Reformfreunde* do not recognize Talmudic Judaism and the practical *mitzvot*. Abraham Geiger was not pleased with the tactics of the Reformers of Frankfurt, but in letters which he wrote at that time to his friends he propagandized energetically for radical religious reform. The main thing, he wrote to Stern, must be publicly proclaimed, and that is that the religious life now existing among us Jews is filled with falsehood. He also wrote to Berthold Auerbach in the same year about the necessity of religious reform. "For the time being," he declared, "we do not occupy ourselves with building. We must first of all destroy and remove the heaps of dust and mildew. I am not fearful that this may produce a split among Jews, as long as we arrive at actual results."[45]

In the community of Berlin, too, the Reformers, led by Sigismund Stern and Aaron Bernstein, organized themselves. They also put forward the thesis that the Jewish religion must be adapted to the demands of modern times and that all national elements must be removed from it.

The Reformers finally decided to arrange a special conference and there reach certain decisions concerning the reforms required. The conference took place in the summer of 1844 in Brunswick. In this connection the following characteristic feature is worth noting: the organizers invited only rabbis and preachers to the conference. Among them were even men who had quite modest competence in Jewish scholarship, but it was

---

to Abraham Mapu's novel *Ahavat Tziyyon* which had just appeared. He endeavors to show that it is impossible to create artistically in a dead language (*Nachgelassene Schriften*, II, 327–329). On his hatred and contempt for Yiddish, see our *History*, Vol. VII, 14.

44. See above, p. 156.

45. *Nachgelassene Schriften*, V, 73: "In God's name, then, something firm will form even by itself."

considered superfluous to invite such distinguished scholars as Leopold Zunz, Samuel David Luzzatto, and others. Whether this was done consciously or unconsciously, in this fact alone one can see a certain symptom of a struggle for power. These modern rabbis were striving to command the sole right to "loose and bind," to regulate religious life in the communities, to be the "shepherds of Israel," the supervisors of all the institutions associated with Jewish spiritual and intellectual interests.

Twenty-two rabbis and preachers, all Reformers, came to the conference—among them, Abraham Geiger. However, he was not the keynote setter of the conference (incidentally, he participated in it only in its final days), but the still more radically-minded Samuel Holdheim.

Born in 1806 in Kempno, a small town in the region of Posen, Samuel Holdheim was educated in the old fashion. He studied only Talmud and rabbinic literature. In this realm he obtained very extensive knowledge and was renowned as an extremely keen student and "prodigy." It was this ingenious swimmer over the depths of the "sea of the Talmud" that the rabbi of Posen chose for his son-in-law. The rabbi's daughter, however, was already somewhat "anointed with culture" and wished to educate her husband, the *yeshivah*-student. She attempted to familiarize him with the German language. The intellectually curious Holdheim devoted himself with great diligence to self-education. The books of secular content "opened his eyes." The former *yeshivah*-student was soon "infected with heresy." He divorced his wife, who was already too pious and old-fashioned for him, and left to study in Prague at the university of that city.

In 1836 Holdheim began his rabbinical career, first at Frankfurt-am-Oder, later in Mecklenburg-Schwerin. In the first years of his communal activity he was much concerned for the systematic education of children in the communities. However, he refused to be content with this. The former prodigy of Kempno dreamed of radical religious reform. In character and worldview, Holdheim was sharply distinguished from Geiger. Geiger was not only a keen dialectician; in him also flickered, as we shall see below, a poetic spark. He himself wrote German poems and published quite successful translations of the medieval Spanish-Hebrew poets. He was also blessed with a strong historical sense and, in consequence of this, was able to produce in his later years, when the Revolution of 1848 weakened the drive for religious reform to a certain degree, his critical-historical masterpiece, *Urschrift und Übersetzungen der Bibel,* of which we shall speak in the next volume. To Holdheim, however, the slightest poetic emotions were quite foreign. Only the mentally acute, the ingenious notion, was dear to him. Spiritually and ideologically he was in close affinity with the heretics and freethinkers of the high Middle Ages of whom we spoke in the first volume of our work.

These were men of brilliant capacities and with sharply honed minds, but without any inner core or firm roots . . . They were basically indifferent not only to faith but also to the values of inquiry and knowledge. It was not the enthusiasm of seeking and attaining truth that was precious to them, but the play of clever thought, invention, mere ideas; they scoffed at everything enveloped in the mantle of sacredness and toward which others had an attitude of reverence.[46]

"To destroy"—this was Holdheim's motto. The scientific concept of historical evolution was alien to him. Everything transmitted by tradition, everything bearing the stamp of the past, must be rejected, for so "reason obliges."

Holdheim confuses political and national considerations in historical Judaism, and on this basis demands that at the present time not only must the Jewish laws that have some relationship to independent political life be rejected, but also everything that bears in itself signs of national consciousness. The well-known Talmudic dictum *Dina de-malchuta dina*, "The law of the state is law [in Judaism also]" was interpreted by Holdheim in purely pilpulist fashion: Judaism must recognize the power of government, the "high German government," as the supreme tribunal in purely religious questions. As inhabitants of a European state, Jews, for example, must reject the commandment of Sabbath rest, for the government does not recognize Sabbath rest and—"the law of the state is law!" The Jewish religion must assume national German forms because this is demanded by the modern "time-consciousness." The Jews in Germany, after all, constitute one German nation along with the other inhabitants of Germany.

Holdheim was the chief spokesman at the Brunswick rabbinical conference. Not much was accomplished at this conference. Certain quite radical reforms that Holdheim proposed were submitted to a special committee to be considered and set before the second convention, which was to take place a year later in Frankfurt. Of the decisions that were reached at the Brunswick

46. Our *History*, Vol. I, pp. 109–10. Holdheim set forth his reform plans in his *Über die Autonomie der Rabbiner* (1843).

conference, the most important is that one may marry adherents of other religions. In regard to ritual reform, it was concluded that the *Kol Nidrei* prayer be annulled.

It was not so much the decisions that were taken as the sharp tone in which several rabbis permitted themselves to issue forth at the conference against the Talmud that greatly enraged the orthodox camp. As twenty-five years earlier, so now the orthodox rabbis came forward with stormy protests which were published in the collection *Torat Ha-Kena'ot* (two parts, printed in Amsterdam, 1845). Most of the protests are written in the same style as *Eleb Divrei Ha-Berit.*[47] *Torat Ha-Kena'ot* is also full of expressions such as the following: "Erring ones and misleaders;" "worthless men;" "an assembly of evil-doers;" "a band of deceivers;" "men of wickedness;" "a breed of sinful men;" "heretics and deniers;" "violent men among our people;" "wicked rascals;" "reckless and foolish men;" "a band of frauds;" "a mixed multitude of asses;" "rebels and transgressors;" "breach of the sinners;" "the counsel of evildoers;" "a group of rebels who break forth;" etc. The rabbi of Cracow, Dov Berush Meisels, marvels at "the great men among the true rabbis in the land of Germany" for not girding up their loins in order to make intercession with the government that these (the participants in the Brunswick conference) be excluded from the community of Israel and be persecuted and pushed away until they completely change their religion and their name will no longer be mentioned among Jews (*ibid.*, 14).

An exception in this collection, in which over seventy rabbis participated, is represented solely by the letter of Samson Raphael Hirsch. In a soft, gentle tone Hirsch notes that the conference in Brunswick is not an accidental phenomenon but a symptom of the disease from which our entire generation suffers (*ibid.*, 3–5).

Several more moderate rabbis, however, found it more useful not to content themselves merely with protests, but to participate in the subsequent rabbinic conferences and help bring it about that these bear a less radical character. The most important of these rabbis was the European-educated *Oberrabbiner* of Dresden, Zacharias ben Jacob Frankel.[48]

Immediately after Bernays issued forth with his protest against the new edition of the Reform prayerbook, the repre-

47. See our *History*, Vol. IX, pp. 253ff.
48. Born in Prague in 1801, died in Breslau in 1875. We shall speak in the subsequent volume of Frankel's important scholarly works.

sentatives of the Hamburg *Tempel-Verein* applied to Frankel with the request that he express his authoritative view. Frankel responded to this with a rather long letter in the weekly *Orient* (1842, Nos. 7–9).[49] Here he issues forth decisively against Bernays and his militant tone, and concludes that the way that the latter sets forth is the "path of war and dissension" *(Zwietracht).* However, he is not at all satisfied by the editors of the Reform prayerbook. He concludes that they are "eclectics," not consistent and not rigorous.

Frankel reproaches them for lacking historical sense and for not understanding that in such matters as worship, it is a question mainly of feeling and attitude, and these cannot be measured "with the coldness of the understanding," with logically established conclusions. But the editors do not grasp this and wish "the warmth aroused through sentiment to be exchanged for the coldness of the intellect." Frankel can in no way forgive the editors their attitude toward the traditional belief in the redemption and in the coming of the Messiah. Not only in eliminating numerous prayers permeated with this belief, but even by so editing the remaining passages in the prayerbook dealing with these matters do the editors show quite clearly how they endeavored to stifle this ideal, to remove from it its elevating power and freshness of life.

"The idea of independence," Frankel emotively exclaims,

has in itself sublimity, strength of life! . . . In the wish that somewhere in a corner of the world (naturally in the land of our fathers, with which the holiest memories are associated) our peoplehood should again freely step forward and that we should there enjoy the respect which is bestowed, as sad experience teaches us, even with all the progress that enlightenment makes, only upon those peoples who possess external power—in this there is surely no injustice.

In this idea, Frankel repeats, one can in no way see signs of hatred or deprecation for the present fatherland or arouse the suspicion that we consider ourselves aliens in the fatherland and desire to flee from it. We wish men to know that, despite millennial sufferings and calamities, we still do not despair and are at least able to grasp the idea of independence, of "an independent revival." In any case, Frankel asserts, this idea is far more elevated than the constant fear of manifesting the least "character-

---

49. The double weekly journal, *Der Orient* and *Literaturblatt des Orients,* appeared in Leipzig under the editorship of Julius Fürst in the period 1840–1850.

istic trait," the slavish adaptation to external circumstances that ends with hollow, flat cosmopolitanism.[50]

"This," Frankel concludes, "is not rarely the defect of our contemporary Reformers . . . that they overlook history, forget that man, with his feelings, is not rooted in the present alone, that what has been inherited and obtained through tradition has found a home in our hearts, in our souls."[51]

Frankel's response was highly displeasing to the leaders of the Hamburg *Tempel-Verein*. The preacher of the Temple, Doctor Gotthold Salomon, came forward with a special *Sendschreiben* in which he charges Frankel with "nationalism," something that can undoubtedly be injurious to the cause of emancipation. How can it be, asks Doctor Salomon?—Frankel speaks of "the idea of independence;" he ought to explain "how this independence can be brought into harmony with the striving for equality of civic rights."

Apparently Frankel himself was intimidated. This is manifested by his speedy and long response.[52] He comes forth with the logical argument: Is the idea of a newly created Jewish state so wild? Is it really in such screaming inconsistency "with attachment to the fatherland?" Was it taken amiss that the Greeks, who live under Austrian domination, expressed the desire that a free Greece rise again? This hope was by no means taken as a manifestation that they wish to cast off the sovereignty of the Hapsburgs. Why, then, must the Jews be suspected of desiring to rebel against the state? "Because the Greeks," it is answered, "propagandized for their unfortunate brethren who were so greatly oppressed by the Ottomans." Why, then, may the Jews not wish that a fatherland be created for their miserable brethren who languish in Sardinia, in czarist Russia, and in other places. *We* have found a fatherland; *the others* lack it, and so they wish "to obtain independence." "We have no desire to depart from the land that is a fatherland to us." But when the home drives out a man only because he calls himself Jew, "*then* the hope for a friendly homeland may revive." We, Frankel adds, have found a fatherland "and are attached to it." But time occasionally takes steps backward. We observed this in the second decade of the present century[53] in many German states. "And should—God forbid—time regress again, then may a fatherland where our name will be free accept us."[54]

50. *Der Orient*, 363.
51. *Ibid.*, 64.
52. *Literaturblatt des Orients*, 1842, Nos. 23–24.
53. After Napoleon's downfall.
54. *Literaturblatt des Orients*, 362.

Only here does Frankel show how unclear the concepts of nation and national culture yet remained for him. A certain role is still definitely played by fear lest the cause of emancipation be harmed. Hence, Frankel awkwardly confuses civic rights with national rights. Certainly, he writes, where the Jew finds a fatherland and the land of his birth recognizes him "as a legitimate son," he renounces particular Jewish nationality; he *must* renounce it, if he wishes to consider himself a son of the fatherland. He himself, after all, demands of the fatherland that it grant this to him, and thereby Jewish nationality ceases "of itself." For, Frankel asserts, "Jewish nationality" is "something adopted from outside." Through the edict of 1812, Prussia recognized the Jews "as its sons." Hence the Prussian Jews now are connected with each other only through religion, like the Catholics or the Protestants. "Outside his religious relationships, the Jew wishes only to be a subject, and that his nationality be absorbed in that of the state."[55]

Frankel, however, soon had opportunity to become convinced that the "religious relationships" are also transformed into a problem of a very vascillating, undefined content. In 1845, even before the second rabbinic conference, there was formed in Berlin a new Jewish *Reformgesellschaft*. Alien strivings and external powers were called into life. We noticed previously that in the 1840s certain anti-religious moods were strengthened among the German intellectuals. At the beginning of 1845 a "German-Catholic Church" with the tendency of renouncing the Roman pope was formed. Among the Protestants were established *Lichtfreundliche Gemeinde* which proclaimed that they do not recognize certain Christian dogmas (the trinity, Christ's divine birth). Under their influence the Jewish *Reformgesellschaft* was formed. This society addressed a summons to their "brother Israelites in Germany," calling upon them to create a new Judaism "according to the spirit of the time" and according to the concepts of a purified faith. A short time later (the beginning of 1846) the *Gesellschaft* established a *Deutsch-Jüdische Kirche*, a German-Jewish Church, where the worshippers prayed with bared heads and, since very few members assembled on the Sabbath, services were held mainly on Sunday.

Samuel Holdheim was invited to become the preacher of this society. Hence, it is not surprising that, given such moods, at the second rabbinical conference which took place in July 1845 in Frankfurt-am-Main, the chief role was played by the radical Reformers. From their circle were chosen the president (L.

---

55. *Ibid.*, 359–360.

Stein) and the vice-president (Abraham Geiger). Frankel was soon forced to the conviction that he would be swamped by numbers and could have no influence on the decisions that the conference would reach. Rabbi Stein and others argued that all prayers in which there is any remnant of national unity or the ingathering of the exiles should be deleted from the order of worship. What sense, for instance, now has the prayer "Umi-Penei Hata'enu Galinu Me-Artzenu" ("Because of our sins we were driven out of our land")? On the contrary, we now consider the political destruction of the Jewish people by no means a disaster. We feel overjoyed that we presently live among educated peoples, and we ought to praise God for this.

Especially heated debates took place when the question of public prayer was treated, whether it is necessary to worship in Hebrew. Two questions had to be decided in this connection: (1) Is it a necessity, according to the law, to worship precisely in Hebrew, and (2) Should we worship in Hebrew for the sake of *strengthening the religion?* The majority of the assemblage responded negatively to both questions. The Hebrew language, Geiger declared, is merely a national bond, not a religious one; the religion does not require the support of Hebrew. Another member of the conference, Adler, issued forth even more sharply. The lovers of the Hebrew language, he says ironically, admonish us that if we do not pray in Hebrew, the holy language will generally be forgotten among Jews, as happened in the times of Philo of Alexandria. But what sort of misfortune is this?, Adler asks. Are the works of Philo, who did not understand the holy tongue, not much dearer to us than, for instance, the Talmudic tractate *Betzah?* It is argued that there are many important Hebrew liturgical hymns and poetic works of great value that are impossible to translate. A new generation will arise and will create beautiful new poetic works in the vernacular. The dead, unpolished Hebrew language has become our misfortune. It is this language that has distorted the religion. Thanks to it, superstition and barbaric follies have multiplied among Jews. The time is long overdue to remove it from our religion.[56]

As soon as the conference reached this decision regarding the Hebrew language, Zacharias Frankel immediately left the assemblage and in a public statement indicated the reasons that prompted him to the decision to take no further part in the conference. He received congratulations and letters of gratitude for this step from all sides.

56. See S. Bernfeld, *Toledot Ha-Reformatzyon Ha-Datit Be-Yisrael,* 193.

The Frankfurt conference and the Berlin *Reformgesellschaft* called forth a whole polemic literature in both languages—German and Hebrew. However, whereas during the first Reform battle, twenty-five years earlier, the best polemic works and brochures were written in the camp of the Reformers, the upper hand now was obtained by the anti-Reform group. A very successful polemic work entitled *Wohin und Woher?* was published (1845) by David Cassel. With a great deal of temperament and with genuine polemic talent, Phineḥas Menaḥem Heilprin issued forth against "Holdheim and his friends" in his *Teshuvot Be-Anshei Aven* (Frankfurt, 1845) which made no lesser impression than Bresselau's *Ḥerev Nokemet* in its day.[57]

Many epigrams, satires and pamphlets were also composed in Hebrew. The author of *Penei Tevel,* Moses Mendelssohn of Hamburg, wrote a parody on the well-known hymn of Solomon Alkabetz, "Lechah Dodi:" "Come, my beloved, to meet the bride; let us welcome Sunday."[58]

A certain A. Pold composed a satire in the traditional *kinah*-style which begins with these militant lines:

A gathering of queers, they are called—a conference of
    rabbis;
    And they are our wreckers and destroyers;
Sons of Jokshan, with raging arrogance, like smoke of the
    furnace
    Have they gone up in our fields.
A horde of spoilers, ravaging foxes, destroying vineyards;
    They have broken down our fences.[59]

In 1846 the third conference of Reform rabbis took place. The fourth was to have been held in 1848 in Mannheim, but the revolution broke out and the question of religious reform temporarily disappeared from the agenda. In *Der Orient,* where Hebrew pamphlets and epigrams against the Reformers had previously been printed, paeans to the revolution[60] and the abolition of censorship[61] and elegies on the tragic death of the revolutionary battler Hermann J. Jellinek[62] now appeared.

57. See our *History,* Vol. IX, pp. 261–62.
58. *Literaturblatt des Orients,* 1846, 538.
59. *Ibid.,* 145, 470.
60. *Der Orient,* 1849, 303.
61. *Ibid.,* 495.
62. *Ibid.,* 39.

CHAPTER NINE

Scholars and Belletrists

The "disclosers" of the beauties of Hebrew literature—Leopold
Dukes and Isaac Kämpf; Adolphe Franck and Salomon Munk—Michael Yehiel Sachs and the significance of his *Die Religiöse Poesie der
Juden in Spanien*—Heinrich Heine's attitude towards Shakespeare's
Shylock—Heine's *Hebräische Melodien*—Grace Aguilar and her novel
about the Marranos—Ludwig August Frankl and his romantic poems
—Hermann Mosenthal and his drama *Deborah*—Berthold Auerbach
and his Jewish historical novels—Leopold Kompert and his portraits
of the ghetto—Aaron Bernstein; the significance of his popular books
on the natural sciences and his narratives about the ghetto—The idyll
is transformed into a tragedy.

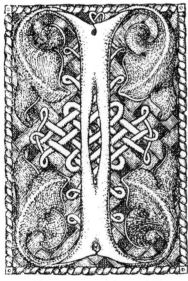N A previous volume[1] we noted
how the Meassefim endeavored
to "disclose the beauties of the
Hebrew language to all other
peoples." We already know that
precisely the "beauties" which
the Meassefim attempted to produce in the language of the Bible
were, with very few exceptions,
of quite limited value. The
founders of the Science of Judaism, led by Leopold Zunz, proceeded from the view that
demonstrating to European society that the Jewish people had "a
philosophy, a poetry, that make
it equal in value to other litera-
tures" would considerably shorten the way to the emancipation
so ardently desired.[2]

Actual life, however, significantly transcended these utilitar-
ian, apologetic tendencies. The national sentiments, not clearly

1. See our *History*, Vol. VIII, pp. 76ff.
2. Zunz, *Zur Geschichte und Literatur.*

formulated and not even entirely conscious, yet firmly rooted in the depths of the soul; the drive of indefatigable speculative thought; the attractive power of genuinely poetic treasures that were revealed—all these helped bring it about that an entire host of scholars endeavored, with enthusiastic love, to familiarize the European world with the authentic beauties hidden for generations in yellowed, dust-covered pages in the manuscript collections of European libraries and private persons.

One of the first of these was Leopold Dukes of Pressburg.[3] While still in his youth he wandered from one library to another, searching and rummaging about in the old manuscripts of the Sephardic poets. In 1837 his *Ehrensäulen und Denksteine zu einem künftigen Pantheon hebräischer Dichter und Dichtungen*, with many German translations of the medieval poets, appeared. Two years later, a special monograph, *Moses Ibn Ezra*, was published and in 1842 *Rabbinische Blumenlese*. In 1845 Saul Isaac Kämpf[4] published *Die Ersten Makamen aus dem Tachkemoni, oder Divan des Charisi.*[5]

In 1843 the French scholar Adolphe (Jacob) Franck made an impression with his treatise *La Kabbale ou philosophie religieuse des hébreux,*[6] written in brilliant style. Three years later the scholar Salomon Munk (born in 1803, died in Paris 1867), who later acquired renown with his classic edition of Maimonides' *Guide for the Perplexed*, which he provided with a rigorously scientific French translation, overwhelmed the learned world with his sudden discovery that the Arabic thinker Avicebron who, with his *Fons Vitae*, played such a significant role in the Christian philosophy of the Middle Ages, and the great Jewish poet Solomon Ibn Gabirol, are one and the same person.[7] The learned Abraham Geiger published, in special monographs, German translations of Jehudah Halevi's and Solomon Ibn Gabirol's numerous poems. The most important achievements in this realm, however, were the work of Michael Yeḥiel Sachs, the antipode and most decisive opponent of Samuel Holdheim.

Born in Glogau in 1808 into a religious family, Sachs obtained a comprehensive education. While he was studying general subjects in the local gymnasium, he obtained in his father's house thorough knowledge of the Hebrew language and its literature.

---

3. Born in 1810, died in Vienna in 1891.

4. Born in Lissa in 1818, died in Prague in 1892.

5. Kämpf published further translations of makamas by Alḥarizi in his *Nichtandalusische Poesie andalusischer Dichter aus dem XI, XII, und XIII Jahrhundert*, two volumes, 1858.

6. A year later Aaron Jellinek published Franck's work in German translation. A Hebrew translation was published in 1910.

7. See our *History*, Vol. I, p. 59.

Sachs devoted little time to Talmud alone, and only in his later years did he endeavor to expand his knowledge in this realm. Endowed with a fine aesthetic sensibility, he was enchanted from childhood on by the poetic beauties in the Biblical writings. He also attempted to compose Hebrew poems himself, and the writer David Zamosc published in his *Resisei Ha-Melitzah* a poem of the thirteen-year-old Sachs.

Sachs obtained his higher education at the University of Berlin where he studied the classical languages and their literature. Next to the Biblical prophets Isaiah and Jeremiah, his favorite authors were Plato and Sophocles. In 1836 he was invited to become preacher in the community of Prague. Sachs, however, was little attuned to the majority of modern rabbis and preachers who appeared in the 1830's in the German communities. To him the Reform tendencies and the love for battle manifested by his colleagues were quite alien. In his character and world-view, he was more like the heroic figures of the Spanish-Arabic period. Highly educated, permeated with the beauties of Greek culture, he was at the same time enthusiastically inspired by historical Judaism, by its extraordinary moral force, in which he perceived one of the most important and powerful factors in general human culture.

To be sure, Sachs knew that this moral beauty had been covered over with dust and mildew by the long generations of terror and homelessness. His fear, however, that incompetent hands would destroy, together with the rot that had accumulated, also such things as belonged to the ethical-cultural treasures, brought it about that he was one of the most convinced of orthodox Jews and led him into close affinity with Samson Raphael Hirsch.[8]

The pathos and enthusiasm with which Michael Sachs was filled to overflowing in regard to Judaism and its historical significance contributed not a little to the enormous success of his preaching. "The streaming flow of his eloquence," enthusiastically relates his younger contemporary, the historian Heinrich Graetz, "the depth of his soul, the ardor of his conviction, the grace of all his movements, the magic which his personality radiated, the beautiful resonance of his voice, the polished form of his speech—in short, every one of traits made him the unsurpassed pulpit orator of his time."[9]

Under the influence of the German poet Friedrich Rickert,

8. On Sachs' pious and orthodox behavior, see the memoirs of A.H. Weiss in *Luaḥ Aḥiasaf*, III.
9. Graetz, *Geschichte der Juden*, 524 (1900).

who acquired fame with his exemplary translations of the Oriental poets, Sachs set himself the task of familiarizing the German public with the unique beauties of Hebrew poetry. In 1885, his translation of the Psalms was published.[10] In it he endeavored to preserve the Oriental colorfulness and style of the original. This first attempt already demonstrated that the talented preacher of Prague[11] was also endowed with the spark of a genuine poet. Sachs later also participated in the new Bible translation which appeared under the editorship of Leopold Zunz, but he did not wish to be content with this. His goal was to demonstrate that even in the generations of exile and homelessness a profound moral consciousness had not been obscured in Judaism and it had produced cultural values of great importance at that time also. For many years Sachs labored on a work which was to familiarize the European public with medieval Hebrew religious poetry, wherein he saw the loveliest and clearest revelation of Jewish moral consciousness, of the firm and unshakeable faith in the goodness and graciousness of the Creator. This work appeared under the title *Die religiöse Poesie der Juden in Spanien* (1845). The author precedes the work with an historical overview of the development of Jewish culture and ethics from the time of the destruction of Jerusalem. He dwells especially on the course of evolution, and on the moral and poetic value, of the *Aggadah*, the primary source of religious poetry. With special affection he portrays the life-path and poetic creations of the great Sephardic poets, and in his translations of the best models of medieval Hebrew poetry he succeeds in preserving the unique rhythm and mood of the original.[12]

As a result of the profound poetic sensitivity and enthusiastic inspiration with which Sachs wrote his work he managed, to a considerable degree, to realize the ideal of the *Aufklärer* of the school of the Meassefim: "to disclose the beauties of the Hebrew language to other peoples." *Die religiöse Poesie der Juden* evoked general interest. The remarkable life of the brilliant Castilian Jehudah Abul al-Ḥasan al-Lawi (Jehudah Halevi), portrayed with such inspired love, made an enormous impression on the modern genius and poet, Heinrich Heine, and shortly afterwards the latter wrote his masterpiece, the marvelous poem "Jehuda ben Halevy."

10. Dedicated to the poet Friedrich Rickert.
11. In 1844 the community of Berlin invited Sachs to occupy the position of preacher.
12. Of Sachs' later works, the following deserve especially to be mentioned: (1) *Beiträge zur Shprach- und Altertumsforschung* (1852–54); (2) *Stimmen von Jordan und Euphrat* (1853)— poetic reworkings of legends and tales from the Talmud and Midrashim.

"The baptismal certificate is the ticket of admission to European culture"—this was one of Heine's aphorisms. He also admitted, as did many others of his generation, that he did not have the strength "to wear a beard and let himself be called "Juden-Moishel." On the other hand, however, because of the fact that, for the sake of the "admission ticket," he had to become an "apostate," Heine could not, throughout his life, forgive the German government or the Christian religion. With the most caustic sarcasm, Heine speaks in his well-known "Disputation" about the religious debates of the Middle Ages and declares in the name of the beautiful queen Donna Blanca that "the rabbi and the monk—both of them stink." The poet himself, however, speaks of the Christian religion in not much more friendly expressions than the disputant "Rabbi Judah of Navarre." "Christianity," Heine declares, "is the most false, the most irrational and absurd religion in the world. A religion of love which is itself nothing but hatred; a religion of freedom that is pure despotism; a religion of humanitarianism from which only the most cruel barbarism has been observed."[13] For the Jewish religion, however, Heine, the philosophically-educated free thinker and skeptical mocker, has the greatest respect. "I," Heine declares in January 1850, "make no secret of my Judaism, to which I have not returned because I never left it."[14]

Heine, however, was very far from Geiger's position of perceiving in Judaism nothing but "theology." He saw in Judaism not a religious community but a national collective of very great cultural scope—and this not only in the years when he wrote *Almansor* and *The Rabbi of Bacharach* but also in the later years when he declared himself to be a Hellene or Greek, and was in love with the Hellenistic world-view for its "restoration of the flesh." Very symptomatic in this respect is his attitude towards Shakespeare's portrait of Shylock.[15]

The *Aüfklarer* and scholars of the Science of Judaism exulted in Gotthold Ephraim Lessing's *Nathan the Wise*, but they were ashamed of Shakespeare's Shylock and took pains to be silent about it, considering it a false libel which the brilliant poet permitted himself under the pressure of the obscurantist and superstitious environment. Heine, however, had the courage to declare proudly that Shylock is, aside from Portia, the "most

13. Dr. Hugo Bieber, *Heinrich Heine, Gespräche*, etc., 1926, 179: *Le chirstianisme, la religion las plus fausse, la plus irrationelle, la plus absurde qui fût; une religion d'amour, qui ne connait que la haine, une religion de liberté qui ne connait que la despotisme, une religion d'humanité qui n'a jamais pratiqué que la plus cruelle barbarie.*
14. *Ibid.*, 297.
15. In his *Shakespeares Mädchen und Frauen* (written in 1838).

respectable character" in the whole play and that all the Christian patricians who move about him are not worth "tying Shylock's shoelaces." It is precisely Shylock's bloody thirst for revenge that impresses Heine, who stresses, "But there is something that he thereafter values higher than money, namely, satisfaction for his offended heart, retaliation for the unspeakable insults to himself."[16] And it is precisely to the people which brought up a Shylock that Europe, he declares, must "elevate itself." "I say elevate itself, for the Jews already at the beginning carried the modern principle which is only presently unfolding visibly among the European peoples." Heine concludes his sketch on *The Merchant of Venice* with the wonderful scene where the poet comes on the Day of Atonement to the synagogue of Venice to look for Shylock: "I did not see him, but at sunset when, according to Jewish tradition, the heavenly gates are closed and no further prayer is accepted, I heard a voice which was saturated with tears such as no human eyes have ever wept before . . . This was a sobbing which could move a stone to compassion. These were cries of woe which could come forth only from a breast in which all the sufferings which a whole people of martyrs had lived through in the course of eighteen centuries were locked up. It was a sobbing of a soul which sinks deathly tired before the heavenly gates . . . And this soul seemed to me familiar; it appeared to me that I had once before heard how it had cried out with such a feeling of despair: 'Jessica, my child!' "

In the magnificent poem mentioned earlier, "Jehuda ben Halevy" Heine portrays the great Castilian not only as "a poet by God's grace" who can "sin neither in verse nor in prose," because

> Pure and refined, without the slightest defect,
> Was his song, like his soul.
> When the Creator made
> This soul—satisfied with Himself,
> He kissed the newborn;
> And the loud echo of that kiss
> Lives in every song of the poet
> Anointed with God's grace.

Heine also stresses that Jehudah Halevi was a Jewish *national* poet:

16. Heine here also acutely notes the purely social foundations of the historical animosity toward the Jews which bears a religious vestment.

He was a great poet,
The light and star of his generation,
The lovely candelabrum of Jacob's house,
A wondrous pillar of fire,
Of song and poetry,
Who went before
The homeless people Israel,
In the darkness of exile.

The Jewish Reformers of the 1840s deemed it necessary to eliminate from the well-known prayer "Avinu Malkenu" the sentence: "Our Father, our King, take vengeance before our eyes for the blood of Thy servants that has been shed." The great poet of "Jehuda ben Halevy," however, identifies himself with the people suffering from exile which produced its mighty poem "By the rivers of Babylon we sat down and wept" with its stormy closing chords of bloodthirsty hatred and revenge. In powerful verses he portrays how "the dark woe," the feeling of vengeance for the millennial degradation and painful sufferings seethes and boils in his heart until finally "the lid springs off" and, like fiery lava, the Biblical phrases, filled to overflowing with venomous hatred, pour forth:

Blessed is the man whose hand
Seizes your young
And dashes them against the rock!

As everyone knows, a profound spiritual crisis came to pass in Heine, who spent the last eight years of his life lying on his painful "mattress grave." The sickly poet was transformed from an atheist into a Deist and, as early as the first year of his illness (1848), Heine, as he himself relates, carried on earnest conversations with God during whole nights of sleeplessness.[17] He no longer felt himself the "great lyricist number two," i.e., the greatest German lyricist after Goethe, but only a "poor, sick Jew." When the painful disease had so shrunk his body that he could be carried on a person's hands as easily as an eight-year-old child, he no longer felt himself a life-loving "Hellene" but an emaciated Jew. He now denied the basic motto of Hellenism and declares that "to be good is better than beauty." The Bible became his favorite book. To be sure, the classic beauties of the Bible already enchanted him in his youth and he praised them

17. Bieber, *op. cit.*, 265.

with high enthusiasm in his well-known letters from Helgoland. "Nevertheless," the disease-wracked poet declares in 1850, "I must write everything anew now that I better understand the poetry and the cultural-historical significance of the Bible, as well as its ethical and religious attitude."[18]

And Heine did, indeed, write "everything anew." World-renowned are the enthusiastic pages of his "Geständnisse" in which the poet pours out his enthusiasm for the Bible, for the people which created and preserved the "book of books," and for the greatest hero of Jewish history and tradition, the man who liberated the people from slavery and gave them the Torah—Moses. Not of a religious community does Heine speak, but of a great nation with enormous, universal cultural value.

Like Samuel David Luzzatto, Heine also speaks of Atticism and Judaism. "I see now," Heine writes, "the Greeks were only beautiful striplings, but the Jews were always men—mighty, unbowed men, not only formerly but to the present day, despite eighteen centuries of misery and persecution. I have since come to know and appreciate them better, and if all pride of birth were not a foolish contradiction, I could be proud of the fact that my ancestors belonged to the noble house of Israel, that I am a scion of those martyrs who gave the world a God, a morality, and fought and suffered on all the battlefields of thought." The history of the modern Jews, Heine keenly remarks, "is tragic, and if one writes about this tragedy he is mocked to boot—which is the most tragic thing of all." "Jewish history," he says further, "is beautiful, but the young Jews wrong the old, who should be placed far above the Greeks and Romans. I believe: If there were no more Jews, and it would become known that somewhere there is an exemplar of this people, they would travel hundreds of hours to see this exemplar and shake his hand. And now—they shun us."

In Heine's generation there were a great many who utilized the baptismal certificate as a "ticket of admission" not only to European culture but, indeed, chiefly to bourgeois European society, in order to "make a living." However, in some communities there still lived in considerable numbers Jewish families descended from the Sephardic Marranos who, out of fear of the Inquisition, concealed their Jewishness but secretly remained faithful to it, transmitted it as a heritage to their children, and finally left their fatherland in order openly and freely to declare their loyalty to the religion of their fathers. A scion

18. *Ibid.*, 344.

of such a family was the gentle, romantically-minded Grace Aguilar.[19] Quite early in her youth death spread its wings over her. Weak and sickly, she hastened to pour out as quickly as possible her sentiments, her love of the faith for which her fathers suffered so much, to transmit to her generation the profound feeling of reverence for the ethic and history of Judaism with which she was filled to overflowing. At the age of seven she began to write a diary. At twelve she composed a drama, and at nineteen published anonymously a collection of poems, *The Magic Wreath.*

Grace Aguilar wrote several ethical-religious works, *The Spirit of Judaism: In Defense of Her Faith and Its Professors* (1842), *The Jewish Faith* (1846), and others. She also composed historical works but acquired renown with her historical novel about the life of the Marranos in Spain and Portugal. This novel, *The Vale of Cedars* (1850), composed in soft, romantic colors, was translated three times into Hebrew, first by J.L. Gordon in *Ha-Melitz* (not completed), the second time with some additions by A.S. Friedberg under the title *Emek Ha-Arazim* (1875), and in the twentieth century (1923) by S.S. Kantorowitz. *Emek Ha-Arazim* was for a long time the favorite book of Jewish young people raised on Hebrew literature, and the author of these lines still remembers the impression which this novel about the Marranos used to make on its youthful readers.

But romantic tones were heard not only by the gentle, dreamy Grace Aguilar. We shall see further on how, under the conditions in Russia, romantically-minded Jewish poets who could not be satisfied by the gray, shameful life of their environment turned their glances to the ancient past which shimmered before their dreamy eyes in the most marvelous colors. A similar phenomenon, but under quite different conditions, was noticeable also among several writers in the German provinces. Typical in this respect is the poet Ludwig August (Abraham Elazar) Frankl.

Ludwig August Frankl was born[20] into a distinguished family in the small Bohemian town of Chrast. He was educated in the gymnasium at Prague and at the same time pursued Jewish studies with his relative, the later well-known rabbi and scholar Zacharias Frankel (see above, pp. 188–192). He obtained his higher education at the University of Vienna, where he studied medicine. While still a student he began to write German

19. Born in London in 1816, died at the age of thirty-one in Frankfurt-am-Main, 1847.
20. In 1810, died in Vienna in 1894.

poems. His first poems were patriotic—*Das Habsburger Lied* (1832) and othes that made a name for him in literary circles. After the March Revolution, Frankl composed the poem *Die Universität* which was disseminated in hundreds of thousands of copies and to which twenty-seven composers wrote music. For his epic-poem *Christoforo Colombo* he obtained the title "honorary citizen of the city of Genoa," and in 1851 the Austrian emperor raised him to the nobility as Ritter von Frankl-Hochwart.

This "honorary citizen of Genoa," knight of Austria, and founder and editor of the popular Austrian newspaper *Sonntagsblätter*, however, felt himself a Jewish poet. The legends and sagas of the Jewish past dominated his poetic imagination. In 1842 his romantic biblical poem *Rachel* appeared. In it are woven the old Talmudic legends wherein the mother of the two Hebrew tribes is portrayed as the symbol of mother-agony and mother-love. The poem in a short time went through ten editions and was translated into Hebrew three times.[21] His poem *Der Primator*,[22] about the history of Jewish suffering in the Middle Ages, also enjoyed great success. In a whole series of poems Frankl celebrates the heroes of Jewish history—Moses, King David, Johanan ben Zakkai, the Maharal of Prague. But his favorite poet was the singer of Zion, Jehudah Halevi. He celebrates the Spanish-Jewish poet in two rather long poems, lovingly quotes passages of Halevi's renowned ode to Zion, "Tziyyon Ha-Lo Tishali," and pours out in poetic verses his romantic love for the historic land "where the prophets rest and the flame of the altars rose to the heavens." National elegiac tones also resound in his poems "The Last High Priest," "The Ninth of Av" (about the expulsion from Spain), "The Emblems of the Jewish People," and others.

Also strongly dominated by romantic moods is Hermann (Salomon) Mosenthal's[23] German drama *Deborah* which was published in 1851 and had colossal success on the European stage. In the title-role was one of the most renowned and best-loved dramatic actresses of that time, A. Ristori. For its enormous success, however, the drama is indebted not to the poetic talent of its author but merely to its extraordinary theatrical effects. The drama takes place in a village in Styria (which belonged to the Austrian crown). The milieu, however, is so schematically portrayed that it is difficult to determine the time when the

21. By M. Stern, M. Letteris, and S. Bacher.
22. Translated by M. Letteris into Hebrew under the title *Nasi Be-Yisrael*.
23. Born in 1821, died in 1877.

events take place, whether in the Middle Ages or at the beginning of the nineteenth century. The heroine of the play, the beautiful Jewess Deborah, who is in love with the Christian Albert, walks as if on stilts and pours forth melodramatic speeches and monologues. Also portrayed without real vitality are the other Jewish characters, along with the teacher, the converted Jew. It is clear that the author, who was raised in an assimilated family, knew very little of the actual Jewish way of life.

The Christian way of life is also portrayed in purely melodramatic fashion. The civic representatives of the village, the pastor, his relative, the mayor and his son—all are ideal persons. Only the people, *der Pöbel*, is wildly fanatical and capable of destroying the innocent Deborah who is as full of virtues as a pomegranate is full of seeds. On the other hand, the author considers it necessary to underscore the tendencies which were especially popular in his day among the assimilated Jews. The young Reuben declares: "Our fatherland is not Jerusalem. The soil which is illuminated along with us by one and the same sun, the soil where the language we speak resounds, the soil where our cradles stood—this our fatherland. This beautiful land, this ground with which my whole existence is grown together—this is our genuine fatherland." And Albert enthusiastically tells about the audience he had with the emperor. One enters the monarch's presence as one enters a church. He has time and attentiveness for everyone. "I will remember all my life the moment I saw him."

The first among Jewish authors who attempted to rework historical themes in purely realistic tones was the later renowned novelist Berthold Auerbach.[24] Born into a pious religious family, Berthold (Mosheh Baruch) Auerbach in his youth studied the Talmud and prepared himself to become a rabbi. Talmudic dialectic, however, was not at all congenial to the future poet. He went to Tübingen and studied law at the university there. Because of the student unrest that broke out in Tübingen, Auerbach did not complete his studies and became a professional writer. His first works had very limited success. Under the effect of Sir Walter Scott's novels, Auerbach decided to write historical romances about Jewish life. "I undertook," he writes, "to provide genre-pictures of Jewish life in various lands and at various times, and on this banner to portray the development of individual characters and personalities."

24. Born in 1812, died in 1882.

Auerbach's first historical novel was *Spinoza, Ein Denkerleben* (1837) which went through more than thirty editions and was soon translated into virtually all the European languages.[25] Its great success, however, is to be explained more by the strong interest in the brilliant thinker of Amsterdam than by the artistic virtues of the novel itself. To be sure, the Sephardic community, the environment in which the great philosopher lived and grew up, is portrayed by Auerbach in broadly realistic features. On the other hand, the central figure of the work is not at all successful. The deep experiences of the thinker, his struggles and world-view, are very sketchily portrayed. The entire figure of Spinoza lacks blood and life.

More successful is Auerbach's second novel about Jewish life, *Dichter und Kaufmann* (1839). The central figure of the novel is the poet Ephraim Moses Kuh (born in Breslau in 1733, died in 1790). The child of a wealthy family (his uncle was the well-known court-jeweler Ephraim Kuh), he did not have to be concerned about earning a living. In his youth he was prepared for the rabbinate. However, the knowledge-hungry Ephraim was early infected with European science and occupied himself much with German literature. He became not a rabbi but a merchant. But business did not satisfy him either, and so he traveled much —through Germany, France, Holland. In Berlin he became acquainted with Mendelssohn, Lessing, and other prominent literati. Kuh himself began to write poems, and his sharp epigrams achieved great success in Mendelssohn's circle. A man of broad culture, of gently feeling poetic nature, but with a weak character, he sensed with special painfulness the rightless conditions and civic disabilities of the Jews. A constant wanderer, he could find rest nowhere. He lost his fortune and finally became mentally ill.

Around this central figure, Auerbach presents a rather extensive gallery of various persons and characters. The poet's father, Moses Daniel, a typical Jew of the old style, with his firm life-principle "This also is for the good;" the poet's rabbi, Ḥananel of Poland, a keen Talmudist and covert *maskil*; Mendelssohn's circle in Berlin; the representatives of the Jewish bourgeois circles already slightly veneered with culture; typical beggars and adventurers in whom the eighteenth century was so rich. The young Jewish females whom Auerbach brings forth in his novel are interesting. Typical is Kuh's sister-in-law Theodolina (Taubchen), a spiritual sister of Reb Chenech's daughter in Isaac

25. The novel was translated (with abridgements) into Hebrew by M. Shapiro in 1898.

Euchel's play[26] whose entire education consists in half-errone-
ous French phrases that she has caught. Especially successful is
Kuh's sister—the gentle, sentimental Feilchen, in love with
Lessing, a maiden who lives through the same drama as many
other young Jewish girls and women of that time with romantic
moods, for whom the sources of Jewish belief were closed and
who were, therefore, drawn to the pomp-filled Christian church
with yearning eyes and languishing hearts.[27]

Least successful in Auerbach is the central figure with his
morbid experiences and spiritual wrestlings.

It is interesting that in all of his later works, which made him
renowned—in his *Schwarzwälder Dorfsgeschichten* as well as in his
wide-ranging novels (*Auf der Hohe, Das Landhaus am Rhein,* and
others)—Auerbach portrayed the present, people of our age.
Only for his Jewish novels did he utilize themes of past life. The
first belletrist who portrayed contemporary Jewish life and
tried to familiarize the European world with the "Jewish
ghetto" of his day was Leopold Kompert.

Born in the Czech townlet of Münchengrätz[28] in 1822 into a
poor family, Kompert spent his youth in poverty and distress.
As a result of his great thirst for knowledge and his brilliant
capacities, he nevertheless managed to obtain a certain degree of
education, and at the age of sixteen set out on foot without any
resources whatever for Vienna. Despite grievous distress and
hunger (at first he spent his nights in a gypsy camp) he prepared
himself for the university examination and was accepted into
the philosophical division. The university professors soon became aware of the richly talented student with his many-sided
learning and when the court steward Count Andrasy requested
them to recommend a suitable tutor for his children, they referred to him the Jewish student Kompert. The beggar-student,
for the first time, had enough to eat. There, in the country, in
the alien environment of the nobility, memories of his childhood years awakened in him. The forms of his own environment, the figures of the Bohemian ghetto, hovered before his
eyes. He decided to familiarize the outside world with these, and
so his collection *Aus dem Ghetto,* published in 1848, came into
being. The success of the work was quite unanticipated, and the
poor Jewish student suddenly became a renowned writer. After
the first collection came Kompert's further anthologies, *Böhmis-*

26. See our *History,* Vol. VIII, pp. 140ff.
27. *Ibid.,* p. 122.
28. Died in Vienna in 1886.

che Juden (1851), *Neue Geschichten aus dem Ghetto* (two volumes, 1860), *Geschichten einer Gasse* (two volumes, 1865) and others.

Kompert was the first to disclose to the European world the Jewish ghetto with its unique inhabitants and extraordinary way of life. In this consists his historical importance. The ghetto pictures are portrayed in him with much love, in somewhat sentimental colors. As a journalist[29] and communal worker, Kompert propagandized a great deal for the recognition of mixed civil marriages by the government without the sanction of the religious leaders. This problem of love-romances between Christians and Jews plays a rather significant role in Kompert's work. The sympathetic female figure in Kompert carries through the match between Jonathan Falk and the Christian girl Christina which ends with a civil marriage ceremony. However, where a civil marriage ceremony cannot be conducted and the demand is made that the Jewish partner renounce his faith and go over to Christianity (the stories "Der Hausierer" and "Des Pächters Kinder"), the attachment to one's own environment overcomes ardent love and the match is dissolved.

The following point is also worth noting. The rationalist-minded Jewish *Aüfklarer* had a certain contempt for the folk-legends, regarding them as "superstition" and "prejudices." Kompert, however, lovingly collected "fairy tales from the ghetto," *Märchen aus dem Ghetto*—those imaginative legends which the masses of the people produced and were transmitted orally from generation to generation.

Leopold Kompert acquainted readers with the ghetto of the Jews in Bohemia. With the ghetto life of the Posen region, Kompert's contemporary, Aaron Bernstein, familiarized his readers.

Born in the townlet of Fordon in the Posen region, Aaron Bernstein was educated according to the old fashion. Until the twentieth year of his life he studied Talmudic literature exclusively and was renowned as a prodigy. His thirst for knowledge drew him to the broader world, above all, to the primary source of Haskalah—Berlin. In the Prussian capital he devoted himself with enormous energy to general sciences. The former *yeshivah* student manifested great interest in such various realms of knowledge as biblical criticism,[30] political economy, astronomy,

---

29. Kompert took part in many journals and was one of the founders of the popular liberal journal, *Neue Freie Presse*.

30. His first published work (in 1834) was a translation of the Song of Songs with a critical introduction.

and chemistry. His work *Das junge Deutschland,*[31] published in 1835, created a reputation for him in literary circles and he became a regular contributor to various journals.

Bernstein manifested especially intensive activity in the 1840's. A great sensation was evoked in 1843 by the publication of his pamphlet on political economy, *Zahlen Frappieren.* At the same time he also published a treatise on the rotation of the planets. Bernstein also participated in the Reform movement and belonged to its left wing. He was one of the major founders and theoreticians of the radical *Reformgenossenschaft* of which we spoke previously (see above, p. 191) and was the author of the well-known summons "Zu die israelitische Brüder in Deutschland."

After the revolution, when reaction became ever stronger in 1849, Bernstein stepped forward into a broader arena.

He became a political battler, established the democratic *Urwahlerzeitung* which became highly popular as a result of his publicistic talent. The journal was suppressed by the censorship and the militant publicist became familiar with Prussian jails. However, he did not surrender and soon established (in 1853) the daily *Volkszeitung* in which he published, besides his brilliant journalistic articles, his famous *Naturwissenschaftliche Volksbücher* which were translated into virtually all the European languages. These treatises on the natural sciences, written in clear, popular language, also played a certain cultural role in the Jewish quarter. As early as 1862 Shalom Jacob Abramowitch (the later Mendele Mocher Seforim) translated into Hebrew and published in *Ha-Tzefirah* the chemical part of Bernstein's work. It was translated in full by Ruderman and David Frischman under the title *Yediot Ha-Teva* (1881–1885) in twenty-one parts that enjoyed great success and went through several editions. Later (in 1908–1909) A. Frumkin and M. Shapiro issued Bernstein's *Volksbücher* in Yiddish also.

However, it was not only as an excellent popularizer of the natural sciences that Bernstein became well known in the Jewish quarter, but also as a talented portrayer of the Jewish ghetto, as the author of *Mendel Gibbor* and *Vögele Maggid.* At the same time that Bernstein established his *Volkszeitung* and wrote his *Volksbücher,* there appeared in Josef Wertheimer's *Jahrbuch für Israeliten* his two just-mentioned great stories. Here the militant battler appears before us in a quite unexpected role. This radical fighter for Reform, who so ardently endeavored to demonstrate

---

31. Published under the transparent pseudonym Rebenstein.

how necessary it is to reform the Jewish religion and adapt it to the new demands of life, becomes the inspired singer of the old, patriarchal way of life in his castaway little town in the region of Posen. He, the founder of the *Reformgenossenschaft* with its Reform Temple, where men worshipped with uncovered heads and Sunday displaced Saturday as the Sabbath, portrays in the tenderest colors, covered with moonlight, the idyll of the "holy Sabbath" when the "angels of rest" *(malachei ha-shalom)* descend upon Jewish homes and, when Noah Bral sits Friday evening with his beloved wife Taubele, two angels bend over their heads and smile at each other.

With love and yearning Bernstein portrays the old-fashioned characters among whom he spent his childhood years.[32] Genendel the wife of the *gabbai;* the blind Malkah with her grandson; the beautiful Henele; the rabbi; the two *yeshivah*-students; Chaim Mikwitzer with his two daughters; Meir Poier; Chatzkel Gibbor; his son Mendel Gibbor with his friend Zalme; and many others—all these are portrayed with a loving hand and good-humored smile. The author adopts an attitude of irony and sarcasm only toward Rabbi Abele with his "little saws" because of his quizzical mannerisms and arid over-subtlety. As a result of this love and gentleness, such scenes as the one in which the blind, proud Malkahle blesses her grandchild Henele and begs that she may belong to the maidens "with strong hearts" attains the level of poetic beauty. This is also the case when Henele shows that she is indeed worthy of her grandmother's blessing when she, who is descended from a great, prestigious family, openly proposes to the good-hearted, gentle Mendel Gibbor that he marry her, modestly employing in this connection the well-known Talmudic dictum: "Step down lower and take a wife for yourself."

Bernstein goes still further. We have already observed, and in subsequent chapters shall have occasion to speak more of this, how ardently the *maskilim* propagandized that the Jewish masses should cast off their insubstantial modes of earning a living and petty trade, and betake themselves rather to productive labor, to artisanry and agriculture. Bernstein, however, is totally opposed to these tendencies. Sarcastically he speaks about the "brilliant" ideas of the Prussian legislators, who permitted only invalids and aged men to occupy themselves with peddling in the villages. As soon as a policeman would "catch" a young Jew capable of work carrying a little pack of merchan-

32. The story of Mendel Gibbor took place in 1831.

dise in a village, he would immediately confiscate the merchandise and arrest the trader. Ironically the author notes:

There was, indeed, great danger in the fact that Jews used to bring on their shoulders into the village kerchiefs, cotton prints, ribbons, pins, corkscrews, little knives, buttons, suspenders, little combs, mirrors, clothes-brushes and other such things, and thereby take away from the peasants the opportunity to make the civilizing journey into town and there purchase these same objects from the urban masters ... According to the firm conviction of the sage legislators, it is, in fact, very lamentable and harmful that the peasants do not need to set aside their work and householderly respectability and drag themselves into town in order there to sell three or four pounds of pig's hair or the skin of a calf but rather sell all these things, without moving from their places, to the Jewish peddlers who deal in everything they produce in their economy—e.g., wax, honey, animal fat, feathers, wool, skin and the like.

"The merchants of the large cities," Bernstein declares with irony, "take this greatly amiss. They conclude that social conditions would be considerably improved if the peasant were forced to buy everything he needs and sell his products exclusively in their stores and workshops."

Bernstein gives us an interesting genre-portrait of how, when Sunday arrives, the Jewish townlet is emptied of its male population. Only old men, children who study in the elementary schools, and students in the *yeshivah* and study-house remain. Fathers of families set out into the "country," into the surrounding villages and peasant hamlets, and there the barter trade begins: the Jew sells cotton prints, colored stones, and all kinds of haberdashery articles that "make Vanya more beautiful in Christie's eyes and Christie obtains favor in Vanya's eyes." And the Jew obtains from the peasant either a skin or bristles or wax, honey, feathers, and the like. On Friday the Jews return from the villages and come to the wholesaler Noah Bral. The latter buys up everything that has come from the "country."

Relationships between the Jewish peddlers and the peasants are quite friendly in Bernstein's work. Sunday when the peasant woman goes to church, the Jew stays in her home rocking the baby. On the other side, the Jew leaves with the peasant woman, with the inscription *kasher*, the pot in which he cooked potatoes, so that when another Jew later comes along, he may calmly use the pot.

It is interesting to note the irony with which Bernstein speaks in this connection of the Jewish "grandees," the bankers, factory owners, and wholesale merchants, who yearn so ardently for emancipation—how they complain so strongly of the fact that Jews occupy themselves little with physical, productive work and the number of proletarians among them is so small. Hence, they preach that Jews should become stone masons and clay-diggers, so that their own wealthy children, who engage in noble professions, may be endowed with equal civic rights. Another characteristic point is worth noting. We have pointed out in Vol. VII of our *History* (p. 14) the contempt with which the German representatives of *die Wissenschaft des Judentums* regarded the "despised" jargon and its literature. Bernstein's fellow-battler for religious reform, Abraham Geiger, declares the language of the Jewish masses to be the most "miserable gibberish" and considers the Judeo-German literature a "model of tastelessness." "A German *Josippon*, a *Tze'enah U-Re'enah*, a *Tam Ve-Yashar*, and the like—truly poisoning the taste."[33] In this particular also the author of *Vögele Maggid* takes radical issue with his erstwhile fellow-battlers. He portrays in the clearest, most sympathetic colors the heroes of his narrative, the clever and voluble younger daughter of Ḥayyim Mikwitzer, Vögele surnamed Maggid. All of her intellectual baggage has been drawn by the wise Vögele from the same literature which is ridiculed so by the brilliant Abraham Geiger. She is always making references to the Yiddish *Menorat Ha-Ma'or, Ḥovot Ha-Levavot, Benot Yerushalayim, Simḥat Ha-Nefesh, Ḥochmat Nashim* and, more frequently than all others, the incomparable *Tze'enah U-Re'enah*. This "women's Torah" was so dear to Vögele that she calls it "my *Tze'enah U-Re'enah*."

The talented publicist and man of science who lived in one of the chief centers of European culture regarded the little town of his birth with longing eyes which were veiled with the imaginative dreams and romantic rose-wreath of long-gone childhood years. The narrow, gray ghetto alley is transformed into an idyll irradiated with trembling, silvery moon-beams on which the "angels of peace," the harbingers of peace and holy Sabbath rest, sway.

Now we shall move on to those who first strove to the sources of culture which the author of *Vögele Maggid* and *Mendel Gibbor* already commanded to an extensive degree. They strove for them and could not attain them, because the old-fashioned way of life which dominated the little town idealized by Bernstein cut down their wings, shut off for them, as with an iron wall,

33. *Nachgelassene Schriften*, II, 221.

the light of European culture and science. The social foundations on which the townlet of Mendel Gibbor and the *yeshivah* student Tzembelburgski[34] was based became rotten and despicable. The rich men and community leaders had long not been such loving, tender men as Bernstein's Noah Bral. This the poor masses felt at every step. The idyll become a tragedy. The "angels of peace" disappear, while the air is filled to overflowing with bitter struggle and venomous hatred.

Of this we shall speak in subsequent parts of our work.

34. In this figure the author portrays himself.

Addenda

To p. 12: Characteristic of Bendavid as a personality is the epitaph, composed by himself, which is inscribed on his tombstone: "My name was Eliezer Lazarus Bendavid. God was my help, granted me that for which I strove: independence. Praised be the name of God."

To p. 17: In May 1824, when the *"Cultur Verein"* was in its death-agony and the epidemic of conversion grew stronger, Heine's intimate friend Moses Moser wrote to Immanuel Wohlwill: "Of Judaism nothing has remained except the pain in some spirits. The mummy dissolves into dust at the touch of the free atmosphere, and the deep meaning of the hieroglyphic script it bears is now transformed into brand new album-maxims, just as if Moses our teacher had been born and raised on the Busta-Strasse (one of the streets of Hamburg) and modernized his style so finely that he is actually worthy of becoming a contributor to the *Leipziger Literaturzeitung.* No one is concerned about Judaism . . . One can learn more Judaism from a dead rabbi-figure in a zoological museum than from the living temple preachers. Judaism must come to an end as soon as the people begin to lose the consciousness of themselves as God's people" (we quote according to Franz Kolbers, *Juden und Judentum,* Vienna, 1935, p. 213).

To p. 105: Of the moods that prevailed in Jewish progressive circles in Galicia in the first days after the March Revolution of 1848, a picture is provided by the Yiddish summons *An Di Isra-elitishe Befelkerung Galitziens,* signed by one Isaac Judah ben Abraham, "a lover of Israel and also a friend of the nations," and reprinted in the *Historishe Shriftn Fun YIVO,* II, 633. This "lover of Israel" appears to be a quite moderate liberal, but is very fond of the "good king Ferdinand" and of the "golden governor" in

Lemberg. But he writes excellent popular Yiddish and understands how to render in plain, clear words the value of freedom of publication and the press, the significance of the constitution, etc.

To p. 108: The first person who utilized the freedom of the press in Galicia in the Jewish quarter was one of the "seers" (see above, p. 84) Abraham Mendel Mohr, who, on May 5, 1848, began to issue a weekly in Yiddish, *Lemberger Yidishe Tsaytung* (published until the end of 1849).

To p. 204: A Hebrew translation of Mosenthal's play was published by David Radner (Vilna, 1880).

BIBLIOGRAPHICAL NOTES

The Science of Judaism
and Galician Haskalah

CHAPTER ONE

CHAPTER ONE

THE SCIENCE OF JUDAISM; LEOPOLD ZUNZ AND HEINRICH HEINE

On Zunz, the pioneering figure in the modern form of Jewish scholarship known as *die Wissenschaft des Judentums*, and on this scholarship itself, see Alexander Altmann, "Zur Frühgeschichte der jüdischen Predigt in Deutschland: Leopold Zunz als Prediger," *Yearbook* of the Leo Baeck Institute, VI (1961), 3–59; Bernard Bamberger, "The Beginnings of Modern Jewish Scholarship," *Yearbook* of the Central Conference of American Rabbis, XLII (1932); Fritz Bamberger, "Zunz's Conception of History: A Study of the Philosophic Elements in Early Science of Judaism," *PAAJR*, XII (1941), 1–25; Hugo Bieber, "Leopold Zunz Un Der Farayn Far Kultur Un Visnshaft Fun Yidn," *YIVO-Bleter*, XXV (1945), 298–303; Samuel S. Cohon, "Zunz and Reform Judaism," *Hebrew Union College Annual*, XXXI (1960), 251–76; Ismar Elbogen, "Ein hundertjähriger Gedenktag unserer Wissenschaft," *MGWJ*, LXVI (1922), 89–97; idem, "Ein Jahrundert Wissenschaft des Judentums," *Festschrift zum 50-jährigen Bestehen der Hochschule für die Wissenschaft des Judentums* (1922); idem, "Leopold Zunz zum Gedächtnis," *Fünfzigster Bericht der Lehranstalt für die Wissenschaft des Judentums in Berlin* (1936), 14–32; Ludwig Geiger, "Zunz im Verkehr mit Behörden und Hochgestellten," *MGWJ*, LX (1916), 245–62, 321–47; idem, "Aus L. Zunz' Nachlass," *Zeits-*

chrift für die Geschichte der Juden in Deutschland, V (1891), 223–68; idem, "Zunz' Tätigkeit für die Reform (1817–1823) mit einem Anhang (1840)," *Liberales Judentum,* IX (1917), 113–20; N. N. Glatzer (ed.), *Leopold and Adelheid Zunz: An Account in Letters, 1815–1885* (1958); idem (ed.), *Leopold Zunz: Jude-Deutscher-Europäer* (1964); idem, "Leopold Zunz and the Revolution of 1848," *Yearbook* of the Leo Baeck Institute, V (1960), 122–39; G. Karpeles, "Leopold Zunz," in *Studies in Jewish History and Literature* (1895); D. Kaufmann, "Zunz, Leopold," in *Allgemeine Deutsche Biographie,* XLV (1900), 490–501; idem, "Die Familie Zunz," *MGWJ,* XXXVIII (1894), 481–93; Michael Meyer, *The Origins of the Modern Jew* (1968), 144–82; S. P. Rabinowitz, *Yom Tov Lipman Zunz: Hayyav, Zemano, U-Sefarav* (1896); D. Rosin, "Die Zunz'sche Bibel," *MGWJ,* XXXVIII (1894), 504–14; Solomon Schechter, "Leopold Zunz," in his *Studies in Judaism,* Third Series (1924), 84–142; idem, "The Beginnings of Jewish *Wissenschaft,*" in his *Seminary Addresses and Other Papers* (1915), 173–195; Luitpold Wallach, *Leopold Zunz und die Grundlegung der Wissenschaft des Judentums: Über den Begriff einer jüdischen Wissenschaft* (1938); idem, "Über Leopold Zunz also Historiker: Eine Skizze," *Zeitschrift für die Geschichte der Juden in Deutschland,* V (1934), 247–52; idem, "The Beginnings of the Science of Judaism in the Nineteenth Century," *Historia Judaica* (April, 1946); idem, *Liberty and Letters; The Thoughts of Leopold Zunz* (1959); Max Wiener, "The Ideology of the Founders of Jewish Scientific Research," *YIVO Annual of Social Science,* V (1950), 184–96; idem, *Jüdische Religion im Zeitalter der Emanzipation* (1933), 177–87.

On Ludwig Börne, see Heinrich Heine, *Über Ludwig Börne* (1840); Sol Liptzin, *Germany's Stepchildren* (1944), 27–44; L. Marcuse, *Revolutionär und Patriot: das Leben Ludwig Börnes* (1929); G. Ras, *Börne und Heine als politische Schriftsteller* (1927); and *Neue Deutsche Biographie,* II (1955), 404–06.

On the *Verein für Cultur und Wissenschaft des Judentums,* see J. Wolf, *Yearbook* of the Leo Baeck Institute, II (1957), 194–204; H. G. Reissner, *ibid.,* 179–93; idem, *Eduard Gans* (1965), passim; M. A. Meyer, *The Origins of the Modern Jew* (1968); and Siegfried Ucko, "Geistegeschichtliche Grundlagen der Wissenschaft des Judentums (Motive des Kulturvereins vom Jahre 1819)," *Zeitzchrift für die Geschichte der Juden in Deutschland,* V (1935), 1–34.

An English translation of Heinrich Heine's *Works,* ed. by C. G. Leland, was published in 1924.

For comprehensive bibliographies on Heine, see S. Shunami, *Bibliography of Jewish Bibliographies,* second edition (1969), Nos. 3661–67; S. Lachover, in *Yad La-Kore,* IV (1956–57), 143–95 (Hebrew bibliography of works by and on Heine from 1853 to 1956); and G. Wilhelm and E. Galley, *Heine Bibliographie*, 2 vols. (German, 1960). Vol. II of the last work includes a chapter, "Verhältnis zum Judentum."

The literature on Heine is enormous. Among the more important works are Hugo Bieber, *Heinrich Heine: A Biographical Anthology* (revised English edition by Moses Hadas, 1956); Max Brod, *Heinrich Heine* (English translation, 1962); Lewis Browne, *That Man Heine* (1927); E. M. Butler, *Heinrich Heine, A Biography* (1956); B. Fairley, *Heinrich Heine: An Interpretation* (1954); L. Feuchtwanger, *Heinrich Heines Rabbi von Bacharach* (1907); M. Fisch, *Heinrich Heine, der deutsche Jude* (1916); Martin Greenberg, "Heinrich Heine: Flight and Return," *Commentary* (March, 1949); H. H. Houben (ed.), *Gespräche mit Heine* (1926); Hans Kohn, *Heinrich Heine: The Man and the Myth* (Leo Baeck Memorial Lecture, 1959); C. C. Lehrmann, "Heinrich Heine, ein deutscher, französischer, oder jüdischer Dichter?" *Bulletin* of the Leo Baeck Institute, 43–44 (1968), 225–47; Sol Liptzin, *The English Legend of Heinrich Heine* (1954); Leo Lowenthal, "Heine's Religion," *Commentary*, (August, 1947); L. Marcuse, *Heinrich Heine in Selbstzeugnissen und Bilddokumenten* (1960); S. S. Prawer, *Heine, The Tragic Satirist* (1961); W. Rose, *Heinrich Heine: Two Studies of his Thought and Feeling* (1956); E. Simon, in *Essays Presented to Leo Baeck* . . . (1954), 127–57; Adolf Strodtmann, *H. Heines Leben und Werke*, 3rd ed., 2 vols. (1884); I. Tabak, *Heine and his Heritage: A Study of Judaic Lore in his Work* (1956); L. Untermeyer, *Heinrich Heine, Paradox and Poet*, 2 vols. (1937); and Antonia Valentin, *Poet in Exile: The Life of Heinrich Heine* (1934).

Most of the writings of Eduard Gans, who served as a professor at the University of Berlin for thirteen years after his conversion to Christianity in 1825, are in the field of comparative jurisprudence and history. His major works include *Scholien zum Gaius* (1821), *System des römischen Civilrechts im Grundrisse* (1827), *Über die Grundlehre des Besitzes* (1839), *Beiträge zur Revision der preussischen Gesetzgebung* (1830–32), *Das Erbrecht in weltgeschichtlicher Entwicklung* (4 volumes, 1824–35), and *Vorlesungen über die Geschichte der letzten fünfziger Jahre* (1833–34).

On Eduard Gans, see H. G. Reissner, *Eduard Gans: ein Leben in Vormärz* (1965); idem, "Rebellious Dilemma: The Case Histories of Eduard Gans and Some of his Partisans," *Yearbook* of the Leo Baeck Institute, II (1957), 179–86, IV (1959), 92–110; and M. Wiener, in *YIVO Annual*, V (1950), 190–93.

On Lazarus Bendavid, see Ludwig Geiger, "Aus Eduard Gans' Frühzeit (1817)," *Zeitschrift für die Geschichte der Juden in*

Deutschland (1891), 91–99; Jakob Guttmann, "Lazarus Bendavid: Seine Stellung zum Judentum und seine literarische Wirksamkeit," *MGWJ*, LXI (1917), 26–50, 176–211; and A. Görland and E. Cassirer, *Hermann Cohens Schriften zur Philosophie und Zeitgeschichte*, II (1928), 117 ff.

Isaac Marcus Josts's monumental *Geschichte der Israelitem* was published in ten volumes in Berlin (1820–47). For autobiographical information about his youth, see "Vor einem halben Jahrhundert: Skizzen aus meiner frühesten Jugend," in J. Pascheles, *Sippurim*, III (1854), 141–66.

On Jost, see J. Auerbach, "Dr. I. M. Jost: Eine biographische Skizze," *Volkskalender und Jahrbuch für Israeliten* (1861), 129–64; S. W. Baron, "I. M. Jost, The Historian," *PAAJR*, I (1928–30), 7–32; idem, *History and Jewish Historians* (1964), 240 ff; N. N. Glatzer (ed.), *Leopold and Adelheid Zunz; An Account in Letters, 1815–1885* (1958), Index; G. Herlitz, "Three Jewish Historians: Isaac Marcus Jost, Heinrich Graetz, Eugen Täubler," *Yearbook* of the Leo Baeck Institute, IX (1964), 69–90; R. Michael, in *Bulletin* of the Leo Baeck Institute, III (1960), 239–58; and H. Zirndorf, *Isaac Markus Jost und seine Freunde* (1886).

CHAPTER TWO

BIKKUREI HA-ITTIM; JEHUDAH MIESIS' *KINAT HA-EMET*

On *Bikkurei Ha-Ittim*, the literary-scholarly annual published in Vienna for twelve years (1821–32), see J. Klausner, *Historyah Shel Ha-Safrut Ha-Ivrit Ha-Hadashah*, 2nd ed., II (1952), 30–37; B. Wachstein, *Die hebräische Publizistik in Wien* (1930), XIII–XL (introduction), R. Fahn, *Pirkei Haskalah* (1937), 100–41; and B. Katz, *Rabbanut, Hasidut, Haskalah*, II (1959), 204–207.

On Shalom ben Jacob Cohen see J. Klausner, *Historyah Shel Ha-Safrut Ha-Ivrit Ha-Hadashah*, 2nd ed., I (1952), 275–90; J. L. Landau, *Short Lectures on Modern Hebrew Literature* (1939), 121–34; R. Mahler, *Divrei Yemei Yisrael . . .* , I, Part 2 (1954), 275–9; and B. Wachstein, *Die hebräische Publizistik in Wien* (1930).

On Jehudah Loeb Jeiteles and the Jeiteles family in general, see R. Fahn, *Pirkei Haskalah* (1937), 134–41; S. Hock, *Mishpehot Prag* (1892), 165–9; S. Katznelson, *Die unsterbliche Geliebte* (1954), Index; R. Kestenberg-Gladstein, *Neuere Geschichte der Juden in den böhmischen Ländern* (1969), Index (also contains bibliography); G. Kisch, in *Historia Judaica*, VIII (1946), 149–80, passim; and F. Lachover, *Toledot Ha-Safrut Ha-Ivrit Ha-Hadashah*, I (1928), 117–18.

On Jehudah Leib Miesis, see R. Mahler, *Ha-Ḥasidut Veha-Haskalah* (1961); J. Klausner, *Historyah Shel Ha-Safrut Ha-Ivrit Ha-Ḥadashah*, 2nd ed., II (1952), 267–82; and G. Kressel, *Leksikon Ha-Safrut Ha-Ivrit Ba-Dorot Ha-Aḥaronim*, II (1967), 343f.

CHAPTER THREE

NAḤMAN KROCHMAL AND SOLOMON RAPOPORT

Kitvei Naḥman Krochmal, critically edited by Simon Rawido-wicz, appeared in Berlin in 1924, with a long introduction by the editor. A second edition of this work was published in London and Waltham, Massachusetts in 1961.

On Krochmal, see J. Guttmann, "Yesodot Ha-Maḥashavah Shel Rabbi Nahman Krochmal," *Keneset*, VI (1941), 259–86; idem, *Philosophies of Judaism* (1964), 321–44; J. Klausner, *Historyah . . .* II (1952), 148–214; F. Lachover, in *Sefer Bialik* (1934), 74–98; idem, "Nigleh Ve-Nistar Bi-Mishnato Shel RaNaK," *Keneset*, VI (1941), 296–344; J. L. Landau, *Nahman Krochmal, ein Hegelianer* (1904), N. Rotenstreich "Tefisato Ha-Historit Shel RaNaK, *Zion,* VII (1942), 29–47; idem, *Jewish Philosophy in Modern Times* (1968), 136–48; Solomon Schechter, "Nachman Krochmal and the 'Perplexities of the Time,' " in his *Studies in Judaism*, First Series (1896), 46–72; and S. Spiegel, *Hebrew Reborn* (1930).

The pioneering biographical articles written by Solomon Jehudah Rapoport, originally published in *Bikkurei Ha-Ittim* (1828–31), were also separately published after his death under the title *Yeriot Shelomoh* (1904; reprinted 1913 and 1960). His *Erech Millin*, a Talmudic encyclopedia dealing chiefly with historical and archaeological matters relating to the Talmud, is a work of major importance. The first volume was published in 1852, the rest in 1914. Rapoport also wrote an introduction to Abraham bar Ḥiyya's philosophical treatise *Hegyon Ha-Nefesh* (edited by Freimann, 1860; reprinted, 1967). Rapoport's correspondence was published in *Iggerot Shir*, edited by S. E. Graeber (1885).

On Rapoport, see S. W. Baron, "The Revolution of 1848 and Jewish Scholarship, Part Two: Austria," *PAAJR*, XX (1951), 1–100; Isaac Barzilay, *Shelomo Yehudah Rapoport (Shir) and his Contemporaries* (1969); S. Bernfeld, *Toledot Shir* (1897); D. Kaufmann, *Gesammelte Schriften*, herausgegeben von M. Brann, I (1908); A. Kurländer, *Biographie S. J. Rapoports . . .* , 3rd ed. (1878); and J. Klausner, *Historyah . . .* , II (1952), 215–266.

On Jacob Samuel Bick, see G. Bader, *Medinah Ve-Ḥachamehah* (1934), 36–37; D. Sadan, in *Mazkeret Levi* (1944), 99–108; M. Weissberg, "Die neuhebräischen Aufklärungsliteratur in Galizien," *MGWJ*, LXXII (1928), 184–201; S. Werses, "Yaakov Shmuel Bick, Der Blondzshendiker Maskil," *YIVO-Bleter*, VIII (1938), 505–36; and N. M. Gelber, *Toledot Yehudei Brodi* (1955), 181–83, 189–94.

CHAPTER FOUR

KROCHMAL'S *MOREH NEVUCHEI HA-ZEMAN*

On Krochmal's *Moreh Nevuchei Ha-Zeman* and his philosophy of history, see the bibliography under Chapter Three. See also the following: A. I. Katsh, "Nachman Krochmal and the German Idealists," *Jewish Social Studies* (April, 1946); S. Rawidowicz, "Nachman Krochmal als Historiker," in *Dubnow Festschrift* (1930); idem, "War Nachman Krochmal ein Hegelianer?", *Hebrew Union College Annual*, V (1928); N. Rotenstreich, "Muḥlat Ve-Hitraḥashut Bi-Mishnato Shel RaNaK," *Keneset*, VI (1941), 333–44; I. Schorsch, "The Philosophy of History of Nachman Krochmal," *Judaism*, X (1961), 237–45; and J. Taubes, "Nachman Krochmal and Modern Historicism," *Judaism*, XII (1963), 150–64.

On Samuel Leib Goldenberg, the editor of *Kerem Ḥemed*, see J. Klausner, *Historyah . . .* , II (1952), 37f.

Professor Gershom Scholem maintains that Eliakim Ha-Milzahgi's unpublished manuscript on the Zohar, *Zohorei Ravyah* (at the Hebrew National and University Library in Jerusalem) is the most important book written on the *Zohar* during all of the nineteenth century. Also unpublished is his commentary on the "Book of Raziel," located in the library of Jews College, London (Ms. 347). Ha-Milzahgi's bibliography is given in G. Kressel, "Kitvei Eliakim Ha-Milzahgi," *Kiryat Sefer*, XVII (1940), 87–94.

On Ha-Milzahgi, see F. Lachover, "Nigleh Ve-Nistar Bi-Mishnato Shel RaNaK," Keneset, VI (1941), 296–344; S. D. Luzzato, *Iggerot Shadal*, ed, by E. S. Graeber, Part Four, (1882), 602–5; and G. Scholem and I. Joel (eds.), *Kitvei Yad Be-Kabbalah* (1930), 40, No. 13.

CHAPTER FIVE

JOSEPH PERL, ISAAC ERTER, AND ABRAHAM KOHN

Yoysef Perls Yidishe Ksovim was published in Vilna in 1937. Perl's *Megalleh Temirin* in Hebrew was first published, under the pseudonym Obadiah ben Petaḥiah, in Vienna in 1819 (second edition, Lemberg, 1864).

On Joseph Perl, see I. Davidson, *Parody in Hebrew Literature* (1907), 61–74; Ph. Friedman, "Yoysef Perl Vi A Bildungs-Tu'er Un Zayn Shul in Tarnopol," *YIVO-Bleter*, XXXI–XXXII (1948), 131–190; Z. Kalmanowicz, "Yoysef Perls Yidishe Ksovim, Literarisher Un Shprakhiker Analiz," in *Yoysef Perls Yidishe Ksovim* (1937), LXXI–CII; S. Katz, "Naye Materialn Fun Dem Perl Arkhiv," *YIVO-Bleter*, XIII (1938); J. Klausner, *Historyah* . . . II (1952), 283–320; B. Kurzweil, *Be-Ma'avak Al Erchei Ha-Yahadut* (1969), 55–95; R. Mahler, *Ha-Ḥasidut Veha-Haskalah* (1961), 155–208; Ch. Shmeruk, in *Zion*, XXI (1957), 94–99; I. Weinles, "Yoysef Perl, Zayn Lebn Un Shafn," in *Yoysef Perls Yidishe Ksovim* (1937), VII–LXX; S. Werses and Ch. Shmeruk (eds.), *Yosef Perl, Ma'asiyyot Ve-Iggerot* (1969), 11–86, with English summary; S. Werses, in *Tarbiz*, XXXII (1962–63), 396–401; and idem, in *Ha-Sifrut*, I (1968–69), 207–27.

Aryeh Leib Kinderfreund's collection of peoms *Shirim Shonim* was published in 1834 in Lemberg. On Kinderfreund, see G. Kressel, *Leksikon Ha-Safrut Ha-Ivrit Ba-Dorot Ha-Aḥaronim*, II (1967), 754.

A new edition of Isaac Erter's *Ha-Tzofeh Le-Veit Yisrael* was published in Tel Aviv in 1944.

On Erter, see S. Bernfeld, *Sefer Ha-Shanah*, II (1935), 134–42; J. Chotzner, "Isaac Erter, A Modern Hebrew Humorist," *JQR*, III (1891); idem, *Hebrew Humor and Other Essays* (1905), 127–39; J. Klausner, *Historyah* . . . , II (1952), 321–49; and M. Weissberg, "Die neuhebräischen Aufklärungsliteratur in Galizien," *MGWJ*, LXII (1928), 184–201.

On Abraham Kohn, see S. W. Baron, "The Revolution of 1848 and Jewish Scholarship, Part Two: Austria," *PAAJR*, XX (1951), 1–100; N. M. Gelber, *Entziklopedyah Shel Galuyyot*, IV (*Sefer Lwow*, 1956), 231, 235 ff.; J. Kohn, *Leben und Wirken Abraham Kohns* (1863); G. Kohn, *Abraham Kohn im Lichte der Geshichtsforschung* (1898); and J. L. Tenenbaum, *Galitzye Mayn Alte Heym* (1952).

A bibliography of the writings of Joshua Heschel Schorr, compiled by E. Spicehandler, is to be found in *Studies in Bibliography and Booklore*, II (1955–56), 20–36.

On Schorr, see Spicehandler, "Joshua Heschel Schorr: *Maskil and East European Reformist*," *Hebrew Union College Annual*, XXXI (1960); J. Klausner, *Historyah* . . . , IV (1952), 58–77; J. Margoshes, *Erinerungen Fun Mayn Lebn* (1936), 54–61; and N. M. Gelber, *Toledot Yehudei Brodi* (1955), 213–218.

CHAPTER SIX

SAMUEL DAVID LUZZATTO AND HIS GENERATION

In 1809 Samson Bloch published a new edition of *Iggeret Ha-Rashba* (the epistle of Rabbi Solomon ben Abraham Adret against the study of philosophy), together with Jedaiah Ha-Penini's *Iggeret Ha-Hitnatzlut* (letter of defense on behalf of philosophy). He also published in 1814 a Hebrew translation (from the German) of Menasseh ben Israel's *Vindiciae Judaeorum* under the title *Teshu'at Yisrael* with an introduction, as well as a biography of the author by David Franco-Mendes.

On Bloch, see J. Klausner, *Historyah . . .* , II (1952), 350–68.

On Meir Halevi Letteris, see J. Klausner, *Historyah . . .* , II (1952), 369–400; G. Kressel, *Leksikon Ha-Safrut Ha-Ivrit Ba-Dorot Ha-Aharonim*, II (1967), 247–49; F. Lachover, *Toledot Ha-Safrut Ha-Ivrit Ha-Hadashah*, 1953 ed., II, 7–11; M. Weissberg, "Die neuhebräischen Aufklärungsliteratur in Galizien," *MGWJ*, LXXII (1928), 184–201; and S. W. Baron, "The Revolution of 1848 and Jewish Scholarship, Part Two: Austria," *PAAJR*, XX (1951), 1–100.

For a discussion of the Italian Haskalah, see I. E. Barzilay, "The Italian and Berlin Haskalah (Parallels and Differences)," *PAAJR*, XXIX (1960–61), 17–54.

On Isaac Samuel Reggio, see A. Milano, *Storia degli Ebrei in Italia* (1963), Index; J. Klausner, *Historyah . . .* , IV (1952), 10–37; H. S. Morais, *Eminent Israelites of the Nineteenth Century* (1880), 296 ff., I. H. Weiss, *Zichronotai* (1895), 153 ff.; and W. Zeitlin, *Bibliotheca Hebraica Post-Mendelssohniana* (1891–95), 296 ff.

The first book by the Protestant theologian Franz Delitzsch, *Zur Geschichte der jüdischen Poesie vom Abschluss der Heiligen Schriften des Alten Bundes bis auf die neueste Zeit* (1836), was the first significant critical-historical study of the history of Hebrew poetry. Delitzsch also aided Seligmann Baer in his edition of the Hebrew Bible, based on the Masoretic text, and edited Moses Hayyim Luzzatto's *Migdal Oz* (1857) and the Karaite Aaron ben Elijah's *Etz Hayyim* (1841), the latter with the assistance of Moritz Steinschneider. Among his other works of Jewish interest are *Jüdisches Handwerkerleben zur Zeit Jesu* (1868, second edition, 1879); *Jüdisch-arabische Poesie aus vor-mohammedanscher Zeit* (1874); *Die biblisch-prophetische Theologie* (1845); *System der biblischen Psychologie* (1855, second edition, 1861); and *Jesus und Hillel* (1866, second edition, 1875). One of his missionary writings, written in his later life when he was active in proselytizing for Christianity among

Jews, *Ernste Fragen an die Gebildeten jüdischer Religion* (1888) also appeared in Hebrew under the title *Ha'amek She'elah* (second edition, 1912).

On Delitzch, see E. Delitzsch, *Franz Delitzsch als Freund Israels* (1910); D. Kaufmann, "Franz Delitzsch," *JQR*, II (1890), 386 ff.; idem, *Gesammelte Schriften*, I (1908), 290; A. Kohler, *Realencyclopedie für protestantische Theologie und Kirche*, IV (1898), 565; P. P. Levertoff, *Delitzch-Bibliographie* (1913); and A. M. Stengel, *Divrei Emet Ve-Ahavah . . . Le-Yom Hulledet . . . Professor Franz Delitzsch* (1884).

Samuel David Luzzatto's voluminous correspondence, *Iggerot Shadal,* was edited by E. Graber, 9 vols., Przemysl and Cracow, 1882–91.

On Luzzatto, see *Samuel David Luzzatto 1800–1865. Exhibition on the Occasion of the 100th Anniversary of his Death,* arranged by B. Yaron, Catalogue (Hebrew and English), Jerusalem (1966); *Rassegna Mensile di Israel*, XXXII (1966), Nos. 9–10 (all articles deal with Luzzatto); S. Baron, in *Sefer Assaf* (1953), 40–63; S. Bernfeld, "Samuel David Luzzatto, ein Lebensbild," in *S. D. Luzzatto, ein Gedenkbuch zum hundertsten Geburtstage,* (1900); J. Klausner, *Historyah . . . ,* II (1952), 47–127; S. Morais, *Italian Hebrew Literature* (1926), 78–152; N. Rosenbloom, *Luzzatto's Ethico-Psychological Interpretation of Judaism* (1965); N. Rotenstreich, *Jewish Philosophy in Modern Times* (1968), 30–42; S. Rostovsky-Halprin, *Shadal Ve-Hitnagduto Le-RaMbaM* (1954); D. Rudavsky, "S. D. Luzzatto's Jewish Nationalism," *Herzl Yearbook*, VI (1964–65); idem, in *Tradition*, VII, No. 3 (1965), 21–44; S. Spiegel, *Hebrew Reborn* (1930); L. D. Stitskin, "Samuel David Luzzatto—Ethics and Feelings" (contains selections from *Yesodei Ha-Torah*), *Tradition*, VII, No. 2 (1965); and S. Werses, in *Me'assef Le-Divrei Bikkorei Ve-Hagut,* V–VI (1965), 703–15.

CHAPTER SEVEN

LIBERATION MOVEMENTS; RIESSER, MARX, AND PHILIPPSON

On Gabriel Riesser, see B. Auerbach, in *Gallerie der ausgezeichneten Israeliten aller Jahrhunderte*, IV (1836), 5–42; S. Bernfeld, *Gavriel Riesser* (Hebrew, 1914); G. Deutsch, "Gabriel Riesser," *Yearbook* of the Central Conference of American Rabbis, XVI (1906), 297–303; N. Frankfurter, *Denkrede auf Gabriel Riesser* (1863); F. Friedländer, *Das Leben Gabriel Riessers, Ein Beitrag zur inneren Geschichte Deutschlands im 19. Jahrhundert* (1926); M. Rinott, in *Year-*

book of the Leo Baeck Institute, VII (1962), 11–38; J. Seifensieder, *Gabriel Riesser* (1920); and M. Silberstein, *Gabriel Riessers Leben und Wirken* (1911).

Bruno Bauer's *Zur Judenfrage* was published in 1842. On Bauer and the controversy he provoked, see N. Rotenstreich, "For and Against Emancipation: The Bruno Bauer Controversy," *Yearbook* of the Leo Baeck Institute, IV (1959), 3–36; Tzevi Rosen, *Olamo Ha-Ruḥani Shel Karl Marx* (1974); and idem, in *Zion*, XXXIII (1968), 59–76.

The literature on Karl Marx is vast. A few of the more important works are: S. Avineri, *Mishnato Ha-Ḥevratit Veha-Medinit Shel Karl Marx* (1967); I. Berlin, *Karl Marx: His Life and Environment* (1963), includes bibliography; J. M. Cuddihy, *The Ordeal of Civility: Freud, Marx, Lévi-Strauss, and the Jewish Struggle with Modernity* (1974); J. Fink, *Die Judenfrage bei Marx und bei uns* (1964); H. Gemkow, *Karl Marx: Eine Biographie* (1968); K. Korsch, *Karl Marx* (English, 1963), includes bibliography; J. Lachs, *Marxist Philosophy: A Bibliographical Guide* (1967); H. Lefeberre, *Marx, son vie, son oeuvre, avec un exposé de sa philosophie* (1964); J. Lewis, *The Life and Teaching of Karl Marx* (1965); A. Massiczek, *Der menschliche Mensch: Karl Marx' jüdischer Humanismus* (1968); R. Mizrahi, *Marx et la question juive* (1972); R. Payne, *Marx: A Biography* (1968), includes bibliography; N. Rotenstreich, *Yesodot Ha-Pilosofiyah Shel Marx* (1964); L. Schwarzschild, *The Red Prussian: The Life and Legend of Karl Marx* (1948); E. Silberner, *Ha-Sotzyalizm Ha-Ma'aravi U-She'elat Ha-Yehudim*, Part Two (1955), 133–64, 448–51, includes bibliography; and idem, in *Historia Judaica*, IX, No. 1 (1949), 3–52.

On Ludwig Philippson, see J. Bass, "Ludwig Philippson," *MGWJ*, LVI (1912), 1–32, 218–49; G. Kayserling, *Ludwig Philippson* (1898); J. S. Kornfeld, "Ludwig Philippson," *Yearbook* of the Central Conference of American Rabbis," XXI (1911), 141–190; E. G. Lowenthal, in *Bulletin* of the Leo Baeck Institute, VIII, (1965), 89–106; J. Philippson, in *Yearbook* of the Leo Baeck Institute, VII (1962), 95–118; and J. Rosenthal, in S. Federbush (ed.), *Ḥochmat Yisrael Be-Ma'arav Eyropah*, I (1958), 399–408.

CHAPTER EIGHT

HIRSCH, GEIGER, HOLDHEIM, AND FRANKEL

Samson Raphael Hirsch's *Gesammelte Schriften*, edited by N. Hirsch, were published in six volumes in Frankfurt-am-Main (1902–12).

Among Hirsch's works that have appeared in English translation are: *The Nineteen Letters of Ben Uziel*, translated, with a preface and biographical sketch of the author, by B. Drachman (1899, revised 1960); *Horeb—Essays on Israel's Duties in the Diaspora*, 2 vols., edited and translated by I. Grunfeld (1962); *Fundamentals of Judaism: Selections from the Works of Samson Raphael Hirsch*, edited and translated by Jacob Breuer (1949); and *Judaism Eternal: Selected Essays from the Writings of Rabbi Samson Raphael Hirsch*, 2 vols., edited and translated by I. Grunfeld (1960–66).

On Hirsch, see I. Grunfeld, *Three Generations: The Influence of Samson Raphael Hirsch on Jewish Life and Thought* (1958), includes comprehensive bibliography; idem, in S. R. Hirsch, *Horeb—Essays on Israel's Duties in the Diaspora* (1962), XVIII–CLXII; I. Heinemann, *Ta'amei Ha-Mitzvot Be-Safrut Yisrael*, II (1956), 91–161; idem in *Sinai*, XXIV (1949), 259–71; idem, in *Zion*, XVI (1951), 44–90; M. Heller, "S. R. Hirsch," *Yearbook* of the Central Conference of American Rabbis, XVIII (1908), 179–216; E. W. Jelenko, "Samson Raphael Hirsch" in S. Noveck, ed., *Great Jewish Personalities in Modern Times* (1960); N. H. Rosenbloom: *Tradition in an Age of Reform: The Religious Philosophy of Samson Raphael Hirsch* (1976); J. Rosenheim, *Samson Raphael Hirsch's Cultural Ideal and Our Times* (1951); N. Rotenstreich, *Ha-Maḥashavah Ha-Yehudit Ba-Et Ha-Ḥadashah*, I (1945), Index; and S. Schwarzschild, "Samson Raphael Hirsch—The Man and His Thought," *Conservative Judaism*, XIII (1959).

A complete bibliography of the published writings of Abraham Geiger is to be found in Ludwig Geiger, ed., *Abraham Geiger: Leben und Lebenswerk* (1910), which also includes a biography of the great nineteenth century German protagonist of Reform Judaism, as well as evaluations of his work.

Selections from Geiger's writings in English translation, and a biographical introduction, are contained in Max Wiener, ed., *Abraham Geiger and Liberal Judaism: The Challenge of the Nineteenth Century*, translated by E. J. Schlochauer (1962).

Several papers, presented at a colloquium marking the hundreth anniversary of Geiger's death in 1974 and held at the Hebrew Union College-Jewish Institute of Religion in Cincinnati, are included in Jakob J. Petuchowski, ed., *New Perspectives on Abraham Geiger* (1975). This small volume also contains a full and comprehensive bibliography, compiled by Michael A. Meyer, of writings dealing with Geiger.

For literature on the Reform rabbinic conferences of the 1840s in Germany and on the early history of the Reform movement in general, see the bibliography for Chapter Nine of Vol. IX of this *History*.

Among the published writings of Samuel Holdheim, the most radical of the nineteenth century German champions of Reform, are *Über die Autonomie der Rabbinen und das Prinzip der jüdischen Ehe* (1843), *Über die Beschneidung zunächst in religiös-dogmatischer Beziehung* (1844), *Das Ceremonialgesetz im Messiasreich* (1845), and *Ma'amar Ha-Ishut Al Techunat Ha-Rabbanim Veha-Kara'im* (1861).

On Holdheim, see S. Bernfeld, *Toledot Ha-Reformatzyon Ha-Datit Be-Yisrael* (1923), 165–81; M. M. Kaplan, *The Greater Judaism in the Making* (1960), 227–31; J. J. Petuchowski, *Prayerbook Reform in Europe* (1968), Index; D. Philipson, "Samuel Holdheim, Jewish Reformer," *Yearbook* of the Central Conference of American Rabbis, XVI (1906), 305–33; idem, *The Reform Movement in Judaism*, second edition (reprinted 1967), Index; W. G. Plaut, *The Rise of Reform Judaism* (1963), Index; I. H. Ritter, "Samuel Holdheim, The Jewish Reformer," *JQR* I (1888), 202 ff; and M. Wiener, *Die jüdische Religion im Zeitalter der Emanzipation* (1933), 87–101.

The major works of Zacharias Frankel, the leader and mentor of the Positive-Historical school in nineteenth century German Jewry, include *Die Eidesleistung bei den Juden* (1840), *Vorstudien zu der Septuaginta* (1841), *Der gerichtliche Beweis nach talmudischem Rechte* (1846), *Über den Einfluss der palästinischen Exegese auf die alexandrinische Hermeneutik* (1851), *Darchei Ha-Mishnah* (1859; with supplement and index, 1867; new edition, 1923); and *Entwurf einer Geschichte der Literatur der nachtalmudischen Responsen* (1865).

On Frankel, see I. Barzilay, *Shelomo Yehudah Rapoport (Shir) and His Contemporaries* (1969), Index; J. L. Blau, *Modern Varieties of Judaism* (1966), 91–95; M. Brann, *Die Geschichte des Jüdisch-Theologischen Seminars in Breslau* (1904), 28–40; D. J. Silver and B. Martin, *A History of Judaism*, II (1974); L. Ginzberg, *Students, Scholars, and Saints* (1928), 195–216; D. Kaufmann, *Gesammelte Schriften*, herausgegeben von M. Brann, I (1908), 258–71; A. Lewkowitz, *Das Judentum und die geistige Strömungen des 19. Jahrhunderts* (1935), 361–75; S. P. Rabbinowitz, *Rabbi Zechariah Frankel* (Hebrew, 1898); D. Rudavsky, *Emancipation and Adjustment* (1967), 192–214; and idem, in *Jewish Journal of Sociology*, V (1963), 224–44.

CHAPTER NINE

SCHOLARS AND BELLETRISTS

Leopold Dukes was a prolific scholar in many fields of Jewish learning. Among his most important works are *Raschi zum Pen-*

tateuch, translated into German (in Hebrew characters) with explanatory comments (five volumes, 1833–38), *Ehrensäulen und Denksteine zu einem künftigen Pantheon hebräischer Dichter und Dichtungen* (1837), *Moses Ibn Ezra* (1839), *Zur Kenntniss der neuhebräischen religiösen Poesie* (1842), *Die Sprache der Mischna* (1846), *Zur rabbinischen Sprachkunde* (1858), *Shirei Shelomoh* (poems of Solomon ibn Gabirol, 1858); and *Salomo ben Gabirol aus Malaga und die ethischen Werke Desselben* (1860). On Dukes, see his autobiography in *Allgemeine Zeitung des Judentums*, LVI (1892); I. Davidson, "The Study of Medieval Hebrew Poetry in the XIX Century," *PAAJR*, I (1930), 33–48; and W. Zeitlin, *Bibliotheca Hebraica Post-Mendelssohniana*, I (1891), 69–71.

Saul Isaac Kämpf's most important work is his pioneering two-volume study of medieval Hebrew poetry, *Nichtandalusische Poesie andalusischer Dichter aus dem 11., 12., und 13. Jahrhundert* (1858). On Kämpf and his work, see S. W. Baron, "The Revolution of 1848 and Jewish Scholarship, Part Two: Austria," *PAAJR*, XX (1951); I. Davidson, "The Study of Medieval Hebrew Poetry in the XIX Century," *PAAJR*, I (1930), 33–48; M. Reines, *Dor Ve-Hachamav*, I (1890); and W. Zeitlin, *Bibliotheca Hebraica Post-Mendelssohniana* (1891–95), 163 ff.

Adolphe Franck's major work in the field of Jewish scholarship is his *La Kabbale ou philosophie religieuse des hébreux* (1843; second edition, 1892). It was translated into English under the title *The Kabbalah: Or the Religious Philosophy of the Hebrews* (1926). Among his other works relating to Judaism are *Sur les sectes juives avant le christianisme* (1853), *La religion et la science dans le judaisme* (1882), and *Le panthéisme oriental et la monothéisme hébreu* (1889). On Franck and his writings, see H. Derenbourg, in *REJ*, IV (1892), 3–11; D. H. Joel, *Die Religionsphilosophie des Zohar* (1923); A. Kohut, *Berühmte israelitische Männer und Frauen;* and M. Steinschneider, *Jewish Literature from the Eighth to the Eighteenth Century* (1965), 299, 301.

Salomon Munk's most important works are *Mélanges de philosophie juive et arabe* (1857–59) and his classical three-volume edition of the original Arabic text (in Hebrew characters) of Maimonides' *Guide for the Perplexed*, based on several manuscripts, with a French translation entitled *Guide des Égarés* and annotations (1856, 1861, 1866). The Arabic text was re-edited by B. J. Joel (1960). On Munk, see P. Immanuel, in S. Federbush, ed., *Ḥochmat Yisrael Be-Eyropah* (1965), 239–241; A. Jellinek, *Salomon Munk* (German, 1865); G. A. Kohut, *Salomon Munk* (English, 1902); H. S. Morais, *Eminent Israelites of the Nineteenth Century* (1880), 247–52; and M. Schwab, *Salomon Munk* (French, 1900). M. Brann published 44 German letters of Munk's, with a biographical notice, in *Jahrbuch für jüdische Geschichte und Literatur*, II (1899), 148–203.

Michael Sachs' scholarly works include *Beitrage zur Sprach-und Altertumsforschung* (2 vols., 1852–54), as well as editions and translations of the *Maḥzor* in both the German and Polish rites (9 volumes, 1855) and an edition and translation of the *Siddur* (1858). His major work is *Die religiöse Poesie der Juden in Spanien* (1845; second edition, 1901). On Sachs, see S. Bernfeld, in the 1901 edition of *Die religiöse Poesie . . .* ; idem, *Michael Sachs . . .* (Hebrew, 1900); J. Eschelbacher, *Michael Sachs* (German, 1908); and L. Geiger, ed., *Michael Sachs und Moritz Veit, Briefwechsel . . .* (1897).

On Heinrich Heine, see the works listed under Chapter One of these bibliographical notes.

The most popular and widely read of Grace Aguilar's Jewish novels is *The Vale of Cedars* (1850), a sentimental romance about the Marranos of fifteenth-century Spain. She was also the author of apologetic works on Judaism, including *The Spirit of Judaism: In Defense of Her Faith and Its Professors*, published in 1842 in Philadelphia with notes by Isaac Leeser, and *The Jewish Faith: Its Spiritual Consolation, Moral Guidance, and Immortal Hope* (1846). On Aguilar, see A. S. Isaacs, *Young Champion: One Year in Grace Aguilar's Girlhood* (1933); H. S. Morais, *Eminent Israelites of the Nineteenth Century* (1880); and F. Modder, *The Jew in the Literature of England* (1939), 182–87.

Ludwig August Frankl achieved recognition at the age of twenty-two with his first collection of ballads, *Das Habsburger Lied* (1832). Two years later (1834) he published a book of poems on Jewish themes, *Morgenländische Sagen*. Also of Jewish interest are his *Elegien* (1842), *Rachel* (1842), *Libanon* (1855), and *Ahnenbilder* (1864). Frankel's *Nach Jerusalem* (two volumes, 1858–60), describing his stay in Palestine, provides valuable information about Jewish life in Jerusalem in the middle of the nineteenth century. It was translated into English under the title *The Jews of the East* (1859). On Frankl, see S. Dollar, *Sonntagsblätter von Ludwig August Frankl* (1932); *Otzar Ha-Sifrut*, V (1896), 129–34, which contains bibliography; E. Wolbe, *Ludwig August Frankel, der Dichter und Menschenfreund* (1910); and Y. Yaari-Poleskin, *Holemim U-Magshimim* (1967), 48–56.

Solomon Hermann Mosenthal's best known play *Deborah* (1849) was translated from the German into the major modern languages. It became famous in English under the title *Leah, the Forsaken*. Mosenthal also wrote a book of stories about Jewish family life, *Bilder aus dem jüdischen Familienleben* (1878). A collected edition of his numerous plays, poems, and stories was published posthumously in 1878 in six volumes. On Mosenthal, see his necrology reprinted in *Allgemeine Zeitung des Judenthums*, 1877, p. 155, and M. Martersteig, *Das deutsche Theater im 19. Jahrhundert* (1904), 402, 423.

The first work published by Berthold Auerbach was a pamphlet entitled *Das Judentum und die neueste Literatur* (1836) in which he defended the Jews of Germany against the charge of radicalism. His profound interest in Spinoza led him to a five-volume German translation of the philosopher's writings (1841), as well as to his first novel, *Spinoza, Ein Denkerleben* (1837). The subject of Auerbach's second historical novel, *Dichter und Kaufmann* (1840), was the German-Jewish poet Ephraim Moses Kuh. His *Schwarzwälder Dorfsgeschichten* (1843) became the major foundation of the peasant-story genre in German literature. The foreward to the English translation of this work, *Village Tales from the Black Forest* (1846–47), was written by the British statesman William E. Gladstone. On Auerbach and his work, see A. Bettelheim, *Berthold Auerbach* (German, 1907); F. Mauthner, *Prager Jugendjahre*, 2nd ed. (1969), 309–17; E. Wolbe, *Berthold Auerbach* (German, 1907); and M. I. Zwick, *Berthold Auerbachs sozialpolitischer und ethischer Liberalismus* (1933), which includes a bibliography.

Two editions of Leopold Kompert's collected writings were published, one in 1882–83 and one in 1906. Some of his stories were translated into English under the titles *Scenes from the Ghetto* (1882), *The Silent Woman* (1890), and *Christian and Leah: Other Ghetto Stories* (1895). On Kompert, see S. W. Baron, "The Revolution of 1848 and Jewish Scholarship, Part Two: Austria," *PAAJR*, XX (1951), 26–27; H. Bergmann, in *Czechoslovak Jewry, Past and Future* (1943), 22–24; M. Grunwald, *Vienna* (1936), Index; S. Hock, in Kompert's *Sämtliche Werke*, I (1906), v–lvii; G. Kisch, in *American Jewish Historical Society Publications*, XXXVIII (1948–49), 185–234; idem, *In Search of Freedom* (1949), Index; R. Michael, in *Yearbook* of the Leo Baeck Institute, IX (1964), 102–07; and J. Shatzky, in *Freedom and Reason*, Morris Raphael Cohen Memorial Volume (1951), 413–37, passim.

Aaron David Bernstein's two novels in the Judeo-German dialect *Vögele Maggid* and *Mendel Gibbor* first appeared in book form in 1860 (reissued 1934–35) and made their author one of the major ghetto novelists. They were translated into many European languages, including Russian (1876). On Bernstein, see S. J. Fuenn, *Keneset Yisrael* (1886), 75–76; A. Geiger, *Jüdische Zeitschrift für Wissenschaft und Leben*, VII (1869), 223–226; and S. Katznelson, *Juden im deutschen Kulturbereich* (1959), 28, 574.

GLOSSARY OF HEBREW AND OTHER TERMS

Glossary of Hebrew Terms

Aggadah (or Haggadah): The non-legal part of the post-Biblical Oràl Torah (see below), consisting of narratives, legends, parables, allegories, poems, prayers, theological and philosophical reflections, etc. Much of the Talmud (see below) is aggadic, and the Midrash (see below) literature, developed over a period of more than a millennium, consists almost entirely of Aggadah. The term *aggadah*, in a singular and restricted sense, refers to a Talmudic story or legend.

Aharonim (Hebrew for "later ones"): A term used to designate relatively recent rabbinic authorities, as distinguished from earlier ones, known as Rishonim (see below). Aharonim usually refers to decisors and codifiers of the law subsequent to the compilation of Rabbi Joseph Karo's *Shulḥan Aruch* (see below) in the sixteenth century, although occasionally the dividing line between Rishonim and Aharonim is placed as early as the eleventh century.

Amora (plural, Amoraim): The title given to the Jewish scholars of Palestine and especially Babylonia in the third to the sixth centuries whose work and thought is recorded in the Gemara of the Talmud.

Baal Shem (in Hebrew, "master of the Name"): A title given to persons believed capable of working miracles through employing the divine Name. The title was not uncommon in Eastern Europe in the seventeenth and eighteenth centuries, where it frequently implied a quack or impostor who produced magical amulets, pronounced incantations, etc.

Bet Ha-Midrash: In the Talmudic age, a school for higher rabbinic learning where students assembled for study and discussion, as well as prayer. In the post-Talmudic age most synagogues had a Bet Ha-Midrash or were themselves called by the term, insofar as they were places of study.

Gemara: The second basic strand of the Talmud, consisting of a commentary on, and supplement to, the Mishnah (see below).

Gematria: A system of exegesis based on the interpretation of a word or words according to the numerical value of the constituent letters in the Hebrew alphabet.

Halachah (in Hebrew, "law"; derived from the verb *halach*, "to go" or "to follow"): The legal part of Talmudic and later Jewish literature, in contrast to Aggadah or Haggadah, the non-legal elements. In the singular, *halachah* means "law" in an abstract sense, or, alternatively, a specific rule or regulation; in the plural, *halachot* refers to collections of laws.

Haskalah: The movement for disseminating modern European culture among Jews from about 1750 to 1880. It advocated the modernization of Judaism, the westernization of traditional Jewish education, and the revival of the Hebrew language.

Haskamah (plural, Haskamot): Approbations or authorizations by respected rabbinic authorities, sometimes inserted in Hebrew books. The practice of inserting *haskamot* became particularly widespread after the synod of rabbis in Ferrara in 1554 decided that Hebrew books should obtain prior approval by Jewish authorities in order to prevent suppression or censorship by the officials of the Church. Later a *haskamah* was frequently solicited by the author of a book as testimony of his work's scholarly value and its orthodoxy.

Hilluk (plural, Hillukim): Subtle distinctions or refined analyses in interpretation of the Talmud or other rabbinic texts.

Kabbalah: The mystical religious movement in Judaism and/or its literature. The term Kabbalah, which means "tradition," came to be used by the mystics beginning in the twelfth century to signify the alleged continuity of their doctrine from ancient times.

Kasher (Hebrew for "fit" or "suitable"): A term usually employed to designate those foods which are regarded as permissible for consumption by Jews according to Talmudic-rabbinic law, as well as vessels considered permissible for use. More generally, it is used to refer to anything ritually approved.

Kelipah (plural, kelipot): Literally, "husk" or "shell." A mystical term used in Kabbalist literature, demoting demonic power or the forces of evil.

Kinah (plural, Kinot): In Biblical and Talmudic times, a dirge over the dead. Later the term came to be applied to a liturgical composition for the Ninth of Av dealing with the destruction of the Temple as well as with contemporary persecutions.

Maaseh Bereshit (Hebrew for "work of creation"): The term refers to the account of creation in the Book of Genesis, the exposition of which was one of the primary concerns of early Jewish mysticism.

Maskil (plural, maskilim): An adherent of Haskalah (see above).

Masorah: The term is used to refer to the collections of traditions, collected by various schools in the Talmudic and Gaonic eras, in regard to the correct spelling, writing, and reading of the text of the Hebrew Bible.

Meassefim: The contributors to the Hebrew journal *Ha-Meassef*, the major organ in Hebrew published by the proponents of Haskalah (see above) in Germany in the last decades of the eighteenth century and the first of the nineteenth.

Midrash (plural, Midrashim): The discovery of new meanings besides literal ones in the Bible. The term is also used to designate collections of such Scriptural exposition. The best-known of the Midrashim are the *Midrash Rabbah, Tanhuma, Pesikta De-Rav Kahana, Pesikta Rabbati*, and *Yalkut Shimeoni*. In a singular and restricted sense, Midrash refers to an item of rabbinic exegesis.

Mishnah: The legal codification containing the core of the post-Biblical Oral Torah, compiled and edited by Rabbi Judah Ha-Nasi at the beginning of the third century C.E.

Oral Torah (or Oral Law): The body of interpretation and analysis of the written law of the Pentateuch created in post-exilic Judaism and handed down orally from generation to generation. The Oral Law consists of the Mishnah (see above) and the Gemara (see above), both of which were combined to form the Talmud (see below). Even after the redaction of the Talmud, the body of tradition contained in it continued to be known as the Oral Law because its roots were in an oral tradition.

Pilpul: In Talmudic and rabbinic literature, a clarification of a difficult point. Later the term came to denote a sharp dialectical distinction or, more generally, a certain type of Talmudic study emphasizing dialectical distinctions.

Rebbe: Yiddish form of the term rabbi, applied generally to a teacher but also, and especially, to a Hasidic rabbi.

Rishonim (Hebrew for "first ones"): In modern times, the term has come to be employed primarily in reference to the commentators on, and codifiers of, Talmudic law of the Gaonic era until the time of the composition of Rabbi Joseph Karo's *Shulhan Aruch* (see below). Later authorities are referred to as Aharonim (see above). On occasion the dividing line between Rishonim and Aharonim has been drawn as early as the eleventh century.

Selihah (plural, Selihot): A special type of synagogal hymn or prayer, the themes of which are an expression of contrition for sin and a request for divine compassion and forgiveness.

Shofar: The horn of a ram sounded on Rosh Ha-Shanah, or the New Year, as well as on other solemn occasions, e.g., the ceremony of excommunication or at a time of epidemic or famine.

Shulhan Aruch: The abbreviated code of rabbinic jurisprudence, written by Joseph Karo in the sixteenth century, which became the authoritative code of Jewish law and is still recognized as such by Orthodox Judaism.

Talmud: The title applied to the two great compilations, distinguished as the Babylonian Talmud and the Palestinian Talmud, in which the records of academic discussion and of judicial administration of post-Biblical Jewish law are assembled. Both Talmuds also contain Aggadah or non-legal material.

Tanna (plural, Tannaim): Any of the teachers mentioned in the Mishnah, or in literature contemporaneous with the Mishnah, and living during the first two centuries C.E.

Tashlich: A Hebrew term meaning "thou wilt cast," and referring to the custom, observed on Rosh Ha-Shanah, or the New Year, of praying near a stream or body of water and (at one time) throwing bread crumbs to the fish.

Torah: In its narrowest meaning, the Pentateuch. Torah is also known in Judaism as the Written Law. In its broader meaning, Torah comprises as well the Oral Law, the traditional exposition of the Pentateuch and its commandments developed in the late Biblical and post-Biblical ages. In its widest meaning Torah signifies every exposition of both the Written and the Oral Law, including all of Talmudic literature and its commentaries. The term is sometimes used also to designate the scroll of the Pentateuch read in the synagogue service.

Tzaddik: In Hebrew, the term means "a righteous man." It is a title given to a person renowned for faith and piety. The concept of the tzaddik became especially important in the Hasidic movement of the eighteenth century, in which the tzaddik was regarded as endowed with extraordinary powers and capable of serving as an intermediary between God and man.

Wissenschaft des Judentums, die: (German for "the science of Judaism"): The modern type of scientific and critical exploration of Jewish history, literature, and religion, initially developed in Germany in the first half of the nineteenth century.

Yeshivah (plural, Yeshivot): A traditional Jewish school devoted primarily to the study of the Talmud (see above), and rabbinic literature.

Zohar: The chief work of the Spanish Kabbalah (see above) traditionally ascribed to the Tanna Simeon ben Yoḥai (second century) but probably written by the Spanish Kabbalist Moses de Leon at the end of the thirteenth century.

Index

Index